neon rose

it's a blue blue rose that grows beneath the neon sun*

place

VOLUME III NUMBER 1

*mel tillis

© NEON ROSE was printed in San Francisco by Stecher-Traung-Schmidt Corp. June 1973. Copyright 1973 by NATURAL WONDERS, INC. All rights reserved under Pan American and International convention.

Distributed by RANDOM HOUSE and in Canada by RANDOM HOUSE OF CANADA, LTD.
ISBN 0-394-70990-X   LC 73-5040

Second class postage paid at Walnut Grove, California.

California Yurt Living

This country's government's done so many awful things lately, that it's hard to think of our 200th anniversary with much of an idea of celebrating; but with the political climate worsening at such speed, people of all ages seem to be opening up to most any ideas.

SUGGESTIONS: A. Stop selling war—outlaw the export of armaments. Treat all the nations of the world as equals; withdraw all our troops and security agents from the soil of allies and enemies alike. B. Declare the United States a free port area of the world, removing all taxes, duties, and tariffs, allowing commodities and manufactured goods to circulate freely around the globe. Allow the prices of goods to establish themselves solely on the basis of cost of production, transportation, and consumer demand. Give the people unhindered choices of what they want to eat, drink, wear, drive, and live in. C. Remove all tax laws, and finance the government entirely of donations from private citizens. D. Encourage and equip the residents of cities, suburbs, and towns to reconstruct their communities in order to make them more spiritually profitable places to live. E. Drop all farm subsidy, soil bank, and price support programs, encouraging the farmers to enter the world market with their own co-operative efforts. F. Keep each country's capitalists in their own back yard—outlaw American ownership of foreign manufacturing facilities and natural resources. Likewise, exclude foreign ownership of American industries and resources. G. In celebration of the bicentennial, begin to move the works of the government to, say, the Ozark Mts. of Missouri or Arkansas, building a new capital in an appropriate style, out of native wood and stone. Do NOT use concrete, asphalt, aluminium, plastic, steel or stainless steel. Recruit a common labor force from all over the country. Have no business or military men, or other pollution within 50 miles of the new capital (politicians aren't born dishonest). Turn the District of Columbia into a Model City-state, making it an educational, historical, world trade city.

Most of us probably chuckle to ourselves some when we think of the Russians being about the same as us. And Arabs, Africans, Chinese, and Argentines and us all being of the same race. There's an uncertainty about this which allows us to be easily talked into believing there's a daemon loose in Asia, or that some country in South America needs help. But governments nowdays are often better suited to be feared than to be trusted; and as we fear our own, it's easy to imagine that other people fear their governments too, as much or more than we fear ours. Knowledge and power come from the natural world, with humans the most critically powerful terrestial beings. People like to group themselves together, with their own power forming the power of the group. It's hard to separate yourself from your group and usually you stick with them till the end, be you a Hells Angel, a ballerina, one of Nixon's Cain, or a Veteran of Foreign Wars.

In a group a bird can get along with a dog without being eaten, and people can get used to any position. They can be paid to leap over a MacDonald's counter for television (outlaw ads on tv), or to design most ingenuous impersonal towers of power.

'Hey mister, how far is it to New York from here?' 'Well it's three lengths of a fool—if you don't believe me, lay down and measure it sometime.'

Groups are like icebergs, with the people on the top being pushed up above the surface. When the group does something through these people, it's where there was nobody doing anything before. New acts of energy happen in places of their own, and cast shadows on what happened before nearby. Groups often go by age and date of birth: throughout the school years one is grouped by age, and these groups are carried on through military experience, social and community organizations and old age societies. People naturally move with their group through these different ages. There's a cycle which becomes a full one, beginning with birth, flowing to maturity, and beginning with another birth. Age groups, as well as poor folks, stick together.

There's a certain set of right answers to old questions, and when an important question comes up, the group changes into a crowd—the people start feeling themselves being on their own. When people come up with the right answers, they prosper; but when a wrong answer is given, the people suffer. As long as they aren't able to reverse their wrong decision it remains a stumbling block in their lives, and causes continual trouble. In people, the number of incorrect answers, or the amount of uncomfortable things in their lives, increases from time to time; and for some builds up to an unbearable situation.

What relieves this pressure is *the beginning of another cycle.* For a society in general, it is the birth of a new generation of people, with the life cycle starting over fresh. To Christians, it is salvation, or a new birth. Coffee, alcohol, avocados, dope, and fresh green peas can also lead one into a new birth. A person, if willing, can have 9x9 born again lives. A simple example is one of my more recent lives into which I was reborne while sitting in a bathtub of the Daniel Boone Hotel, Boone, North Carolina, in December, 1969. I was in my early 20s, and due to a personal pseudo-calamity, my consciousness was disarrayed sufficiently for me to catch a glimpse of my legs, lying, like morbidly truncated boas, lifeless, in six inches of rusty hotel bath water. For six years I had taken showers, washing myself while standing up, feeling antiseptic sureness that the stinging hot showers were getting me cleaner, quicker than would a tub; but sitting in that Daniel Boone bathtub I began noticing that, laying out there in front of me were my legs, which I hadn't really looked at in the six years I'd been taking showers. This happiness of mine in a bathtub is just a facet of the general rebirth I'm trying to relate to you.

So, give up your shower for a bathtub once in a while (you'll get clean enough), and try to come up with the right answers to all the old questions. Remember, people have more fun than, and that little old lady sitting out in her back yard knows as much as . . . anybody; and life lasts up to the very end.

Jim Holdorf

CONTENTS

GOOSEDOWN

Send us a pound of goosedown and we'll send you PLACE for a year. Or send whatever amount seems fair, depending on you and your goose. Any other lightweight natural wonder will also be considered as an exchange item. See Subscription Page for details.

My first issue of PLACE came to me while I was in the mountains with the Kids (the mountains being Carolina's Blue Ridge, the Kids being the students and teachers of Amity Community, a free school co-operative. Five days in the mountains away from city, radios and newspapers a soft mellow experience tempered by the newness of children.) Back we were at Amity, a fine old Victorian house haunted by its previous and only owner, a fine old Victorian. On the front porch sat the accumulated news of five days in April of 1972 and in the mailbox a few letters and a surprise package. What was soon to be a regretable action I opened the newspapers first, in reverse order, to discover Mr. Nixon's latest grandstand play, the mining of North Vietnam harbors. The affect of the news, shocking but not disabilitating was more curious interest in somehow missing five days of work-a-day world and not actually missing much at all, noticing how each newspaper contradicted what was said the day before, and todays only destined to be nullified by tomorrows.

Newspapers away I opened the package to behold *A Workingman's Guide to the Universe*. I hadn't expected anything so glossy and polished, so fine in concept and execution. But here it was, and on subsequent days I sat on the porch rolling in my hammock reading about an America I barely knew. Many times as I relocated my soul to obscure corners and holes in the country I planned submitting an essay, verbal or photo on Raleigh, on its old homes, its corner groceries, its neighborhoods, its changes. But time and again I put it off. First I was busy with the school, it was my life and while I lived and worked there I was at peace as I had never been before.

May came and things changed and the school was caught in political turmoil, our peaceful place amidst chaos was succumbing to the chaos around it and squeezing myself and the other teachers out. So as a family we moved and began looking for a school in a different place that could use us and we them.

Holed up in a hot treehouse apartment, working in the kitchen of a jazz club riding my bicycle to swimming holes and country farms the summer melted on with a prospect in Arkansas, one in Rhode Island, one in Chapel Hill. Among the fragrant lindens and drying day lilies and gathered mulberries *Star Route 1* arrived. Now with sweat beads forming on my beard, hair piled on my head to try to keep cool I read Border Incidents and Cabeza De Vaca and I began to see that from out of rural America was springing a new literary group who sang songs to the simple life, to the past, to childhood, but also to a renewed consciousness, a new awareness of the entire oneness of the universe of man and land.

We didn't go anywhere as a group, deciding to stay in Raleigh (it is a good place and we know it pretty well now) and start another school which we did. But I was itching, so I hopped on my bike and started west, alternately thumbing and pedaling until I reached Doniphan Missouri and the home of long lost friends. A sunset shower greeted me and I had found a new place. I didn't stop though, something drove me on, and I continued North up to St. Louis where the city shocked me into a sleepless soul searching night.

From St. Louis it was East to Pennsylvania and North to Rochester New York and friends in a trailer park, and a side trip to Toronto, a place to turn around and look back at America (The United States since Canada *is* America too!) I was very confused with what I saw and kept on moving. Now to New England and country again the peacefulness tugged at my road weariness. Like a steel ball falling down the slope of the pinball machine, hitting here, bouncing there, so I bounced and rolled down the coast to Raleigh.

I walked out of the Greyhound Station at dawn and slowly walked home. Feeling Carolina around me seeing its great sky around me, I was home, my itching cleared up, my psyche at rest.

Amity Again sprang up from hard work and opened this time outside the city limits, in the country, "our year in the woods" we would come to call it and it too was fine.

Again I moved, this time into a fifteen room white house across from old Amity. In my room above the library and in the living room before the fire, I read *See America First*. I haven't read it all, yet. One day I put it down and someone else picked it up and I've just now gotten it back. This house, with its fifteen rooms, twelve foot ceilings and garden. With its solid construction and spreading cherry tree, this house is soon destined for removal, making way for the offices of influential lobbies in the state government, located just two blocks away. With this area going under and vast wooded areas on the outskirts of town being cleared for shopping centers and apartments the charm of Raleigh is falling to the almighty dollar, needless to say I'm sad.

An invitation from my Missouri friends, to come stay for awhile, be a dirt farmer, try out some of my fantasies, prompts my decision to leave town. So I ask Pam (now living on a small farm just outside the city limits, recently rezoned and sure to come under the dozers) to come with me, and she says yes.

Rogue's Gallery arrived, and found me anticipating my move from city to country from free-school to rural high school possibly. And the stories don't appeal to me, they confuse and depress. The photos are quaint and seem to be searching for a new definition of the art form, looking to age as some bestower of knowledge.

Admittedly *Place* is leagues ahead of establishment magazines but it seems headed for established format. Its promoting a regular group of writers much as *city lights journal* did in the fifties and sixties and in time, with an article here in the *Times* there in *Esquire* it will move beyond its purpose and succumb to the richness of notoriety. So I'm not renewing my subscription, looking instead for a publication that serves as useful in my upcoming rural days. Maybe later on we'll meet up again, when either of us or both of us has changed. I do want to thank you for being a part of this past year, for making me think some, and especially for trying something new. I think you've succeeded maybe its time to move on?

Jeff London
Raleigh N.C.

Bergdorf, Idaho

dear sedentary places,

boy are you a lousy bunch of correspondents, not one single juicy newsletter tho we did get two copies hot off the press which makes up for something i guess. sure looks nice, tho i note still somewhat afflicted with creeping typo.

monday we make a last foray into town, all thirteen of us, to take a final peak at a pizza and receive the benefits of modern medicine in the form of shots of gamma globulin (could it be their putting us on, and merely saying happy halloween in portuguese,) in our collective ass, since we've been exposed to the hep in true hippy style. No money left—spent the last on a gallon of Vino Fino and a halfgallon of brandy for our st. bernard. four inches of snow on the road and down to 10° sometimes in the morning not the languorous moment one might wish, but we've figured that out, letting the fire go out cold in the heating stove, which is an executive-size Ashley right next to the bed, then stoking it full of sawdust soaked in diesel fuel and logs, so in the wee morning hours you just lean over and throw a match in. there seems no alternative, however, to our outhouse, which threatens to overflow in midwinter and isnt the least bit homey. during the day the squirrels shoplift the toilet paper, at night the trees creak and giggle.

election day was pretty uneventful here, except for Larry going to town on a booze run to find all the liquor stores closed because for some reason booze and politics arent to be mixed. without t.v. it all becomes a little hard to contemplate tho it was still a shock to tune in the radio at 4 and already hear the networks predicting Nixon landlording. never did hear whether he took Calif. tho i assume he did. well that blows several theories dont it.

its interesting to think that, were it not for the snowmobile, we would be entirely a law of our own here, though it aint all that pure, since we are now everyone of us wards of the state, having proved ourselves poor enough to qualify for food commodities, which is just a simple handout of what the govt buys up to keep the farmers in the fields, plus a cookbook of inventive hints for canned pork, prunes, and peanutbutter.

We drove up to Grangeville to pick it up, where its stock-piled in the basement of the bowling alley. on the way out in early morning snowdrizzle, we met two basque sheepherders with their pack on a pole between their shoulders, walking out of the mountains, mildly surprised when we told them how far it was to town. we drove them to the bus station where they were headed for another job in Washington and they filled Deltas hand with quarters when we weren't looking.

love, pam

My Favorite Place is Baars' House

One time I was over at Lori Baars house, and we were walking in their pasture. A baby cow, which Lori called Squirt, walked up to us. We fed him an apple. Then we had a great idea. I walked over and held Squirt while Lori jumped on his back. He just stood there for a moment, but all of a "sudden" he started bucking! Lori fell off but she wasn't hurt. We both laughed.

The next day we were in the barn when two men drove up in a truck. We walked out to where the men were standing. One man said that they had come to get a cow for butchering. We didn't know it was going to be Squirt. When they put Squirt in the truck he cried and tried to get away, but he didn't. After they left, Lori started crying. After, she stopped. Lori has forgotten Squirt now because she has a horse!

Christy Laman, age 13
Ludington, Michigan

Hello.

Here is my entry in the *Why I'd Like Armstrong Linoleum All Over My Whole House* contest. Sure hope it wins, because I really *would.* I'm not entering this contest just because I'd enter any old contest that came along. No, *sir.* I'm entering this one because I *really like* Armstrong Linoleum. When we lived in the city, Armstrong Linoleum was the only thing that saved that awful, dingy little kitchen or I guess I should say saved *me* from just plain old going crazy trying to cook a decent meal for my family, that's just me and my husband of course, he was a dishwasher at the time. We got a scrap of the red tile pattern, it cost us 2.34, I believe, and put it on the floor and had enough left over to cover the countertop where it was beginning to rot away from the sink a little. It really looked nice, and it was real easy to clean, too. That's the first place we lived after we were married, and I remember cooking a Thanksgiving dinner of roast chicken, pumpkin pie, baked sweet potatoes and dressing and acorn squash, green beans and homemade bread in shifts on a two burner stove, right there in that old tiny kitchen nook that we made real pretty with that Armstrong Linoleum. It was our first Thanksgiving, of course.

Now, after going through a lot of different changes, we've moved to a little old farm just outside of Excelsior Springs, Missouri the World Famous former Mineral Spa. I mean, it still has the minerals it just isn't a spa anymore. It seems like folks just don't care anymore about taking mineral baths and such, and I'll tell you plain, I tried drinking some of that iron water up at the Hall of Waters that they sell, You know? Like it was a soda fountain? And it tasted just awful, just like drinking old rusty nails. It was terrible.

Anyway, our house is just a little old house, just four rooms downstairs, I wouldn't want linoleum upstairs in my bedroom, no, not even the red tile pattern, the kind that goes all the way through, not the photograph in plastic. That'd be asking too much, I guess. To have it in my bedroom, I mean.

It sure is a funny house. There ain't a single place that's level, and I don't mind telling you when I first moved here I used to get kindly what you'd call seasick, just walking across the kitchen floor to the sink. Well, anyway, when we spill something we know which corner to run to to clean it up.

But why I really want Armstrong Linoleum all over my whole house is because this house was built 150 years ago, the living room, anyways. It's a log cabin. The rest of it just grew like that old story about Topsy—first the dining room but of course it was a bedroom then—then the kitchen and a porch in the little ell between—then when the baby came along (not mine, the folkses who lived here thirty years ago) why then they just closed in that old back porch and made it into a real little girl room, with pink curtains and pink flower wallpaper and pink woodwork and pink flower linoleum—not Armstrong Linoleum, though. Well, one reason I want Armstrong Linoleum in my Whole House is because I don't even like pink all that much. And pink flowered linoleum with a different kind of pink flowered wallpaper is kind of icky, you know it? And besides, that linoleum is thirty years old, I know that because the girl who used to be that same little baby came by here just the other day to fish in the pond and to tell us how the Old Place has Gone Down since she lived here, and that girl is thirty if she's a day.

Anyway, so that linoleum *is* thirty years old, and when you spill something on it the finish comes right off, right down to the brown backing if you don't wipe it up right away. Probably didn't cost much in the first place. And, too, the old wringer washer is in there, making spills, and so's the kitty litter pan, and it's nice to have something durable.

That's another reason I'd like Armstrong Linoleum All Over My Whole House—because we've got these 23 cats. We did have 36, but we gave 14 away and we're expecting a lady just tonight that wants a kitten. Well, the thing is that we can't afford to get all our mama cats fixed, and so we keep on getting kittens, and they don't always figure out right where the litter pan is at first. It's alright, we use it on our compost heap, but it would sure be nice to have a good old durable, easy to clean Armstrong Linoleum All Over This Whole House.

Another thing is that it *is* 150 years old like I said. It's settled a lot and there are big old cracks in the wood floors. I don't know if you know this or not, but when they made log cabins, they didn't make any subfloors, and didn't even know about builders paper yet, so every winter we've got to put bales of hay all around the house to try to block some of the wind out from under the house. Remember that old movie where Marilyn Monroe stepped on the vent and her skirt blew all up; Well, that's how it is around here in the winter. Armstrong Linoleum would sure stop *that* quick enough, though Lord Knows I'm no Marilyn Monroe.

Even in the kitchen where we've *got* linoleum—and it *sure* can't be Armstrong Linoleum, because it's new (I think the people that sold the farm to the fella *we* got it from must of put it down to make the place look modern, but since the outhouse is out back, it didn't really work for what they mean when they say Modern in the real estate ads is just that it's got inside plumbing, not that it looks like some kind of high rise office building.) By the way, the outhouse *does* have Armstrong Linoleum in it, the old fashioned red tile pattern like I told you I like so much, though it doesn't go all the way through the way I meant for it to. They didn't have a big enough scrap of that to fit the two-holer. Well, as I said, it can't be Armstrong Linoleum in the kitchen because even though it's new, every time it gets scraped just a little old bit, there's the old black

backing and it starts moldering away under there. And last winter, it was cold enough in the kitchen to freeze spills right on the floor, at least near the front wall. Armstrong Linoleum wouldn't let it do *that* would it? One time we almost froze to the floor getting out of the old zinc tub.

So I guess that's enough reasons to win that "Why I'd Like Armstrong Linoleum All Over My Whole House" contest—sure do hope you all think so too.

Very truly yours,
Cathy and Sleepy Johnson
Excelsior Springs, Missouri

ie; Biloxi, Mississippi

When I learned our family business interests would cause us to move permanently to Biloxi, Mississippi I caught my breath. This is a section of our great country I always wanted to know and now I would. From the map I learned the population of the city was some forty-five thousand strong and located on the Mississippi Sound in the Gulf of Mexico. The Biloxi Lighthouse which has an exciting history sits in the sound and I can picture long hours of sitting on the beach dreaming of the past it has known. The smell of the damp warm air had already penetrated my nostrils through my thought channels.

On free days we will travel west along the beach to the area between Bay St Louis and Waveland to view the Pirate House where Jean Lafitte hid in this plantation-type cottage built in 1802 by a New Orleans businessman. Hiding was necessary one century ago, after Lafitte struck terror along the Gulf Coast as he captured & scuttled ships from almost every country.

We will visit Fort Massachusetts and Ship Island in the sound; Ingalls Shipbuilding Corporation, the largest on the Gulf Coast. This operation covers over 150 acres along the Singing River, the Pascagoula; then a little to the north east we will find the Church of the Redeemer built in 1890 in memorial to Jefferson Davis' family. The church is noted for its beautiful windows and the chapel in the rear containing a pew draped with a Confederate Flag where Davis worshiped.

The hot humid climate will be a drastic change from the cold dry weather we have enjoyed in Wyoming.

Just one thing I will insist on in our new home—Air conditioning!

Dorothy J. Harper
Rawlins, Wyoming 82301

Jimmy Pierce ETR 3
FPO NY 09501

Dear Place,

The weather is sunshiney, but somewhat windy. We are now in Barcelona, Spain.

I received a flyer about your magazine from Ann Marie at Whole Earth and I felt that it is an excellent idea. I'd write about places I've been over here, but being in the navy the way I am, I don't get to see the really good places or away from the places that have become many towns or the parts of towns and cities that don't have many nearby.

One thing I will wright about is where I lived at home and where I live when we are back in Norfolk Virginia.

Here's a little about myself if you're interested. I'm 24 years old. I was born in Austin, Texas June 27, 1947 at 1:40 AM in a hospital, I don't know its name. Item: a UFO or flying saucer was sighted near the hospital that night. I found this out about four years ago during a study reading process that took place at a library. I lived on a farm outside Rogers, Texas until I was five years old. Sharecropping must have disagreed with my father because he left and we haven't heard from him since. My mother and I lived with her mother and father until I was fifteen, when my (step) father was transferred by the army. My mother remarried when I was seven. I have two sisters ages seven and fourteen that I love very much and have never felt anything, but that they and I were as brother and full sisters and will not allow harm to come to them. We have traveled a lot of places, but my recollections of the places where we lived are not all that clear, but after I return to the states and I get my photo albums from my folks, the pictures will help memory out of its rut. My home town is Belton, Texas, the county seat of Bell County. The 1970 census finally put the population count up to 10,000. A small creek flows through the west and south part of town but it is almost dead as there is a small chemical plant about 10 miles upstream.

There is a small park about five acres on one side of the creek. It was used a lot when I was younger, but about since 1965 it hasn't been used for anything except things like the Old Fiddlers Contest every fourth of July. The minimum age for entrance is age 65! I received a letter from my aunt last summer letting me know that the winner was a man as spry as can be at age 91! We also have the annual Rodeo Carnival at one end of the park, and fourth parade. There are several riding and roping clubs in my area also. Belton is situated just north of a place called Three Forks where the Leon creek, Lanpasas river and the Salado river meet. About 10 miles south of Three Forks is a hilly area called the Knobs. This is where supposedly Maximillian lost a few millions in gold and church ornaments when the freight wagons that were hauling it were attacked by Comanche Indians. They had time to bury it and so people have been looking for it about 100 years now. In the spring of 1967 a man in Salado (about five miles south of Belton, which is 160 miles south of Dallas) found about $1,000 dollars worth of old spanish square gold dollar pieces, but there was a government man talking about taxes so the man and his gold disappeared! The old Chisolm Trail passed right through my home town for the main reason of the artesian wells that were there and is still how the downtown areas gets its water. They are going year round and have never dried up as far as I know I guess I'll close for now because when I got to reminiscing about the past history of my home and forget I'm writing a letter and start acting like I'm writing a novel so I'll close for now and I hope everything goes well with you and above all Take care and don't let people hassle you unnecessarily.

Sincerely,
Jim

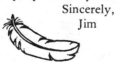

Hello place.

If you're traveling chickens are hard to keep. But chickens are fantastic things to get to know. Constant and easy personalities to see and be with. They are productive folks as well. It's a gas when your rooster thinks you are trying to make it with his hen and he comes rushing at you with spurs and feathers everywhere. And watching an egg get laid is a hot steaming rush.

Larry Maurer
Fullerton, California

Hi Jerry

Hows everything with you? Been busy here and there. As for the answer on the job this spring and summer I don't think I'm going to. I've been thinking of selling everything and get a steady job not having everybody under me. I've got all messed up with some checks and am in jail right now for 15 days. And am going to sell out and move to town someplace I guess. Sorry about the jobs but the wife wants me to go straight all together and the only way is to have nothing to do but work at a job and take care of things once. You know what I mean. Did you get your bird house up yet! that toy I mean 250 by 40 wasn't it? If you write back sent it home I should be their then. If not I'll see you sometime I suppose.

As ever
Just
Jim

Why Bums Drink

I've never been a bum, but I do have times of melodrama when the curtain of the future draws back and I'm alone and old in the city, broke and thirsty too, working a bunch of strangers for sweet wine money. It must take place in the city because to be a bum, you must be anonymous. Borrow money in the country and eventually you have to pay it back, and its hard to panhandle around a small town bar without pissing someone off. Age is important because young panhandlers are just out of work, whereas old men sleeping in alleys and drunk tanks don't have work left to do. There must be women who are bums, but I've never met one, probably because they approach women for handouts. Here are a few bums I've met.

BOSTON ONE

I was working in a bookstore in bargain basement Boston, on Washington Street, sitting up high by the cash register, listening to ponderous bookstore classical FM musak, watching for paperback book thieves, and eating shit food. In from the slushy sidewalk came a fellow in a bum's uniform, overcoat, baggy pants, scuffed shoes, grey hair, and hungry grin. His right eye was swollen shut and dripping something yellow down along his nose. He put a slushy black nylon rat-tailed comb down next to my hamburger, and began genuflecting all over the front of the store, doing little stoned curtsies, saying that I was King John come back after these many years to deliver the country, and that he'd brought me a gift as greeting. I gave him fifty cents, and, as his king, commanded him to go to Boston General about his eyes. I promised him a dollar if he could bring back proof that he had seen the doctor.

He came back the next night with the bad eye smeared over with Vaseline. He claimed the people at the hospital had given him a tube of salve and told him to get out. I believe that sort of thing can happen in this country, so I gave him the dollar and asked him his name. He said it was Raymond L. Ditmars, and wandered out the door. When I was in high school I had read the biography of a herpatologist named Raymond L. Ditmars, and didn't remember the part about our meeting in Boston. I never saw the bum again.

PINOLE

Natchez isn't a city but its got a big numbers game running through it in the mornings, and a real ritzy set of rich white people living days in the court house and nights in big pig homes on the banks of the Mississippi. Pinole lived there. He said his real name was Robin Hockett, because he robbed it, then he hocked it. He was between thirty-five and fifty five, when I met him, and was carrying a rope over one shoulder. His sweatshirt had TREE KING crayoned on the back. His teeth were about gone but he talked fast and hustled hard. His daughter thought he was crazy, and told him so frequently. He had been busted for public intoxication so many times, and he owed so many days to the City of Natchez, that the cops would come and find him when they needed work done in the dump. But when Pinole got tired of working, he would just walk away from the dump and start bumming wine money around the juke joints.

I drank two pints of muscatel with him, me buying. He asked for paper cups with the wine, and we sat at a cafe table. He poured his whole pint in the paper cup and just leaned back and let the wine pour into him. I asked him what he was. "I am an understander of all things. I know the meaning of every word in Webster's dictionary, except for one word. Say, what is the meaning of IT?"

BOSTON TWO

Peter Veres and I were on a cultural outing, watching women, sitting on a bench in the Fens close to the Museum of Fine Arts, when a bum wandered down the path by the pond and plopped down beside us. He had two-thirds of a pint of Wild Irish Rose Wine in his left hand. He took a little hit, passed the bottle to me and roughed out a whisper: "Pope John was a wonderful man." He was crying a snotty sob when we passed the last third back to him.

Pretty soon he was shuffling around in front of the bench with an empty bottle and singing a crying song like:

I love you trooooooooooooly,
Honest to God I do.
I love you trooooooooooooly,
Father, I was made for you.

That went on for a few minutes, then, in the middle of his act he just flashed, like a bird waking up, and changed into a very alert, dry person. He looked through us and said: "What I really want to do is suck your dicks."

The wine was gone. Peter and I went to the museum.

THE CIRCLE GAME PANHANDLING CONSPIRACY.

The idea is to collectivize the process of living on the city streets with no money, and introduce the concept of sharing into a stingy (stin geee) scene. It works like this: Lets say we are ten bums living and working in the same neighborhood. Even with an unlimited stream of total strangers pouring down the sidewalks, we are going to have more trouble getting money for what we need if all ten of us are trying to keep up with the traffic than if just one person is out there hustling hard at the few people who are probably going to come across anyway. So, we draw lots, numbers from one to ten, and draw a circle on the sidewalk, or use a trash can if we prefer. Number one gets the circle, and gets to tell what he wants from it. Lets say a bottle of wine. Number two goes out to hustle for an hour, and everybody else hangs close to the circle. When number two comes back, he puts his earnings in the circle, and if there is enough, number one gets his wine, number two gets the circle, and number three goes out to hustle for an hour. Number one must report back to the circle when he can, say four hours, or whenever he has to go hustle for number ten. It will only work if it lasts longer than three or four pints of wine, and if there is an area set aside, a turf, where people in the game wouldn't be hustling unless it was their turn.

Somebody, maybe Tom Grissom, told me this was being done in SF.

DRINKING.

If you drink to get stoned, or to participate in the general metamorphic trends, but you don't like to get sick or hung over, just blasted and temporarily truthful and happy, then drink straight hard liquor and beer chasers. Mixed drinks will kill you with twitches and nervous conversation. Wine is healthy and natural, like vanilla, and not so sudden as whiskey, but when wine is used as a food and fuel, it burns out your memory and gives you the runnies. Don't worry about all the cigarettes you smoke when you drink, because the alcohol is harder on your body than the smoke. Try smoking only when you are drinking (science). If you don't like what you are drinking, then don't drink it (philosophy). Buy someone a drink (economics). Pass the bottle around (politics).

Bums drink because, to them, it feels good to be drunk. Beggars can be boozers.

Last night I slept on a subway grate,
In a windy part of town.
Came in once on a westbound freight.
Dammed old city's got me down.
Wake up mornings with nothing in my coat,
But a few more bugs and me.
Wrote a check I shouldn't have wrote,
in Nashville Tennessee

Bums in the alleyway
Waiting for a new day
Baby, don't you ever say,
You saw me there.

and so forth

I can't get no further right now

J.D.

"PEBBLE BEACH'

The Stanfords are kind to me. They live in Pebble Beach and as I hoe and pull and trim their weeds and such, they will always bring me a cup of fresh hot coffee with real cream. Then while I drink I can glance way across the golf course to the ocean—about the distance of a V.W. bùs and 10,000 air mail postage stamps end to end.

This area of the coast is remarkable as a 'wild life' sanctuary: antelope watch me pull weeds, pigeons and gulls play territorial games, and seals bark to the rising fog. "R R R."

Parked behind the fancy gates of the driveway is a flag pole with an American flag which has been waving full-time recently.

I believe this is so that if strangers land on the coast—night or day—they will know that they've landed in America and a free cup of coffee.

Wally Partymiller
Seaside, California

Rascal Flats, Oklahoma

Shed not the bitter tear . . .

Okalahoma tallies a long and bloody account with badmen. Back in territorial times, dozens of U.S. deputy marshals were gunned down here by ugly desperadoes.

I have seen their lairs. Just a sawed off six-gun shot from Tulsa, outlaws skulked in a pecan grove called Rascal Flats. Atop a rocky robbers roost in the Panhandle, bandits kept vigil over the Santa Fe Trail's Cimmarron cutoff and galloped out to prey on passing wagon trains. Yes, and the vengeful Daltons rode through the land of the redman, Black Jake, Oklahoma Al, and Fast Steve rode in the local fearsome Fieldhouse gang scouraging the territory at will, and the train and bank robbin' Doolin outfit, the vicious Buck gang . . .

I know where pistol-packing shotgun-totin' Belle Starr rests in eerie loneliness, though her epitah adjures one not to weep. She died in the saddle with her silver tip boots on, this formidable horse thief and consort of renegades, friend of the James Brothers; someone shot her in the back. They buried her face down on her own land not too far from Hooker in eastern Oklahoma. Some knew her affectionately as Rosie; pretty as the petals and sweet as the scent but tougher than the thorns. The grave lies past a plum thicket, beyond an alfalfa patch, through a grassy field fringed with sycamores and blackberry vines, to a forgotten and scrub-tangled knoll above the river. I couldn't find no trace of the old cabin though it had stood within feet of her tombstone. Ah, Belle, I thought aloud, lying amid weeds and wildflowers, do you know the words they buried you with?

> Shed not for her the bitter tear
> Nor give the heart to vain regret
> Tis but the casket that lies here,
> The gem that filled it sparkles yet

Frederic David
Plainview Press

**NOW THE MOST AMAZING
FISHING DISCOVERY EVER**
A revolutionary new fish lure
that swims under its own power
flops on its side like a crippled minnow
buzzes like a dying insect
it plunges through the water
driving pan fish game fish
salt water fish into a frenzy
Get savage bites that can't pull loose
from your hook no need to pull it
or tug it its completely self-propelled
simply cast or drop this fish catcher
in the water and start hauling in those eyepoppers
it'll be the fishing thrill of your life
order now and reccive a free waterproof carrying kit
get the limit every time and amaze your friends
with the lure that swims under its own power

Under rocks ware rocks cant be found you may fien if the dezier stong ennufe, a hole. It is sed that he who fineds the hole of mistory is that of a selected few. It would seme that thies few allso are the only people that would go looking for shouch a thing in the first place, and this is very true. If we as on lookers were to go on a hunt shouch as this, curiosty would be the greatest reison for us to atemted a surich of this naither. But our harts would not be with us in the serach and we'd sone give up. For what is a hole that we know nouthing about. It is to us apposutly nothing. It is for this reacen that most cant be part of the few that at lest find this mistory hole. I say at least find, for a fery good and logegell reacen becase apon the deaskory of this hard to come by hole. De-pinsen on the manor of how the indeasle reates to what he or she as the case maybe just put their foot in.

Up to this earth saking cliamak that has you on the edge of your seats I think it only faer to fealin the large gap of not knowing But to do this Ill have to explane a lot more about this dam hole. first, why is it under a rock?

Steven Tussey

Ellsinore Mo.
R2 Feb

Dear Sir—

I don't exactly understand just what you would want, but I could write from now on, on a 1000 subjects all true and of 1000 places.

But you know after knowing 12 murderers that got by with it then the 17th of Jan these murders of Bob Kitterman & Bertha & Roberta folks I've known and loved for 14 years I am ready to commit murder.

I'd just love to shoot Dealy Cowin Rector.

Most young folks will work if they get a chance.

But as you know this child labor law is 99% the cause of so much restlessness rioting and such. Oh here I go again.

But really I know any child even 4&5 needs to have a few simple chores he can feel responsible for and given more as they grow. (Darn if I am to write. I must stop eating or you will get half of my foods on this letter Ha)

No really—when I was young I could see so many injustices just as of today. So my form of rebellion took the form of marrying a handsome "stinker from the sticks" and leaving Indianapolis, Indiana.

I firmly believe I am safe in saying I've walked at least 20,000 miles after dark, for relaxation and a few times from or because of emergencies in these 50 years.

Just recently I took a moonlight walk of two miles instead of taking a sleeping pill or laxative it works believe it or not.

Well if you should have any preference for a subject for other editions. Select one and I will try to give you your moneys worth for I can use any & all extra. I will list things I can tell you about then you can choose for I don't imagine you'd want 2 murder stories a month or 2 animal stories you see what I mean.

good wishes from
"Ozark Mert'

1. 12 murders (would fill 10 books in my life)
2. Reaming open wilderness by hand here in '73
3. Raising all FOOD or FLOWERS or CROPS
4. Raising COWS—HORSES—HOGS CHICKENS—DUCKS—SHEEP—pheasant—TURKEYS—HOUSES—
5. Terracing land to save our precious top soil—just as those indians in PERU S.A. did 400 years ago did it still works
6. Digging ponds even on a steep hillside. I've done it, one 20 yrs ago still holds like a jug.
7. I have built five house & cabins in 4 states this one is the worst. For both my TIME & CASH were short
8. "Jingle Bell sleighing with 2 horse hook up in winters oh man what kids nowdays miss
9. "Camping out—really camping" My two oldest girls and I used to camp out 1 or 2 night a week rain or snow for years
10. I did one night this winter as I got lost crossing or trying

to cross country to a friends as my old car played out and thats a fall story

11. Ive delivered 55 babies 4 of my own 22 grand kids and one 2½ lbs great grand daughter that the doctors said was NOT EVEN THERE.

12. Haunted house & his aunt that was a Seer or WITCH.

I'll get you a bunch of picture for future use. But now all I have are colors.

Mrs. Myrtle F. Bain

I've lived ever since 6 or 7 years old under an alias and did not know anything about it till April of 71.

13-14-15

I drove a truck for 10 years over 8 states for over 2,250,000 miles from 49 to 60 and never hit anyone. I WAS hit 8 times in a 22 mon. period nothing serious NO BLOOD

I wore out 6 trucks 13 cars and about ready for another truck this time from 1939 to 73. Of course I've driven lots in the last 3 yrs My old 66 Ford Ranch wagon has about quit. I need a truck for I always have a load going out or coming into.

But I'll say now girls or wives that could STAY HOME & keep things in order & have time to sew, crochet, paint, or do what they want and aren't doing so are sure crazy.

Even tho I dont have too much money Man I am so happy to be able to stay home. Oh I know some consider me crazy. But as long as it doesn't HURT I don't care course I dont lead the order I'd like but so what I dont care I have a 6 yr old 3 legged cat—as sure as I straighten the throw rugs she proceeds to have a rassling match and balls them up and smiles at me.

So I told her honey if you are having fun go ahead momma doesnt care.

Ive always called myself Moma to ever CAT, DOG, SHEEP, CALF, pig, chick & all things Ive raised.

As a child mom would not allow us to have a pet of any sort "superstitious" but I promised myself if I lived to be grown Id have pets. Ive bent over backwards at it.

This spring I had 15 cats (3 adults) 11 dogs a pup, + a mother thru 9 pups. I did. I did not keep them long. Tho now I just have ming toy and one of the nine thats almost as big as a horse NOW and 3 adult cats.

I will list more later.

I could write a 100 or most factual stories about Indiana Kentucky and these Ozarks and no FICTION at all.

1959—About my grandfather whom daddy never saw but he outlived dad several years. I accidently located him after dad dies here in these Ozarks.

Also 2 YEARS AGO I found my grand mothers uncle who came to Ripley County way back in the 1800s and disappeared but I found him and his family in '71 all dead of course.

Also the most incredible thing from 3 yrs old I felt there was a difference somewhere, some way, a mystery oh Man WHAT A ONE! Over the years I'd overhear a few words or a *sentence*. On my 48th birthday I heard parts of 2. Too much for 6 or 7 years I nearly died often. Then 4 MONTHS AGO I had the most incredible experience—I WALKED UP TO MYSELF yep thats really the LIVING end really as a month ago my OTHER SELF dropped dead. I aim to write this all out next. the LAST first, etc.

Here comes grandma 'preaching—

you see I just read where the "Good news" paper went FLUNK died.

Now if you use this slick expensive "aristocrat" paper you cant print any more interesting or important "Place" talk than up you used common newspaper paper or quality of this cheap sheet and you would come nearer selling yearly subscriptions as well. I take the organic G.G.T. from Rodale Press, Penn. it on a cheap paper but its a top class magazine its a book (or mag) with a REASON a good reason.

See what I mean?

I do glory in the NO ADVERTISING tho.

Hugh Martin is starting a homesteading school in Oakhurst, California (93644, Box 862), and he wrote "Ozark Mert," offering her $5,000 to come and teach. So she's hired, and here's part of her letter to him.

2-20-73
R2 Ellsinore, Mo.

My dear sir—

After my other letter I was really surprised to hear from you. For you see I truly thot you was playing on folks desires to get back to the natural ways of living.

Yes indeed I've done all the things I told you and maybe a few more. They never seemed odd or fantastic as some seem to think. I can teach you or any other really interested persons.

Oh not at all one "setting." That's why I said 2 yrs. For altho I've been told I gat 90 miles an hr. I know my mind is not that fast. Ha, I've already got a row of oriental onions out and was planning on planting more vegetables Mar 17, if God's willing.

But if you really want me to come out there and can advance me the $5,000 by return mail you get me a map of the location or better still plan to meet me at some well known easily found truckstop. For I hate to drive in cities especially with a loaded truck.

So as my station or Ranch wagon needs new ring job I will trade it in on a new truck and build a high rack so I can bring all my canned foods my deep freeze in case we can get some service in or a large generator. Also I will bring my hens thru. I have framing + wire + plastic to make a four decker coupe. I wont bring much only clothes + bedding + necessities and camp for a bit also + build a camper rig to fit my truck.

But as I said keep your mouth shut or I'd lose my dab of Social Security.

Yes I can feed them 2 meals a day for $1000.—2 yrs. Of course various teams, will have to take K.P. duty at various times also boys and girls alike for thrift in the kitchen can make or break any well set up home.

Sure I will be glad to teach you as well as anyone else, bless you, but I'll tell you now I am a HARD TASK MASTER Ive been told, by some born lazy peoples Ha

Right now I am recuperating from a fall I got 4 wks ago and caught with my left shoulder against the door frame and now that I am getting better I learned I'd cracked the left side of the collar bone and tore the muscles (2½") all loose from the outside of my left arm about half way between elbow and shoulder. Dr. wanted to put me in a cast I said Heck as it was mending OK another couple weeks would not amount to much—as I was not going to go play football or such I could not stand no cast that would be worse and wuss as my mother-inlaw used to say. Oh she was grand.

Be sure to send me the best road map and well marked

route, South.

First I'd better learn where Oakhurst is north of S.F. or east west or crooked from L.A. I know where Santa Clara and Cupertino San Diego and L.A. and S.F. on the maps. I have a niece in S.F. one in Santa Clara and a nephew in between. I say a nephew way I hear it any more he looks like a cross between a bear and a walrus. Last time I saw him he was about 10 now after 3 or 4 wives 7 or 8 kids some married with kids I'll bet he aint a bit prettier than I am. Ha Ha I hope you wont be too disappointed when we meet. For I am the ugliest old hill billy you ever saw So prepare yourself so it wont exactly floor you.

For you see I dont want to be arrested for voluntary man-slaughter right off.

How much are horses out there? Whoa now not race horses just common work stock.

In the mean time you get all the sincere WORKERS up to 1000 persons for you see NO ONE can learn everything at once and as I said before there are 100 phases or more to a successful farm and unless you have diversified farming you can not have a real organized setup.

So with a 100 persons that will only be 10 to start clearing 10 to cut fence post 10 to line out TRUE and dig post holes 10 for trimming poles for the community building frame and 10 more peeling them 10 or 20 start in on the gardens and ever 2 or 3 day or a week rotate 5 or 6 of each group 10 at scalping see it wont be hard to keep 1000 busy an rotate that way all get a chance at all phases of work of course first things come first let me have a graft of your weather there (for its very different from here to Ky.) even so I will know before hand and can plots dates and jobs for the best results. Also let me know do you have severe wind storms there, where we will be.

You know, its really pitiful how peoples in the past 50 years have 90% of them grown up right here in the U.S.A. that are so down right ignorant for all their H.S. diploma and their college degrees. Ph.D.D. MD and all the rest of the alphabet while most any 6th grader of today can tell you how to get to the moon. Most of them even 50 yr old would starve to death or die of fright turn them loose, even this close to a town.

I've had lots of fun in my old life and can tell others how even tho I may not be able to do all I know how to do, again. But I sure hope I can.

I'll leave here by Mar 15 that was my dear daddy's birthdate and I am sure even with a load I can be there by the 29th or 30th. I'll write you every week and call you at say day before I hope to be at the meeting point Say 3-30 about noon or would that inconvenience you at your work. Say better meet OUTside of town so no NOISE about my chix—give me a phone number, TOO.

Before I forget it always have all doors or at least one open-ing inward in case of a landslide or a snowstorm blocking you from opening outward as I had happen to me 5 years ago over in Ky. We had 60" drifts against our door and we were all day getting it opened, never again. Unless there is another door on another END, or SIDE.

11P.M.

As I strained my arm and got it hurting so I can't sleep I am up again, listing jobs so students can choose if they desire what they want to join in doing first to help get our organi-

zation rolling as fast as possible. Instead of waiting till I am out there to do it all while they sit about waiting.

As for the details of our deal there wont be too much to that you can make 2 copies of this other page you sign both and send to me and I'll sign both and send one back to you notarized also.

You know really as many women need to learn this as men for really 9 times out of 10 if a wife wont help and do and can and save foods—as Ive always told mine and Bill admitted time and again if a woman wont make a home not many men will. Today most young folks expect to start in where mom and dad left off instead of starting out small, as most parents did, and gradually building up and avoiding a pack of sky high debts right off.

Thats exactly why there are so many divorces.

Oh gosh here I go preaching again but I think you can see I am right, at least on the out edges.

Oh its another lovely day but I overslept but thats OK for now and my arm has done a little work without paining of course it will take more time for the soreness to leave it.

I shall have to get a store of commissary liscence to buy what few things we will need wholesale. Call and find out what one will cost. HERE its only $12.50.

Thats another rush job a storage building. All such can be pole framed. I do hope part of the land, at least 2/3rd is in usable timber. Of course it would be nice to have some open virgin soil for a quick garden. But usually open land has been wash away almost.

I—Myrtle Bain, agree with Huge Martin—for $5,000 advance to go to Oakhurst California in March to teach as many sincere students up to 1000 for 2 yrs ALL the fundamental phases of organic gardening without POISONS of any kind for $1,000 per student and see that each will get 2 meals a day of good nurishing foods maybe not the fancy garbage as Greta Garbo calls fancy dishes

Signed
Signed
Notarized
   Type 2

Delta Incidents:
The Devil and the Drawbridge

Driving en route to the Sacramento Delta—passing scene after scene, each familiar, or if unfamiliar, not unexpected—is like watching a pleasant, predictable movie until the continuing, unsettling presence of Mt. Diablo starts to addle your sure grip on a scrutable reality. Then the freeway abruptly funnels into the old, rattling, narrow, harrowingly steep ascent of the Antioch Drawbridge. The movie's over and you're caught off guard by the stunning sunshine outside the theater. You immediately forget where you parked.

When you climb uneasily to the giddy 80 foot crest of the span . . . *waaarp* . . . geographies rush apart, land floods horizons, and an accustomed sense of time and space no longer bears as the vista is revealed: downstream the majestic confluence of the Sacramento and the San Joaquin, and waiting immediately, irrefutably below and stretching beyond into unbroken distances: the Delta.

You come off the bridge like off a slide and go winding down the macadam till you've topped a levee and are calmly careening alongside the Sacramento, against its current, the road and the river like two slow freights on parallel tracks, headed different directions, and seeming to merge as they pass. On the far bank lumpy Mokelumne hills melt like lime sherbet into flat pastures and the Delta becomes a two-dimensional plane, interrupted only by stacked clouds piling a high white sky, and the levees like raised veins but aimless as moletracks. Pheasants barely avoid, and falcons note, your progress, and you may observe geese negotiating heaven, or hear them making ready. In winter orchards the bare branches of pear trees are really *roots* seeking the rich air of that climate that has also closed in around you. The light's soft as a solar eclipse: dull gleams spangle the water; a yellow-green patina gilds the land. The serenity is *charged*, and everything seems to be slightly stirring.

This thousand mile maze of connected waterways accomplishes the drainage of more than a third of California, and sectors the Delta into dozens of islands. Each island has its own economy and character; each is largely ignored by and worlds away from five million Bay Area neighbors next door. The Delta exists as a self-contained mini-universe of micro-worlds in collision, and in transit: a 1000 mile square (actually, and appropriately, triangular) alluvial plain of blackland,

Baine Kerr

clay, peat fields, bogs, and tule marsh, that is given forms and functions by levee-walled rivers, sloughs, bayous and lakes. The triangle is principally described by the San Joaquin's route west from Stockton, and the Sacramento's meanderings south from its namesake city. Near Antioch the rivers converge, ebbing almost at the skirts of Mr. Diablo.

From Walnut Creek in a clockwise crescent to Antioch, a homely exurban sprawl hugs Diablo's base but is forbidden by law to trespass further. In the north of the mountain, guttering the shore from the Carquinez Straights, to Suisun, Grizzly and Honker Bays, to the mouth of the Delta, are the factories and refineries of such behemoths as Standard Oil, Shell, PG&E, Johns Mannville, U.S. Steel, and Dupont—a foul-breathed skid row of unregenerate industry whose needs for the wine of the Delta's saltless waters are cravings that can't be slaked. Threading the cities and plants together is a lifeline system of interstates issuing through this valley, up to Vallejo, down to San Jose, and across to Oakland and the thumping heart of the Bay Area.

Strangely inscrutable is the fact that high above this belt of progress Mt. Diablo is alive with mountain lions, more lions than ever in the last two centuries, padding wooded slopes, prowling the edges of cliffs, overlooking the mechanisms of empire on one side, the Delta on the other, and, joining the two, the new rival to Diablo as watchtower and gateway: the black span of the Antioch Bridge.

Only ocean going vessels are allowed to pass beneath the bridge coming from the Delta. Heavy industry respects the same boundary from the other direction. Highway 4 proceeds as far as the entrance to the bridge's precipitous span, then ceases. Since the world, for reasons known only to itself, no longer dares to transgress the Delta (its farmland may be too rich to exploit, or its danger of fire and flood too great), at Antioch you cross not the San Joaquin but oceans, and you're set down in another continent. The Delta's tricky enough to spare change a pickpocket. Nothing is constant. The kaleidoscope turns of itself. Trees seem to move like Birnham Wood. Featureless horizons can close like a wrench, or completely release. The Lower Delta, its peat fields oxidyzing, is always diminishing, while in the Upper Delta the mountain is coming to Mohammed by the ton from the Sierras; the meek flatlands are inheriting the earth. None of the two lane roads follows a straight line: nor do the sloughs which all look alike, and in fact are the same eddying waterway that alters at every bend.

This freshwater is moon driven, with four tides daily that can vary by 5 feet. Islands can flood on the brightest Spring day; if the wrong levees break everything could go— all the Delta, even the capitol city, reclaimed by water. Tule fog comes in on panther paws, blotting out the very nose on your face, striking you blind. But climb a sapling and, across sheer whiteness clung to the ground like gauze, you'll see forever.   * * *

"Night Scene on the San Joaquin River—Monte Diablo in the Distance." Scenes of Wonder and Curiousity in California. J.M. Hutchings. Courtesy Bancroft Library. From DELTA WEST, Scrimshaw Press.

"You imediately forget where you've parked..."

Mt. Diablo has traditionally been a place where men of reason were seized by dreams of Eldorado, the still undiscovered land of limitless treasure, the city of gold. The Diablo Range commands the first view of California's interior, and the vista from Diablo's summit has corrupted many a once sound mind. The first Europeans to behold this panorama were members of the Crespi-Fages expedition 200 years ago. Fray Juan Crespi's reaction, as he gaped from the prospect of the mountain's western peak, was prototypical: looking east at what no white man had ever seen before, the good Father envisioned infinite empire.

Rancher Bill Shelton in his pear orchard.
Photo by James Motlow

It wasn't sight of the Delta that suckered thousands into romantic greed. Except for Jedediah Strong Smith (who preferred the Delta's furs to mountain's metals, and who, having been the first man to make it overland to California, already knew the score) nearly everyone literally overlooked the brimming Eden at Diablo's base. Seekers, instead, would lift up their eyes unto the distance, goggle at the dazzling, crystal chain of the Sierra Nevada, and oggle the rolling blue hills of the Motherlode. In less than a year, forty thousand forty-niners slugged across the Delta or steamed in style up the Sacramento, not giving a tinker's damn about the graceful flatlands they passed, chasing bright chimera dancing on a jagged, sparkling horizon. Years later, after the fever abated and Eldorado had returned to hiding, John Muir, likewise smitten for the first time by the spectacle of the Sierra, declared: I would name them THE WALL OF LIGHT.

The name Diablo, as you might surmise, is a whole nother story. The mountain was christened in 1806 after the Balgones tribe routed a Spanish battalion at its base. As a certain General Vallejo told it: "There was a hot fight, which was won by the Indians. Near the end of the fight, a person, decorated with remarkable plumage, and making strange movements, suddenly appeared. After the victory, the person called *Puy* in the Indian tongue, departed toward the mountain. The soldiers heard that this spirit often appeared thus, and they named the mountain DEVIL."

I (with less eloquence than Muir) would name it SENTINAL, the guard at the gate of the Delta. Or DRAGON, the Keeper of the Fleece; or OLD INSCRUTABLE, all covered with mist, where *Puy,* standing watch over the memory of his murdered people, waylays Argonauts and wards off encroaching America from a lost and gentle land.

* * *

During and after the gold rush great paddle-wheel steamers plowed the Sacramento to and fro the Motherlode. The massive *Navajo* is still wedged and rotting in a cut in a levee where its side paddles were used as emergency pumps to drain flooded Mandeville Island. The famous *Delta Queen,* now a relic berthed in Cinncinnati, was named for her reign over this western delta. Navigating the Delta has always been a bizarre and chancy affair. Those houseboats whose pilots dare stray beyond sight of marinas are continually getting lost, or left high and dry by low tide. Every summer, they say, you'll see some dummy in a houseboat dangling by its moorings from a tree, or perched on pilings that were submerged the night before. And many a plush riverboat, full to the gills with gamblers, gold dust and demon rum, with miners, forty niners and fallen Clementines, would miss hours, even days, circling off the beaten slough, and could, despite guiding dead on Mt. Diablo, somehow wind up stranded in an unchartered backswamp, paddles hopelessly clogged by tules, the very symbol of Eldorado Lost.

In '49 one Bayard Taylor took passage from the gold country on the stately *Senator,* a huge, expensive, red-carpeted riverboat brought west from staid Boston to service a wilder wealth. "After passing the town of Sutter . . ." Taylor wrote, "We steamed rapidly down the river, with Monte Diablo far before us. Owing to the twists and turns of the stream, it was but an uncertain landmark, now appearing on one side and now on the other." Once in the Delta the *Senator* promptly followed a false channel up tapering steamboat slough, running "in among the boughs of trees," backing into banks. She finally emerged on the river and churned on out of the labyrinth, into Suisun Bay, where that old devil, "Monte Diablo . . . wore a blue mist over his scarred and rocky surface, which looked deceptively near."

Except for the gigantic spire of the teevee relay tower behind Locke, Diablo remains the signal landmark of the Delta, abruptly rising above the plain almost 4000 feet—a vertical spread as great and striking as that of most mountains three times its height. But Diablo is "uncertain," is, in fact, about as constant as a March snowflake or an icecube on the sidewalk in July. In the summer its meadows yellow; in spring Diablo's green would turn Ireland brown with envy. Its three faces-of-Janus are cast in shapes and shades that vary by the hour. It is now a vague looming cloud-like form; soon a beautifully intricate alp; then a stark apparition,

1. The Niger   2. The Amazon   3. The Orinoco   4. The Mississippi   5. The Sacramento

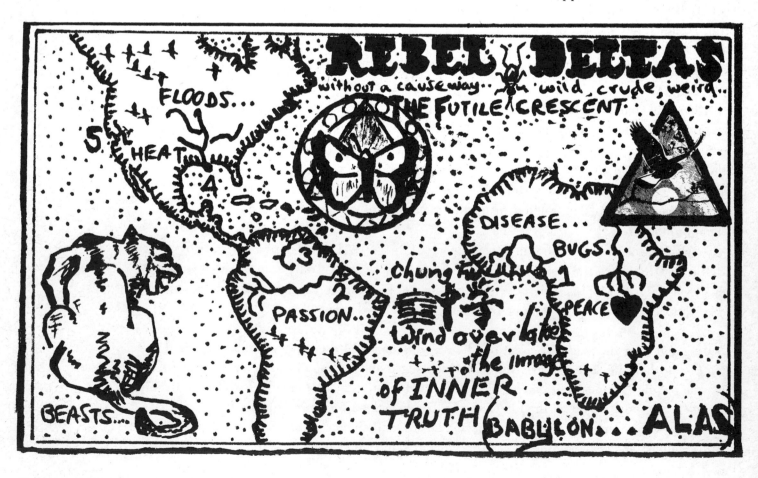

some lone cone rising from the sea; next a fierce, gothic, forbidding Teton rupturing earth and sky—a mountain that has been dreamt before, and imagined as a child; at times lush, benign and beckoning; at other times, invisible.

The gifts of Proteus—mobility, prophecy, the capacity for infinite change—don't suit a landmark. Diablo, rather than mark the land, seems to respond to it, and perhaps to preside over it, ministering its needs. It's said that you can keep a sense of direction in the Delta by referring to an imagined, roughly north-south axis between Diablo and the teevee tower. But as far as I can tell, unless you happen to be astride that axis you're liable to be up shit's slough without side paddle-wheels.

The problem might only be parallax: the phenomenon of apparent motion or change in direction, such as your finger jumping from side to side when you look at it with one eye then the other; such as stars seeming to move in orbits when stars are fixed and we're the ones moving.

Mt. Diablo makes parallactic leaps all over the place. One minute it's on your far right, the next, your far left; it'll be straight in front, then suddenly sneaking up behind. And it has this magic ability to approach "deceptively near" or retreat, shrink into the distance. The Locke tower is worse. It seems to wander at will, like the mast of a ghost ship, an electronic *Flying Dutchman* that has taken the place of the *Delta Queen*.

When Dudley and I returned from our first few feckless days in the Delta, at the foot of Diablo we missed, three times running, the same freeway exit to Oakland. Inscrutable? Or was something pulling, keeping us from leaving? And why would it take weeks longer than planned to get to the Delta again unless something was pushing, not wanting me to come?

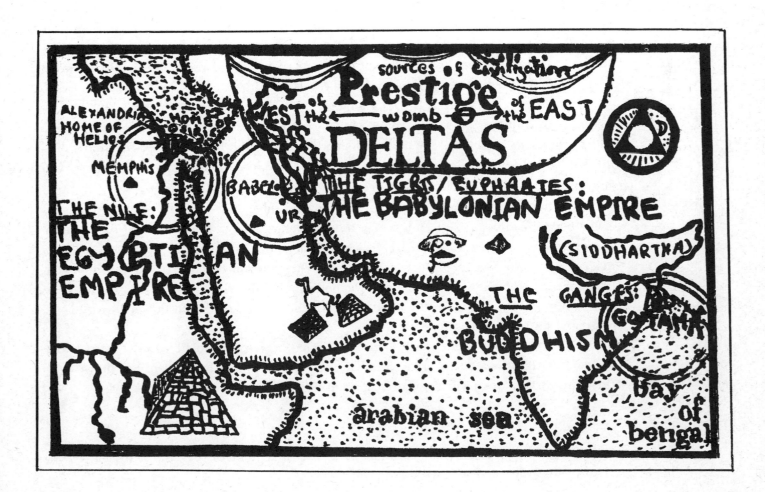

Was he lusting for the same mysteries the leopard sought in the death-white, glistening snows of Kilimanjaro?

I have a hunch we're dealing with something far more profound than optical illusion. One's compass goes haywire in the Delta, according to my hunch, because a magnetic field governs the area. The source of its force is Diablo, a 4000 foot lodestone that has thrown the Delta into scrambled patterns, that attracts homeless cultures, and repels empire.

Driving back, after a recent trip, Diablo looked its most unearthly: immense, its top half obscured by a furious blue-black roil of clouds—a storm—though the rest of the sky was subdued and mostly cloudless. The late sun behind the mountain threw four or five shafts of apricot light through vents in its Olympian anger. As I approached the Antioch Bridge, watching Diablo, I wondered about an incident that I'd heard about that morning.

An enormous mountain lion had appeared on the bridge, brazen in the bright moonlight, at the height of the span, driven by some feral desperation from the fastness of the mountain. But drawn, I wondered, to what: to cross to the far shore, to the Delta? Or did the panther, most perfect of beasts, strain for something more magnificent than he, for some wild dream of Eldorado? When he fell writhing and wailing from the drawbridge, shot by a highway patrolman's rifle, was he lusting for the same mysteries the leopard sought in the death-white, glistening snows of Kilimanjaro . . .

Or was it *Puy*, the Indian Spirit, demon of Diablo, who caterwauled into the cold night at the cold world below, at the broad pale San Joaquin, the Dupont plant and bay downriver, the cities further west; who screamed . . . taunting his enemies, crying his loss.

From a book in progress about the Sacramento Delta and the Rio Grande border by Baine Kerr, with photographs by Dudley and Barbara DeZonia.

THE LAND AT LOCKE

I would be born again
   at a nesting ground
   where birds come
from the farthest corners
     from every cold
which way
   and in this delta sky
they are all still
all at home,   *singing.*
     For people
there's shame in sight *of*
the realistic beauty
     of a sunset a spectrum
of winter sky
in a kindly climate—
there is an aura *that does not burn*
   all over the horizon
   a pink ripeness
   it's like watching
   an old father grow young
   a fantastic process this
   orderly losing of everything
   we were never meant to have.

       Vicky White

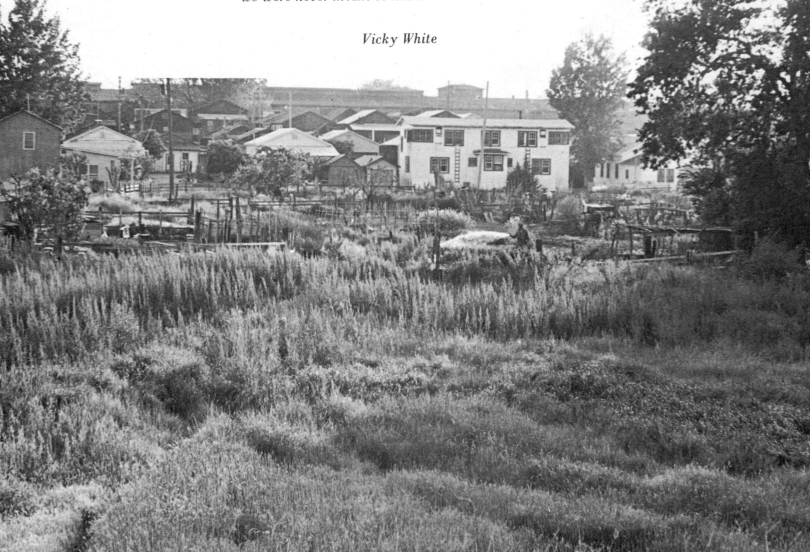

Zen Bastard to the Rescue
An Introduction

PAUL KRASSNER IS THE MAN WHO, as the curtain closed on the opening-night performance of the anti-war play *Mac Bird,* leapt to his feet and shouted, "Fuck you, Walter Kerr!"; the man who soul-kissed a nun (actually former hooker Margo St. James) in the lobby of the San Francisco International Airport while dozens of dumbstruck travellers stood a-gaping; the man of whom the late American Nazi Party kommandant George Lincoln Rockwell once said, "You got balls of steel. For a Jew you shoulda been a Nazi."

Paul Krassner is also the best satirical journalist in America.

The terms ordinarily applied to satirists—"irreverent," "iconoclastic," and the like—are as inadequate to a description of Krassner as "felon" is to describe Charles Manson, or "religious" to describe Jesus Christ. Next to the social, cultural, and political satire he has been publishing for the past dozen years in his magazine *The Realist,* the work of such popular wits as Russell Baker and Art Hoppe seems as bland as mush, milktoast turning soggy in the curdling milk of sacred cows. Krassner is a latter-day Mark Twain, a stoned-out Ambrose Bierce, a priapic H.L. Mencken; in his own time his only peer was his dear friend Lenny Bruce—whose obituary Krassner wrote and published a full two years before Bruce's death, so that (as he told Bruce at the time) "when you *really* die, my reaction will be pure, I won't have to think, on some level of consciousness, 'Oh, shit, now I'll have to write an obituary.' "

The Realist—of which Krassner is founder, publisher, editor, chief correspondent, and (according to the masthead) "Zen bastard" —made its debut in 1958, at the height of the first post-McCarthy wave of anti-communist hysteria ("I've come to ask you to stop harping about H-bomb tests," says John Foster Dulles to Bertrand Russell in an imaginary dialogue in one of those early issues. "You're only aiding the Communist cause . . ."), and it has been determinedly, ubiquitously chronicling the Twentieth Century Nightmare ever since: in the early Sixties Krassner published crusading superatheist Madalyn Murray O'Hair's attacks on the repressive authoritarianism of the Catholic establishment, himself conjecturing that "So-called 'flying saucers' are actually diaphragms being dropped by nuns on their way to Heaven." In 1962, when Adolf Eichmann was languishing in an Israeli jail cell awaiting execution, Krassner published the "rumor" that Eichmann had written a song entitled "If I Knew You Were Coming, I'd Have Baked a Kike," and marvelled in print at "how all the Caryl Chessman fans finked out on Adolf Eichmann." He was on hand again in 1964, when Leary and Alpert were offering weekend consciousness-expansion seminars at Millbrook ("I'm a terrible failure when it comes to meditation," he confessed. "All I do is sit there and say to myself, 'Well, here I am, meditating . . . yup . . . that's the way it goes . . .''). And he was with the Yippies in Chicago in 1968, wondering "how many years can [we] go on listening to General Westmoreland say that we have to continue the bombing as long as they keep using those antiaircraft guns?" and fantasizing an apocalyptic TV spectacular (" . . . Joe Pyne engages in a wooden leg duel with Al Capp . . . The Flying Nun goes down on Johnny Carson . . . Nelson Rockefeller cheekily applies the new TV pancake makeup Bishop Sheen to Richard Nixon's jowls . . . The Federal Marshals' Atonal Chorale and Percussion Ensemble, accompanying themselves on their children's skulls with nightsticks, sing the everbeautiful 'Where Have All the Flowers Gone?' . . . ") and at last concluding, wearily but intrepidly, "Fuck them, oh Lord, they know exactly what they do!"

But *The Realist's* most audacious caper was the 1967 publication of a piece entitled "The Parts That Were Left Out of the Kennedy Book," in which Krassner describes, brilliantly recreating William Manchester's turgid, homogenized prose style, Jacqueline Kennedy's discovery of Lyndon Johnson standing over the President's coffin performing an act someone has described as "necrophilia" upon the wound in her slain husband's throat. "It was," Krassner wrote later by way of explaining why he'd perpetrated the hoax, "the mutual simultaneous culmination of Jackie's and Lyndon's unconsciousnesses." And of course the reaction to the piece was exactly what Krassner, taking Jonathan Swift's *A Modest Proposal* as his catechism, had known all along it would be, which is to say that it ranged from cautious acceptance ("One can never be quite certain," wrote one critic, "how much of the revealing journalism is Krassner's imagination, and how much is plain fact . . .") to querulous disputation ("The body of JFK was supposedly in a casket," a London doctor solemnly declared. "Therefore, short of lifting out the corpse, an act of inverted para-fellatio would be physically impossible . . .") to outraged *denial* ("The incident, of course, never took place," sputtered UPI columnist Merriman Smith). Thereby proving once again (as one of Krassner's readers pointed out), that when William Blake said, "Everything possible to be believed is an image of the truth," he damn well knew whereof he spake. But, as usual, it is Krassner himself who gets the last word: To an interviewer who asked if he "really condoned necrophilia," he replied, "Yes, but only between consenting adults." And besides, he added later, "For all we know, it might have been an act of love."

In the main, though, Krassner is so acutely alert to the already existent madness which rules all our lives that he has little need to invent occasions to inspire more of it. "Was it *my* fault," he pleads, his shrewdness masked in wide-eyed innocence, "that when Pope Paul visited this country, the band at Kennedy Airport played 'Hello, Dolly'?" Thus it was that, in 1966, when *Time* magazine "discovered" a faintly malodorous American literary phenomenon it labelled "black humor," and identified Krassner as a leading exponent of it, he explained, again a little wearily, that "black humor is in bad taste by definition because it's about the way life *is,* and life happens to be in bad taste."

Incredible times, remarkable man.

—ED McCLANAHAN

All quotations are from **How a Satirical Editor Became a Yippie Conspirator in Ten Easy Years,** *by Paul Krassner.*

HIP ODD COUPLE
by Paul Krassner
With Annotations by Stewart Brand

How a Yippie Conspirator Left the Big Apple and Learned the Truth about Frying Marbles

MY, UH, ROOMMATE, STEWART BRAND of *Whole Earth Catalog* dropout fame, left a handwritten note for me on the table beside my bed in the hospital:

9:30 pm
Hello Paul—
Since you're merely flipped out (stoned) and not dying, I'm gonna go meet my date. Background: You passed out in the hallway—at 7:30 pm. I brought you to UC Emergency Hospital at 8. You started coming around at 8:30 and let us know you'd had some THC (and LSD?). Wavy (Gravy) or others may drop by later. I'll call in from time to time and I'll check by later.

—Stewart
P.S. You promised to tell the American people the truth. You also remarked that "It's OK!" Hope you remember details.

When I came to, as they say in comic books, I tried to fly. That's how I can always tell whether I'm dreaming. If I'm able to fly, then I know it's a dream. But if I can't fly, that doesn't necessarily mean it *isn't* a dream. For instance, maybe the only reason I couldn't fly out of that hospital bed at 11:30 that night was because I was attached to it by restraining devices. Moreover, I might have only *dreamed* that someone had placed those leather straps upon my wrists and ankles.

I realized I was awake, but I had no idea where I was or how I had gotten there.

I'd been investigating the Charles Manson case for almost a year then. I had come to the conclusion that Charlie and his combination victim-executioners were taking the rap for a scenerio that could be considered the American equivalent to Nazi Germany's Reichstag Fire. So it was only natural that I should now assume that I was in some government laboratory being debriefed by the CIA.

I remembered a doctor asking me, "Okay, tiger, what'd you take?" I started to answer, "T-H-" I was tempted to spell out T-H-E U-L-T-I-M-A-T-E D-R-U-G, but my motor control was not exactly a tightrope walkers's prayer, and I had to struggle just to utter T-H-C period.[1]

---

[1] Affording us bedsiders enormous relief. We didn't know what the hell Paul was down with. At the THC announcement the doctor smiled and relaxed, "Let him enjoy it." On other subjects Paul had been equally loquacious. In answer to any question whatever ("How you doin, Paul?"), he would intone, "My name is Paul Krassner. I am editor of the REALIST. P-A-U-L-K-R-uh-A-S-uh-S-N-R-E." (the hospital is an appropriate place to be sic.) —S.B.

2

THC. TetraHydroCannabinol. Four Wet Cannibals. —S.B.

3

I had been building a bed while Paul stood in the hall door reporting the latest turns in his hassle with Scientology and L. Ron Hubbard. After a prolonged peculiar silence I peeked in the hall to find that Paul was gone, replaced by a vacant-eyed robot which opened and closed its mouth, made a drifty gesture with a tube of toothpaste, and said "Nn . . . Gn . . ." Terrifying. All I could think was that the Scientologists must've finally zapped him. After a while the thing toppled like a tree, crash, and commenced baying into my buffalo rug. I phoned a friendly shrink for consultation. He listened to symptoms—Paul was by now into a howly slow-motion laugh, "Haaaaaa haaaaaaa haaaa aaaaa"— and suggested I take him to UC Hospital (the most benign emergency room in San Francisco) for evaluation. I told the stunning nurse, "He's editor of the REALIST." "Is that so?" she said politely. Paul spelled his name for her. —S.B.

4

You were doing fine with the buffalo rug. —S.B.

Roommates Paul Krassner (*rt.*) and Stewart Brand at the Whole Earth Demise Party.

"...A hallowed tradition of brotherhood.

Damon and Pythias.
Archie and Jughead.
Huntley and Brinkley.
Stanley and Livingston.
Amos and Andy.
Simon and Garfunkel.
Don Quixote and Pancho Sanza.
Yin and Yang.
Bound and Gagged.
Tarred and Feathered.
Drawn and Quartered.
Brand and Krassner..."

This photo and the one on preceding page by Christopher Springmann/STAR.

At 7 o'clock that evening, just as Walter Cronkite was once again sharing his impersonal mantra, *Andthatsthewayitis,* with senior citizens of all ages, I was gluttonously snorting the last of my THC stash.[2] Too much, as they say. Over a hundred acid trips and I'd never really lost my balance between participation and observation, but now I felt a touch of perverse pride. I was having my first overdose.

A couple of my friends, Margaret Duratt and Dan O'Neill, were leaning over my hospital bed. I managed to ask two questions: "Have they been taping what I've been saying?" And, "Did they inject me with any drug?" I suppose that's the way a media freak brings things into focus.

Stewart Brand's note on the table also helped.

He had brought me to the hospital with the aid of a pair of students from the Zen Center where he goes to worship every Saturday morning with his own black pillow, like a professional table tennis player who carries around a custom-made ping pong racket.[3]

"If I had known it was just dope," he said to me the next day, "I would've put you to bed, but I thought you were having an epileptic fit."

"Did you stick a TV Guide in my mouth like you're supposed to?"[4]

I WAS THE ONLY ONE ON MY BASEBALL TEAM TO USE A SHOEHORN . . .

I'm probably the only person I know who saves old copies of *TV Guide*. It doesn't matter what my basic motivation is. I don't care if my parents toilet-trained me at the age of one month with a whip and a potty-chair. The simple fact is that if you want to know what program you missed six weeks ago, I'm not especially ashamed to admit that I can readily look it up for you.

Stewart, on the other hand, throws things away all the time. He is very neat. He even has filing

cabinets. I have filing cabinets too, but they remain empty. I happen to be a living touchstone for people who need to know that there is somebody around who is even more disorganized than they.

Perhaps it's a possessiveness syndrome. I still have my old shoehorn from junior high school days. I was the only one on my baseball team to use a shoehorn to put my spiked shoes on. I used to get in trouble with the coach because my infield chatter wasn't sincere enough.

Stewart is a cookie freak. He has even been known to eat, unbaked, frozen cookie batter. However, one time I came home with a case of terminal munchies and ate a whole section from his box of sesame graham cookies, leaving only the empty cellophane wrapper as evidence.

Another time I came home looking forward to relaxing in a Carrot Bubble Bath, but the tub was filled with Stewart's potted plants so that they could nourish themselves on water while he was away on a speaking tour. I didn't have the audacity to distrub them.

The closest Stewart and I have come to double-dating was when he cooked dinner for four. He was seeing Carole Levine, and I had gotten a call from Ann Beatts, whom I'd met once at the *National Lampoon* office in New York, so I invited her over. She had curly hair then, but now it was straightened, and I didn't recognize her, so she stood in the kitchen talking to Stewart while I sat in my little bedroom-office watching the TV news. Only after a while did the realization strike us all as to how the choreography had been screwed up.

The prostitutional aspect of the dating system—whereby the male traditionally pays for the female's food and entertainment—has fallen into perspective on those few occasions when Stewart and I have gone out to eat and there is no sex/money role for either of us to play.

Once, at a movie, I remarked to him that even though you were supposed to put your popcorn container or ice cream wrapper on the floor to be swept up by a theater employee, I found it difficult to do so. I want to destroy the government, but I'm a failure at littering. Stewart told me of his trip to Mexico with Stephanie Mills, where the streets were paved with garbage, and there they were, this pair of renowned ecologists, both getting their rocks off throwing stuff on the ground.

Stewart and I are also different in physical appearance. He is tall (6 feet). I'm short (5'6"). He has closely-trimmed blond hair. I have hippie-length curly brown hair. He wears a wristwatch when he sleeps. I don't even wear one when I'm awake.

I am a subdued fanatic against cigarette smoking.[5] Stewart smokes an occasional cigarette. I'm a teetotaler. However, he has turned me on to hot buttered rum. He gave me an $.87 jar of batter for Christmas. I meant to give him a book on *Body Time* but I couldn't find where I'd hidden it.

I will tell Stewart of my latest conspiracy theory. He in turn will give me a copy of *Scientific American* with an article on the mathematics of coincidence.

We often have mini-dialogues. Sample:
Stewart: "What's wrong with being an elitist?"
Paul: "Well, it's not spiritual, I guess."
Stewart: "But all those spiritualist guys are elitists."
Paul: "Well, it's hypocritical, then."
Stewart: "Oh."

It is this constant striving for objectivity that provides Stewart with the impetus to purchase a container of chocolate chip yogurt. He has a strange sweet tooth. In college, his favorite snack was a slice of white bread with butter and white sugar on it.

Stewart is carnivorous and he eats meat. I'm a vegetarian and I eat meat, but only about once a week, usually his leftovers while he's worshipping at the Zen Center.[6]

Stewart drives a car. I've had a car for two years, but I still haven't learned how to drive it. I can operate the glove compartment and the windshield wipers, though. I figure, start with the accesories and work your way up.

Stewart has a telephone-answering machine. So do I. Once I called him and my telephone-answering machine left a message for his telephone-answering machine.[7]

Stewart and I follow a hallowed tradition of brotherhood. Damon and Pythias. Archie and Jughead. Huntley and Brinkley. Stanley and Livingston. Amos and Andy. Simon and Garfunkel. Don Quixote and Pancho Sanza. Yin and Yang. Bound and Gagged. Tarred and Feathered. Drawn and Quartered. Brand and Krassner.

I STOOD THERE WITH MY BARE ASS SMILING OUT OF THE WATERFALL . . .

How had this schizoid partnership come about?

It goes back, for the sake of a sentimental milestone, to the summer of 1963 and my official fake wedding. The ceremony was real enough, but—as planned—the minister was unlicensed in New York. Therefore the marriage wasn't legal. Jeanne and I didn't want to involve the state in our personal relationship; neither then nor when we separated three years later.

5
I'm fairly certain that Paul is the only human being to ask John Lennon to take his cigarette outside. There are but two rules in a Krassner home: 1) No tobacco smoking, 2) No subject is forbidden to discuss.   —S.B.

6
I took Paul along once. We both spent the entire lecture admiring the ear lobe of the girl in front of us, Paul full of complicated moral thoughts on the matter. —S.B.

7
Until it was interrupted by the Phone Company's tape recorder telling our tape recorders to please hang up. Tape recorders are always polite with each other, and I can't say why that bothers me.
          —S.B.

"I was working on the Last Catalog..."

For our, well, honeymoon, we came to San Francisco. I was working with Lenny Bruce on his autobiography, *How to Talk Dirty and Influence People,* and that's where he was. We were supposed to meet him at the Swiss-American Hotel.

Jeanne and I walked around North Beach, passing a barber shop in Chinatown, inside which three Oriental barbers—their scissors, comb and brush having been replaced by a violin, guitar and bass fiddle—were jazzing up a rendition of *Bei Mir Bist Du Schoen,* the old Andrews Sisters' hit song.

Lenny Bruce would've enjoyed that little scene, except that he hardly ever left his room, knee-deep in legal briefs. He was already soul-deep in court cases.

"I'm fighting for ten years of my life," he said gently.

I had been a stand-up comic before starting *The Realist,* and I was scheduled to do a benefit for Lenny at the hungry i. The first new friend I met in San Francisco was Garry Goodrow at The Committee. Jeanne had known him as a saxaphonist and actor in The Living Theatre production of *The Connection.* Now he was a performer in a satirical troupe. I decided to switch from the formality of the hungry i to the funkiness of The Committee. I felt at home there. They even had blown-up cartoons and posters from *The Realist* framed on the walls of their lobby.

It was, incidentally, on the basis of the sale of our red-white-and-blue patriotic *Fuck Communism!* posters that *The Realist* was able to finance the first journalistic probe into why we really got involved in Vietnam, by Bob Scheer, who had co-authored a book on Cuba and was then working as a clerk in the City Lights Book Shop, never dreaming that he would some day marry the waspish daughter of a telephone company executive who would eventually end up living with Tom Hayden who would finally marry Jane Fonda and live revolutionarily ever after.

Anyway, somewhere between the honeymoon and Lenny Bruce and The Committee and City Lights and that Oriental Nairobi Trio, I made a vow to move to the west coast. For eight years I kept busy making that same vow over and over.

Living in New York was breathing involuntarily two packs of cigarettes each day, although you didn't smoke yourself. It was being afraid to go out in your own neighborhood late at night. It was reading an apologia in the *Village Voice* each week on "How I Was Mugged and Learned to Hate Niggers"—signed, *A Former Black.* It was being beaten in the street by a crazed white. It was being robbed at gunpoint while on LSD by six Puerto Rican kids in the NYU Men's Room at a free Hog Farm celebration.

It was beginning to understand that the spreading fear was an orchestrated prerequisite to making a police state desirable. That what was happening was actually what government intelligence agencies *wanted* to happen. Those rotten karma manipulators. You wished it were only paranoia.

Living in New York also had its positive aspects for me. Lots of friends. A wide choice of movies I frequented. Plenty of museums I seldomed. A community radio station—listener-sponsored WBAI-FM—with a standing invitation to go on the air whenever the urge to communicate immediately with a large audience overtook me.

But the ties began to dissolve.

My ex-wife and daughter had decided to leave New York.

My girlfriend's sister was in an airplane accident, and they decided to move to the Virgin Islands on the insurance money. One evening she got a ride from her apartment on the upper east side down to my loft in Greenwich Village, from an organized criminal who had to make his collections on the way. It took four hours. They made stops along the route as if they were conducting a random sample of advertisers in the Yellow Pages. The mob was financing everything from a gay sauna bath to a health food restaurant.

WE DID A LITTLE OM ON THE RANGE . . .

I was scheduled to be a TV talk-show host on Channel 13, but my first appearance was also my last, because I refused to tell the viewers that the woman I was interviewing as Timothy Leary's mother was in reality a character actress, Marily Sokol.

"Welcome to *Free Time,* Mrs. Leary," I had begun. "That's a lovely coat. What kind of fur is it?"

"Oh, it's made of Algerian Camel Hump."

I had first met Marilyn when she was with the San Francisco Mime Troupe. I'd visited the Bay Area as often as I could afford—a peace rally, an abortion conference, a research project, a speaking engagement, a trips festival—but I made my Definite Commitment finally in 1970, while camping out in the Sierras with a few nude cohorts: Margo St. James, a former hooker who is now attempting to unionize prostitutes; Frank Werber, who went from managing the Kingston Trio to managing the Trident Restaurant in Sausalito; Roger Sommers, an architect with the most uproarious laugh I've ever heard.

I found myself confronting a waterfall. I wanted to get under it, but the water in the pond leading to it was freezing painfully cold. Yet a couple of dogs were walking in it quite calmly. I knew that only if I could surrender to the existential impulse right then and there, would I ever leave New York. So I just did it, with one screaming naked plunge. I stood there with my bare ass smiling out of the waterfall, calling out an incoherent chant to commemorate the beautiful illusion of free will.

We visited Gary Snyder, who was building his non-electric dream house with the aid of a bunch of disciples and electric tools. I took a tab of acid to enhance the change my consciousness was already undergoing. Just as it was coming on strong, Gary asked each guest to pump the water-pump one hundred times. I could do that all right. Keeping count was the hard part.

That night all of us sat around a fireplace as if we were rehearsing for a vision of the future. We made our own music, passed along Indian legends, and did a little *Om* on the range.

We talked philosophy. I imprinted on a concept of Robert Duncan that Gary quoted: that if there are no limits, it means there are also no *lower* limits. This morning on the john I was trying to reconcile that notion with some passages from *MAGIC: A Treatise on Natural Occultism* by Manly P. Hall:

> The law or reaction immediately starts incorporating into the organisms the fruitage of the outpoured endeavor, in this way slowly transmuting the entire chain of vehicles into intelligent symbols or images of the path chosen by the consciousness. As one pole or the other slowly grows within the being, the atoms of the opposing substances are slowly crowded or forced out, or sloughed off, for lack of cohesion. The battle of these opposing qualities in the various organisms of life forms the groundwork for the great Indian battle of Kurukshetra, or the Armageddon of Christian theology.
>
> Through this subtle process, the student who lives the white path slowly starves out or else transmutes the powers of the black ray within himself—that is, if he is able to stand the conflict which must first take place in his bodies. On the other hand, the student who takes the black path slowly eliminates or destroys all of the finer principles within, until he becomes a very demon incarnate. Once having destroyed conscience, he does evil for the joy of it . . .
>
> Motive is the key to the problem of magic. Even the greatest of white magicians can become a degenerate in an instant if his motive becomes unworthy. The white magician serves humanity; the black magician seeks to serve himself.

We also talked politics. Gary Snyder told me of someone from the Rand Corporation who had a story to tell. I asked him to pass along my address. The individual turned out to be Daniel Ellsberg. He was an old reader of *The Realist*.

Back in 1967, I had published "The Parts Left Out of the Kennedy Book," whose climactic scene consisted of Lyndon Johnson leaning over the casket as Air Force One dreamed it was flying from Dallas to Washington; LBJ was performing an act of sexual intercourse upon the corpse of John F. Kennedy—in the throat wound, as a matter of metaphor, thereby attempting to change the entry wound into an exit wound by enlarging its perimeter—and among the intellectuals who believed this to be literally true was Daniel Ellsberg. Veresimilitudinous context aside, to have accepted that image as credible was to have admitted your belief in the President's insanity, unless you were a practicing necrophiliac.

But Ellsberg continued to work on Maggie's Funny Farm.

In terms of respectable and widespread impact, it's better that *The New York Times* eventually got the Pentagon Papers, but had I been the recipient, I would have published the material all in one issue of *The Realist* rather than serialize it as the *Times* did. Instead, I published a photo of a Vietnamese woman and her napalmed child crying out in a horror unknown to us. I called it "The Parts Left Out of the Pentagon Papers."

One afternoon in New York, I was watching the news on TV and it was so depressing that when my phone rang I answered by saying: "Whoever this is, you better not be feeling sorry for yourself." The call was from Stewart Brand. He was inviting me to come west and co-edit with Ken Kesey *The Last Supplement to the Whole Earth Catalog.* My verbatim answer was: "Yes, yes, yes, yes, yes."

"I found myself confronting a waterfall..."
Photo: Frank Werber

I HAD NEVER USED THE MASSAGE TABLE TO BE MASSAGED ON . . .

In a letter of confirmation, Stewart wrote: "For two prime origins of the *Catalog* to help finish it is nice. Even tidy."

In addition I was offered a radio program on KSFX, the ABC-FM station in San Francisco. I accepted on the condition that I could use the name Rumpleforeskin. They agreed. The telephone company would later refuse to list me in the directory. They were willing to settle for Foreskin, Rumple. But I insisted my name was one word. There were precedents—the Cockettes and Magnolia Thunderpussy—but you know how bureaucracies are.

Still in New York, I had 180 cardboard cartons full of Stuff. Until the day I left, I would go through this procedure: Put a carton in the middle of my massage table, with a metal garbage can (the Fire Department had made me buy a pair) on either side, and then just sort out the useless junk from the junk I wanted to save, till I was totally out of sorts. I eliminated about a hundred cartons' worth of accumulation.

I had never used the massage table to be massaged on, not even once, and now I was leaving it behind, along with my vibrating lounge chair which I always turned on during television commercials. I still vibrate automatically whenever a commercial comes on TV. Does the name Pavlov ring a bell?[8]

8
A retired stand-up comedian is known as a sit-down comedian.
—S.B.

My last two acts in New York were a veritable study in contrast. I went to see the Andy Warhol production of *Trash* at a Times Square movie house which had a sign saying, "The last three rows are reserved for unescorted ladies." And I took my daughter to an indoor ice-skating rink, and she brought a cushion which she kept inside next to her sweet little ass as a shock-absorber.

I have never been out of the country, except for Canada, Cuba and the final Bratwurst Festival in Sheboygan, Wisconsin. I had never even been away from New York for more than two months at a time, and that was only when I was working at summer camps during my college years. The ghetto slums may have become inner cities, but I was still an urban blight.

I had learned how to trip on acid during the rush hour in a subway, but I had forgotten how to breathe. I walked around constricting my lungs as if I were always immediately behind a farting bus. If people realized how much precious energy gets dissipated blocking off foul air, noise, hostile vibrations, and how that energy gets shunted, like an electrical circuit, away from creative imagination, there would be an instant cultural transformation; that is, if we had any energy left.

That's the real energy crisis. And it is often treated with yet another energy crisis: when everybody is too stoned to get up and change the record. What moving to the west coast taught me is that decisions are a form of energy.

Doing *The Last Supplement* with Ken Kesey was going to serve as a decompression chamber after surviving the psychic bends all those years on the east.

ONE MORNING KESEY COULD BE OBSERVED POURING SOME WHITE POWDER INTO HIS CROTCH . . .

Stewart and Lois Brand drove me from San Francisco to the Whole Earth Truck Store in Menlo Park, and from there to the house in Palo Alto where Kesey was staying. The reunion was perfect. Kesey was talking about the anal sphincter, and I handed him a printed card with wisdom on that very muscle which I had happened to put in my pocket while sorting out those 180 cardboard cartons 3000 miles away.

I was to stay at the Psychodrama Commune led, more or less, by Vic Lovell, to whom Kesey dedicated *One Flew Over the Cuckoo's Nest*.

Hassler, a stalwart from Merry Prankster days, was to serve as our unofficial managing editor, chauffeur, photographer and general buffer zone. He earned his name.

A ritual developed: Hassler and Kesey would come by the Psychodrama house each morning and wake me up. We would all drink Ginseng Tea for breakfast. Then, sharing a joint in an open-topped convertible, we would drive up winding roads sandwiched by forest and end up at this garage near Skylonda, filled with production equipment. Kesey and I would pace back and forth like a pair of caged silver foxes discussing an idea. Gourmet meals were cooked on a pot-bellied stove. Sometimes a local rock band rehearsed with full amplification, drowning out the noise of our typewriters.[9]

9
I was working on the LAST CATALOG and rarely visited the SUPPLEMENT production. During one brief look-in I noticed that while Paul was talking to Kesey and me he was absent-mindedly turning over thumbtacks on the windowsill that had their points up. I remarked that as near as I could tell Paul Krassner spent his life going around turning over dangerous thumbtacks. He blushed. —S.B.

One morning in the Psychodrama kitchen, Kesey could be observed pouring some white powder, from a box he found on a pantry shelf, into his crotch.

"I've used cornstarch on my balls for years," he explained.

It seemed like an organic commercial in the making, so the next day Hassler brought his camera. I had left a note in the box warning Kesey that he was being watched by the Cornstarch Liberation Front. Our public service ad appeared as the inside back cover of *The Last Supplement*, with Kesey delivering this pitch:

"Y'know how it is when you're swarthy anyway and maybe nervous like on a long freeway drive or say you're in court where you can't unzip to air things out, and your clammy old nuts stick to your legs? Well, a little handful of plain old cornstarch in the morning will keep things dry and sliding the whole hot day long. Works better than talcum and you don't smell like a nursery. Also good for underarms, feet, pulling on neopreme wet suits and soothing babies' bottoms. And it's bio-degradable."

10
I let spellings like "neopreme" stand. —S.B.

Stewart Brand had assured us freedom in doing the *Supplement,* and he kept his promise. [10]

When that euphoric month was over, Kesey went back to Oregon and I moved to San Francisco.

I stayed there for three months, then moved to a house on the beach near Watsonville with Hassler and his famous wife Poopsie. Now, instead of subways, I had the roar of the ocean. I started talking about waves of liberation and repression.

I would go into San Francisco on weekends to do my Rumpleforeskin radio show, eat meat, see a movie, go to a party, breathe bus fumes. The usual city trips.

I had a room in the basement of a yellow-painted mansion that belonged to a trio of dope attorneys—Rohan, Stepanian and Shapiro. Whenever anybody in the building flushed any toilet, the sound carried through the pipes in my room. But there was compensation. The caretaker, Myron Cohen, was a practicing jazz drummer, and I used to enjoy balling to his accompaniment from the carriage-house. Did you ever come with a live drum roll?

Around that time, Stewart Brand's marriage was breaking up. He took a room in the basement too. [11] I gave him the key to my room so he could use the refrigerator, my phone till he got his own, and the use of my king-size hot water bottle when I wasn't there. I had not intended this to be bread cast upon the waterbed, but when the house was sold, Stewart found an apartment and agreed to let me use a small room in it as my San Francisco headquarters.

It would be on a trial basis, he said, "as long as our life styles don't conflict."

As you walk up the stairs to our apartment, you pass Stewart's styrofoam sailboat hanging on the wall. At the top of the stairway is a closet filled with his records. On that door is a full-length mirror, so you can see yourself coming up the stairs, and this Christmas card from Gerd Stern:

Bosatu or Bodhisattva (in Sanskrit) means the Way-seeker, Kan-jizai Bosatu or Avalokitesvara Bodhisattva is said to observe human suffering and change Himself, whenever necessary, into 33, hence an infinite number of, different guises to save mankind. Whenever He feels it best, He even appears as a harlot or a demon to truly save man. For this reason, anyone who appears before you should be regarded as the personification of Avalokitesvara Bodhisattva who has appeared to save you, namely, to guide you to spiritual enlightenment, in that appearance. Then you can, and must, be thankful to him no matter how harsh and unkind he may appear.

All I remember from my entire formal education is a professor saying that "Philosophy is the rationalization of life." But it's fun to play that game. In fact, once you accept the premise, it even works. So there is Stewart in his room transcribing an interview he did with Gregory Bateson, and there am I in my room talking to Squeaky of the Manson Family, an X scar on her forehead staring at me as though it were a third eye. I have no doubt that I've learned as much from Squeaky as Stewart has from Bateson.

The walls of my room are lined with bookshelves that Stewart built for his library. One night the heaviest shelf fell down. Had I been there, I might've been killed by his double-volume set of *The Ancient Art of Warfare* alone.

On one wall is a poster with this quotation—"To a crisis of the spirit, we need an answer of the spirit. And to find that answer, we need only look within ourselves"—underneath a portrait of its author, Richard Nixon. Yes, *the* Richard Nixon. One day I noticed that the President's eyes were looking toward the right, but his face was still learning toward the left. It had that spooky effect of the Christ-in-an-ashtray whose eyes follow you as you pass a novelty shop window. I looked closely and could see that the original eyeballs had been erased from the sincere middle and new ones had been drawn in at the right corners.

I checked to see whether the eyes in my daughter's photo on another wall had also been changed, but no, Holly was still looking directly at me. So was my American Indian guide. Only Nixon had been altered.

It seemed slightly out of character for Stewart to have done this, but I asked him nevertheless, and he told me that Kesey had been around. I should've realized when I saw that telltale trail of cornstarch . . .

MY FALSE HUMILITY GLAND BEGAN TO SPRING A LEAK . . .

I still take a Greyhound bus into San Francisco about once a week, although I got fired from my radio show by the guy who replaced John Turpin, the station manager who had hired me. The new man, George Yarhaes, told me how much he respected my work, and that he even used to read *The Realist* in college, but they were going to switch to all music 24 hours a day, and for me to do nothing but play records would be a waste of my talent. Once they got rid of me, they put another talk-show in my old time slot.

I miss the unseen audience that built up over seven months.

One Sunday evening I was eating dinner at Hippo's hamburger place before going to do my show, and I sat at the counter watching the young black chef with an almost serene expression on his face

11
During my first night in the room, as I lay there awrithe with loneliness, three young girls came down from a party upstairs and started a party of their own in the toilet on the other side of my thin board wall. It was interrupt, eavesdrop, or kill myself. They discussed their first Lesbian encounters, and how they learned to get off sexually on water fountains in high school, and compared notes on the bed habits of their host, and then one said, "You know who has a room in this basement?" "No, who?" "Paul Krassner." "Paul KRASSNER! (Ecstatic moan) He's with the Jefferson AIRplane!" —S.B.

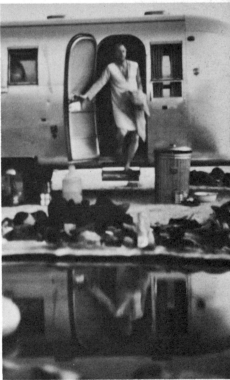

29

as he put one round piece of chopped dead meat after another into the open fire to cook for one somebody he didn't know after another somebody he didn't know. I talked about it on the air that night, inviting listeners to tell how they managed to survive boring, menial, repetitive jobs. The answers covered a spectrum of escapes that ranged from becoming a machine oneself to disengaging in astral projection.

Another time Garry Goodrow—my old friend from The Committee—called to find out if I knew a pickpocket who could serve as a technical adviser to him for his role in the film *Steelyard Blues.* I asked for any listener who was a pickpocket to please call in. One did, and the connection was made.

Recently, The Committee decided to close, as satire began to lose its race with truth more blatantly than ever. It was on the night of their final performance that I OD'd on THC and missed what I had planned as a personal pilgrimage, only to experience one I hadn't planned.

Stewart had hoped in his note that I would remember details. Suffice it to say that for a few hours I was in a space beyond good and evil, but clinging hard to the paradox of human subjectivity. God is Absurdity. While my body was writhing with ecstacy in that hospital bed, my consciousness was in another place that felt like pure energy, where everything was related to everything else precisely because it existed.

Previously a name had come to me once in the dark: *Thomas Eagleton Seagull.* Now I knew that it was more than just a play on words.

I began to write what turned out to be a 10,000-word satire with that title, about a seagull who became Potential Second Best Human Being. I dedicated it "To my psychic friend Mary Jo Baron who, upon seeing Senator Thomas Eagleton's first appearance on television at the Democratic National Convention, immediately stated: 'He's a pawn, and he'll never make it to November.' To which she added: 'And they all know it.' And to those outcast FBI agents who have disregarded L. Patrick Gray's memo urging them to read *Jonathan Livingston Seagull.*"

I showed the manuscript to Stewart Brand. He had only two reactions:

1. In response to the sentence—"It was a quarter to three when Thomas Eagleton Seagull looked at his embryonic Micky Mouse watch and shouted, "It's a Stigmata!" "—Stewart pointed out that Stigmata is plural (excuse me; *are* plural). Although "It's a Stigmata! had the flavor of a little Italian sports car, I changed it to "The Stigmata!" for the sake of correct grammar.

2. In response to the sentence—"Thomas Eagleton Seagull regurgitated himself with supreme peristalsis at the very moment that a reporter from *Speck* magazine was taking a leak and checking it out"—Stewart wanted to know if I had intended this as a deliberate pun. I immediately changed my intention to deliberate. [12]

But I had no idea whether Stewart *liked* my story or not. For the first time, I felt insecure about something I'd written. In *The Last Whole Earth Catalog,* he had stated: "Paul Krassner approaches every moment in his life as a potential source of humor and moral dilemma. He is seldom disappointed. Neither are his readers." So of course I had tremendous respect for his judgment. But Stewart had said "*seldom* disappointed." Maybe this was one of those *other* times.

When I had previously shown him a piece I'd written called "I've Got a Secret to Tell the Truth or Consequences"—about how the President is forced to commit suicide on a network TV game show—Stewart read it three times, pointed out a confusing paragraph which I corrected, and he said: "It's another 'Parts Left Out of the Kennedy Book.'" Now his *non*-commital stance was emphasized by comparison. Hmmmmm . . .[13]

Wavy Gravy of the Hog Farm is now Resident Fool at Pacific High. His role is to show that reverence and irreverence are different sides of the same coin. And the same students who celebrated Gook Night were collecting money to rebuild Bach Mai Hospital. When Wavy invited me to speak at the school one night, I decided to read parts of *Thomas Eagleton Seagull.*

Baba Ram Dass came along for the ride and ended up speaking after me. He said: "Paul Krassner is the Kahlil Gibran of the Seventies. He has written a truly holy book. Paul's humor is so exquisite that it's seductive to try and be funny." Golly-gosh, that certainly was reassuring.

(Excerpts from *Thomas Eagleton Seagull* will appear in *Playboy* this September before it's published as a book with an introductory Warning by Ken Kesey. Hey, Stewart—*nyah, nyah, nyah!*)

As my false humility gland began to spring a leak, Ram Dass was getting a trifle too abstract, and one of the students editorialized, simply: "Words." This particular fellow had fucked a goat, so his attitude was understandable. Later, I told Stewart, and he replied: "Deeds."

I ASKED FOR THE KIND OF MARBLES THAT WERE BEST FOR FRYING . . .

It was my translation of certain words into a specific deed that inspired Poopsie once to call Stewart and me "The Hip Odd Couple." An underground news service, Zodiac, had issued this

12

Retroactive intention is an interesting concept. —S.B.

13

Paul's previous indifference to my 10,000 word article on Computer Science in ROLLING STONE is not surpassed by my silence on his excellent Eagleton satire. —S.B.

report late last September:

The conspiracy trial of six members of Vietnam Veternas Against the War (VVAW) in Gains-
ville, Florida, has been postponed until after the November election.

Federal Judge David Middlebrook ruled in favor of the defense, which claimed that the
Vietnam War would be a political issue in the upcoming election and that the war would also be
a major issue in the conspiracy trial. Judge Middlebrook said that the trial would be postponed
"indefinitely"—until at least after the November election.

Prior to the judge's decision, the trial had been scheduled to start early next month. The six
VVAW members have been accused of plotting to use a variety of bizarre weapons—including
fried marbles, sling shots, cross bows, cherry bombs and scuba divers—to violently invade Miami
Beach and attack the Republican Convention in August.

Fried marbles? That's what it said, folks. *Fried marbles!* Maybe if you sneak up on the words
when they're not watching? Nope, they *still* say *fried marbles* with a straight face.

Now, I've taken a couple of workshops with John Lilly—one at Esalen Institute in Big Sur and
the other on Alan Watts' houseboat in Sausalito—and I got closer to the nature of what Lilly calls
the human biocomputer. That's what a mind is. Well, when *fried marbles* were fed to my biocomputer,
my conspiracy metaprogramming digested them and out came the conclusion that this was a frame-
up. Remember: no *lower* limits. It's important not to underestimate the insidiousness of those in
power. There is a gigantic sociopolitical chess game taking place, with all the concomitant second-
guessing. The logic of those in power is that if they accuse the Veterans o having fried marbles as
a weapon, the public will think it's too bizarre *not* to be true.

When I heard once that Richard Nixon's favorite meal is cottage cheese with ketchup, I went and
tried it. Operation Empathy. It seemed a fitting dish for a President who had invaded Cambodia because they wouldn't let him grow sideburns. So now—the decision had made me—I was going to fry
some marbles.

Stewart Brand is accustomed to my weirdness. All he did was advise me not to use his tefflon
pan.

I went shopping on Market St. Found a place that sold marbles. Asked for the kind that were
best for frying. The clerk laughed at what she had to believe was my little joke. I returned home and
melted butter in my saucepan.

The phone rang and I answered: "I can't talk to you now, I'm in the middle of frying marbles."
"Sure, Paul, call me back later."

Under the influence of eggs and Noah's Ark, I fried two marbles. Apparently the purpose in
weaponry is that when a fried marble is catapulted from a slingshot it will shatter upon hitting the
target. The poor person's cluster bomb. [14]

Five months later, in a letter to *Harper's* magazine, Larry Rottman, Past President of the National
Executive Committee of the Vietnam Veterans Against the War, confirmed my original instincts:

There have been hundreds of instances of known and attempted FBI infiltration into the
[VVAW]. As early as "Operation Dewey Canyon III," the VVAW march on Washington in April
1971, at least six agents, wearing fatigues and trying to cause trouble, were discovered trying to
pass as vets.

Since that time, in nearly every state, FBI agents and informants have been attempting to
destroy or discredit the VVAW by encouraging militant demonstrations, planting illegal drugs
in veterans' homes and cars, offering VVAW members money for favors, for information, pro-
mising new cars in exchange for mailing lists, and even threatening blackmail over sexual encount-
ers or traffic violations if cooperation wasn't given. An agent once told me he had the power to
have me called back to active duty if I didn't answer certain "nonself-incriminating" questions . . .

Bureau involvement has now escalated into the condoning and encouragement of much more
violent tactics. In Ohio, the ACLU has recently filled suit against an alleged informant, Reinhold
Mohr—as well as the campus police chief—charging that Mohr tried to plant a machine gun and
grenade launcher in the Kent State University VVAW chapter. And such insidious attempts have
become almost commonplace.

Yet, despite countless cases of provocation, harassment, assault, and arrest, no bona fide VVAW
member has ever responded with force [italics his]. As our nation's agents of pain and suffering
in Indochina, we (unlike our government) learned the horror and futility of violence. We leave
violence to those who enjoy it and profit from it—whether at My Lai or Southern University.

And no amount of federal indictments, grand juries, or special investigations will stifle our
rage against injustice or still our voices for truth. . .

For when you awake, America (if you ever do), we will still be here.

14
In Tony Randall's voice: "Paul!
You SAUTEED those marbles.
A warm buttery marble is hardly
an instrument of aggression. You
should've added SLICED MUSH-
ROOMS. At least give your
readers the correct recipe: DEEP-
FRY the marbles in fat hot enough
to smoke slightly and then PLUNGE
them in cold water. Zzkk. Orna-
mental little weapons." —S.B.

No wonder the returning POW's are serving as such as diversionary circus, milking the Vietnam soap opera dry of any possible plot. I carried that pair of fried marbles around for a while, like a cross-fertilization of Captain Queeg from *The Caine Mutiny* and Linus from *Peanuts*.

MY RELIGION IS COINCIDENCE, BUT THIS WAS POSITIVELY WIERD . . .

Meanwhile, the laughter and other feedback at Pacific High had tempted me to return to show business. Stoneground was closing one Sunday night at the Boardinghouse in San Francisco, and Deirdre LaPorte introduced me to the audience. There was time for me to do only ten minutes before their next set. But there was a certain spark missing.

"You can't live your whole life on applause," Lenny Bruce said recently, speaking through a trance-medium at a seance in Los Angeles.

Unsure about the function of my audition, I headed back to the apartment. I thought I'd meditate to some late-night television. I have a little black-and-white set in my room, but since Stewart wasn't home I knew he wouldn't mind if I watched the color set in his room. But he had taken it with him to his trailer where he was working on an article.

I noticed a black-covered notebook which I assumed was his transcription of the Gregory Bateson interview. As a lazy version of tossing the *I Ching*, I always use whatever's handy—a radio, a dictionary; even the *National Enquirer* can help crystallize a direction. I opened the notebook at random, circled my index finger in the air and then landed on this—*Paul, you're studied and off*—in Stewart's handwriting.

"*YAAGGGHH!!!*" I whispered.

My religion is coincidence, but this was positively *weird*. It must be Stewart's diary or a journal or *something* personal. I stood there, frozen, muttering several more low-keyed *yaaggghhs* in succession.

Stewart had written to himself what he couldn't tell me. My impulse was to confess this accidental discovery immediately, but I didn't know when he'd be back. There would be a message on his telephone-answering machine, but I couldn't call because my own phone had been shut off; I hadn't paid the bill. [15]

Still, I just had to tell somebody. But who? Wavy Gravy! He'd be sure to understand.

"His *diary*?" Wavy asked. "Paul, a diary is *inviolate*. But that's your role, the Cosmic Yenta."

"But I didn't *know* it was a diary. Does being inviolate mean that you don't want to hear what he wrote about *you*?"

"All right," said Wavy. He knew I had him by his stuffed yak. "What did he write about me?"

"He doesn't even mention you."

I never did tell Stewart. He won't know that I appreciate his perception until he reads it here. I hope he won't consider this a conflict in our life styles. I mean it's not as if I had *fried* his diary.

Oh well, never mind. I'm getting out of show biz anyhow.

[15]
Paul, with his talent for condensation as well as trespass, has at last compressed Crime and Punishment into a single act. He blundered into (was Called by?) a notebook in which I occasionally exercise ideas and exorcise demons (vice versa when it doesn't work). The occasion of the damning statement was a low mood of vile self-opinion which projected itself onto a gallery of friends and family. To dispel the demon I wrote out the charges (an exercise I now recommend). Apparently one angel strayed into the line of fire. Fortunately Paul knows better than to take such a thing personally. At least I know now why he's been looking at me lately like his Nixon portrait. Paul, come home. All is forgiven. ABC says they'll renew the contract. —S.B.

" . . . I mean it's not as if I had *fried* his diary."   Photo by Lucy Hilmer.

Paul Krassner is Editor and Zen Bastard of THE REALIST ($5 for 12 issues) and author of HOW A SATIRICAL EDITOR BECAME A YIPPIE CONSPIRATOR IN TEN EASY YEARS ($7)—both available from The Realist, Main PO Box 4027, San Francisco, Calif. 94101. He is currently putting together the 15th anniversary issue of The Realist, featuring *"An Impolite Interview with Baba Ram Dass"* **and** *"The Parts Left Out of the Lenny Bruce Book."* **He is also working on a couple of novels, plus an autobiography to be called THE ADVENTURES OF RUMPLEFORESKIN.**

WOUNDED KNEE 1890~1973
Michelle Vignes

"You can count your money and burn it within the nod of a buffalo's head but only the Great Spirit can count the grains of sand and the blades of grass of these plains. As long as the sun shines and the waters flow, this land will be here to give life to men and animals."
— Blackfoot Chief [excerpt from a Treaty speech, 1824]

It was within the nod of a buffalo's head, on the morning of February 27, that the American Indian Movement, with the support of about half of the Oglala residents, occupied the village of Wounded Knee, seceded from the U.S.A., declared an Independent Oglala Nation, and set up frontiers on the three roads leading into the village. Within the next 48 hours the U.S. Dept. of the Interior and the F.B.I. also set up road blocks, and the long standing roles were reversed—with Indian people held to seige in a ready made fort, surrounded on all sides by hostile Federal agents.

A.I.M. members occupied Wounded Knee with the purposes of coming to the assistance of the parents of Raymond Yellow-Thunder (an Oglala man who was brutally murdered by whites some weeks before); and to contest the position of Tribal Council chairman Richard Wilson. Wilson and his Council had run the Pine Ridge Reservation for ten years, with no apparent change in the level of extreme poverty among the Indians. The government employees lived in neat cottages and modern house trailers while the Indians were in shacks and abandoned army huts, many without running water or other utilities.

Inside the barricaded village, Dennis Banks, a Korean Vet A.I.M. leader from the Chippewa reservation in Northern Minnesota commanded a rigourously trained militia. Bunkers were dug,

lookouts posted and food rationing organized. In the first few heady days, illicit night traffic across the prairie was a positive rush hour as supporters dogged the Feds to maintain food and arms supplies. The feeling between the opposing camps ran from benign irritation to outright contempt. The Indians would perform traditional coups, touching one's enemy, sneaking up to the armoured personnel carriers and tying the nation's banner (a red ribbon and a feather) to their rumps. In return, the Federal marshalls would pepper the village with some 1000 rounds each night. Using tracers and flares to sight the bunkers, they would usually spray the houses too, trying to intimidate the people into surrendering.

An elderly resident of Wounded Knee, who lost both parents and clan in the 1890 massacre asks, "How many times shall we die, how many times shall we dance for you. What does it take for us to appear real to you white folks."
—Anna Ray Jones

Dennis Banks, A.I.M.

"We are fully prepared here at Wounded Knee for a full scale military confrontation with the Federal forces. Man to man we'd beat 'em! We are strategically and morally better placed than they are. Our morale has been and still is continuing to be very high. We are fighting a holy war, to continue our existence as a free nation and not wards of the Federal government. Those guys out there don't know how to fight; they're city people-desk people. This is a weekend assignment for them, they are not by tradition warriors. The F.B.I. are used to night-raids, breaking down doors and sneaking around, killing their enemies that way. Indians have been involved in street-fighting all our lives, we've fought in bars and backalleys, in cities and on the reservations and we can withstand any kind of special operations group that the F.B.I. cares to lay on us. Morally and physically we are way ahead of them."
　　　　—Dennis Banks, A.I.M.

"I'm here for our treaty rights like my grandfather was. I've been hearing about treaty violations ever since I was a kid. What's happening, here at Wounded Knee, is the only way to win the attention of the US government, to get what we think is right for our people. That's the only reason I'm staying to stand up and face the guns. So my people can be what they have a right to be, to be recognized in their own country. I fought in World War Two and defended the U.S. I called both red and white people my people. I fought for them at D Day, Normandy and I came home to the reservation to find things worse than when I left. We Indian people don't fear death so it doesn't matter what the Federal agents want to do to us--but we will change things. The government don't know how to deal with us; everytime they take a step they're in deeper."

—Resident of Wounded Knee (liberator)

"You know everyone comes and goes in the Western Hemisphere. We watched during the thirties when the Unions were rioting, watched through two world wars, through the fifties and sixties, now its our turn to get it on! The Black Panthers they came and went and all the other freedom and peace groups. But the Indian remains as a constant factor—just like an old chief down in the Southwest once said to whiteman, 'The Spaniards were here for 400 years and they are gone—you'll be gone!''

—Russell Means, A.I.M. Leader

HICKMAN, KENTUCKY, July 20, 1972—

"Today, Bob Gillespie and Ed [Burns] Ellison might very well deserve the title of river rats. They are once again on their way down the Mississippi River after having been waylaid in Hickman for longer than they had planned.

"The story of Bob's and Ed's visit to Hickman began last Saturday as they approached the harbor, having begun a journey from Iowa City, Iowa, on June 21, with aspirations of eventually arriving in New Orleans. Little did the two men know, as they approached their night's resting place, that this stop would result in their longest sojourn thus far on their travels.

"Bob and Ed found their way to the Hickman Cafe Saturday evening for a hearty meal. There they met Elbert Woodruff, Rt. 4, a well-known retired mason and lifetime resident of Hickman. After finishing their meal, Woodruff showed the travelers parts of Hickman and returned the men to their campsite on the river bank. At 7:30 Sunday morning Bob and Ed were rudely awakened by a swift rush of water which was uplifting their canvas pup tent. By the time they were fully awake, they were flooded by three inches of water which was hint enough to 'get up and at 'em.' At this point in remembering the incident, Ed replied, 'I heard a car horn and said to Bob, without even having to look up, it's Elbert and he has come to our rescue.'

"After a short while Ed, Bob and Elbert found themselves at the Hickman Cafe for breakfast where Ed ordered and enjoyed his first platter of brains and eggs.

Pictured above at left is Elbert Woodruff who rescued Burns Ellison, middle, and Bob Gillespie, right, Sunday morning as they camped out in the Hickman Harbor.

"For Sunday dinner they enjoyed a homecooked feast at the home of Mr. and Mrs. Woodruff where the novel taste for both Ed and Bob was purple hull peas. Before sending them on their way, Mrs. Woodruff gave the boys several homegrown tomatoes.

"Ed Ellison, 38, is a former oil worker on the north slopes of Alaska and is now living in San Francisco.

"Bob Gillespie, 33, is teaching at Colby College in Waterville, Maine."

From *The Hickman Courier,* Vol. 114, No. 15.

RIVER
by Burns Ellison

Pretty soon it darkened up, and begun to thunder and lighten; . . . Directly it begun to rain, and it rained like fury too, and I never see the wind blow so. It was one of those regular summer storms . . .

I wonder if there are thunderstorms anywhere in the world as wild and awesome as those that take place on the Mississippi River that is "in all ways remarkable." Someday I might try to describe in my own words one of those "regular summer storms," such as the one that morning in Hickman, or the one we encountered that night outside of Helena, Arkansas, when once again we had to be rescued, or the one that descended upon us the night we camped on Jackson's Island, but for now, listen to Huck:

It would get so dark that it looked all blue-black outside, and lovely; and the rain would thrash along by so thick that the trees off a little ways looked dim and spider-webby; and here would come a blast of wind that would bend the trees down and turn up the pale underside of the leaves; . . . and next, when it was just about the bluest and blackest—fst! it was bright as glory, . . . and now you'd hear the thunder let go with an awful crash, and then go rumbling, grumbling, tumbling, down the sky towards the under side of the world . . .

The myth of a boy on a raft. Of going down the river, of being on water. A return to innocence, a flight back to Eden. But there are other myths too, more recent ones. EASY RIDER has also entered our mythology, and so to a certain extent Bob and I were a pair of Uneasy Canoers. After all, we were entering enemy country. Country inhabited by crackers and rednecks and yahoos—by folks who didn't cotton to hippies and longhairs. And if Bob was a teacher in college, and not some California freak, well, "pointy-head" school teachers know what kind of reception they too can expect in EASY RIDER country.

And if the cards are stacked in EASY RIDER, there are other variations on the theme. One need look no further than DELIVERANCE, or NIGHT OF THE HUNTER. The river can symbolize a return to innocence; it can provide a means of escape. But there are also monsters haunting the river's edge, and lurking beneath the water's surface. Twain relates how "A big catfish collided with Marquette's canoe, and startled him; and reasonably enough, for he had been warned by the Indians that he was on a foolhardy journey, and even a fatal one, for the river contained a demon 'whose roar could be heard at a great distance, and who would engulf them in the abyss where he dwelt.'

I know how Marquette must have felt when he collided with that catfish. One day I accidentally hit an alligator gar with my paddle. It thrashed and slapped its tail and I nearly shot straight up from the canoe. It scared the hell out of me. Later we reached Grand Tower, Illinois, and the great whirlpool that is said to have destroyed countless boats in its day. Indians used to make sacrifices to the monster that lived in that whirlpool, no doubt the same one Marquette had been warned about.

One can get pretty Freudian about the Mississippi. The River as Metaphor. The River, and what lies beneath. The hints, auguries, that come as on a breath of wind, or a surge of current. For the most part the river had been good to us, but it was entirely capable of being other than that. If not, why did we keep getting those warnings? Stay close to the shore. Heed the signs. Watch the rising wind, the darkening sky. Watch out for towboats and the wakes of passing barges. Watch out for submerged rocks and logs. Watch for undertows, for whirlpools. For all those monsters lurking beneath.

Which sometimes appeared on the surface. Out of

Cape Girardeau we came upon a dead dog. Floating on the water, bloated, its pink belly and anus exposed. A foul stench arose from it. The carcass was hairless, but for a few small patches. Eyeless, empty-socketed, jaws parted, revealing small white teeth. As we canoed past, it looked as though it were grinning at us.

Later we came upon a dead alligator gar, a good four feet long, it too bloated and stinking. Gaping jaws, needle-like teeth. It had plated white scales on its belly, which had been gutted open. Sometimes swimming we'd feel something nibbling at our toes, but the water was always too muddy to see what it was.

The river was lulling; it was very easy to lie back spread-eagled to the sun, close your eyes, and just float and drift and dream. But there was death in the river. We made the front page of *The Memphis Press-Scimitar,* where we were billed as "sun-bronzed adventurers." In that same newspaper, but buried in back, there was an article about four fifteen year old boys going down the river on a log, somewhere north of Hickman. They had all drowned.

Below Memphis we saw two kids in the middle of the river on air mattresses. They waved, and we started over to see if they were in trouble. But they were only having a good time and waved us on. About five miles further a helicopter whirled down over us and a Coast Guard Patrol boat pulled up alongside. Had we seen two kids on rafts? It had been reported that their rafts had overturned and they were looking for them. We never did hear whether or not they found them.

Then, in Helena, I read about the body of the drowned man found at MILE 693, thirty miles north, on the same stretch of water over which we had passed the day we arrived.

Yes, the river was lulling. It was like being borne down a great oceanic womb. Overhead, the sun and blue sky, and white cathedrals of cloud. On both sides a wall of trembling-leafed cottonwoods, sycamores, maple, willow, a wilderness of green. Beaches immaculate as those shown in South Seas travel posters. Dense-timbered jungly islands overgrown with creepers and vines. One pulled up to a sandbar and plunged into the water, let the arms of the current take one away. But sometimes that current was more insistent: fingers of rushing water *grabbed,* and pulled one out and away, further than you wanted to go. Then try to swim back *against* that current. And what of those lines of water extending out from the shore? Steer clear, veer around, those lines signified jagged rocks that could rip out the bottom of one's canoe. Deceptive river, one with many faces. One that could change within minutes from a big placid lake to a heaving, churning white-capped sea.

Huck had his close calls on the river, and Twain had his. He also recalled the drownings of friends. In a childhood game of seeing who could stay underwater the longest, "Dutchy" failed to come up. Twain and the others drew straws to see who would dive down to find out what had happened. "The lot fell to me, and I went down. The water was so muddy I could not see anything, but I felt around . . . and presently grasped a limp wrist which gave me no response—and if it had I should not have known, I let it go with such a frightened suddenness."

On another occasion he accidentally dislodged the body of a drowned runaway slave. The body sprang up headfirst from out of the water and seemed to be chasing him as he fled from it. Is it any wonder that he was haunted by bad dreams?

One night as a boy he heard a drunken would-be rapist announce he was going to raid the house occupied by a widow and her daughter. Twain and a friend followed him up Holliday's Hill to the house. The man stood outside screaming obscenities. The widow came to the porch with a musket loaded with slugs. She counted to ten: " 'Seven . . . eight . . . nine'—a long pause, we holding our breaths—'ten!' A red spout of flame gushed out into the night, and the man dropped with his breast riddled to rags. Then the rain and the thunder burst loose and the waiting town swarmed up the hill in the glare of the lightning like an invasion of ants . . . I went home to dream, and was not disappointed." How similar that is to THE NIGHT OF THE HUNTER: the old woman in her house in the darkness, shotgun across her knees, defending the children from the murderous Preacher, informing him she would count to three . . .

Bad dreams. Huck had them, and so do I. One night, camped near Louisiana, Missouri, I dreamed that I was going home for a visit. I was living in a house with people I had never seen before. Except for Ernest Hemingway, he was there. As I was about to leave, he went into the bathroom and stepped into the bathtub which was full of muddy brown water. In it he discovered the decomposed corpse of a boy I had grown up with. He had supposedly gone home earlier in the week, but instead he had killed himself. Hemingway was indignant about the body being in the tub, and insisted I take it home with me and return it to the boy's family. I put on rubber gloves and reached reluctantly into the tub. Hemingway was talking in that abbreviated Indian-English of his, but he was making no sense whatsoever, and I realized that his mind had snapped. At that point I woke up.

What lies beneath, and what is revealed in dreams. To go down the river is to enter into a dream. It can be a dream radiant and golden and lovely, but it is somehow always on the edge of nightmare. Along with the beauty there is an element of terror. Heed the signs, the hints, the auguries. And those warnings concerning the land and the towns, as well as the river.

A druggist in Caruthersville, Missouri asked where we were camped. We told him and he advised us to find another site. "I'm just trying to be helpful to you fellows," he said. "I sure wouldn't camp there. That's a bad place." Drawing us aside to warn us, he drew too close. His face was chalky white, fat and froglike. "Watch out for them niggers," he said.

That same evening in Caruthersville a man invited us to his home and we spent it with him and his wife and son drinking his bourbon and talking about the river. He was very kind and generous, and he was also tactful. "How may I tender this," he asked, "without offending . . . because I know what a fellow would probably like more than anything else after coming off the river. Now I trust you won't be offended . . . but wouldn't you all like a shower?" His wife was mortified. "Oh, John, how that must sound!" At the end of the evening he drove us back to our camp and before he left, he said: "Let me ask you if I may. *Don't* you all carry a gun? I don't want to needlessly alarm you, or make you feel unsafe . . . but my goodness, shouldn't you at least have one on hand? I would worry about that, if I were doing what you fellows are. I carry one myself. I feel you just never know. Oh, I don't wish to sound like an alarmist. Most everybody is good and decent, they're going to treat you fine. But I am talking about—suppose you were attacked by some crazed degenerate. I mean some kind of murderous kook. Don't you think about that some?"

Didn't we think about that some?

Cairo, Illinois is located at the confluence of the Ohio River and the Mississippi. Cairo, where Huck and Jim missed their turn during the night and found themselves going south instead of north. We had been warned about Cairo; there had been racial violence, shootings in the streets; there were bars you did not go into. We pulled into shore a few miles upriver from the town, late on a hot, sunny afternoon. We had had a hard time finding a decent-looking place to camp. The banks were steep and muddy and rocky, choked with timber and brush. It was an area of marshy backwaters, alive with mosquitoes. Turtles plopped from logs, there were undoubtedly snakes. I scrambled up the bank through a tangle of vines and poison oak. Above it was a dirt road with a beat-up old jalopy parked in the middle of it. Alongside the road was a shack with a black woman standing in the yard. There were two white men inside the car, and they watched me as I approached. I asked how far it was to town, and they just looked at me. They were both drunk. One of them mumbled something, but I couldn't understand him. I went back to the canoe, wanting to get away from there. They were a pair straight out of DELIVERANCE.

We finally found a place and beached the canoe. The rocks were wet and slippery, we stumbled and fell, we sank ankle-deep in mud. We carried up our sleeping bags, duffel bags, boxes of food-stuffs, pots and pans, fishing gear, river maps, tent, ice chest. A towboat pushing a string of barges went by. We looked around just in time to go floundering out after our Coleman lantern and knapsack as they were being washed away by the incoming waves.

I pitched the tent while Bob started a fire and fixed dinner. We had finished eating and we were drinking our coffee when the shooting began—the zing and whine of bullets passing over our heads, the thonk of them hitting the bank on the other side. Zing! Thonk! leaves floating down from the trees above. What the shit was going on? Hey, we shouted up at whoever it was, and crouched behind a huge uprooted cottonwood, sheltered within its spidery snarl of twisted white roots. Who was doing the shooting? What was he shooting at? We never found out. Probably somebody doing some harmless target-practice.

In Helena, Arkansas we decided to end our trip. It was a long ways from New Orleans, but then we had never cared that much about whether or not we reached New Orleans anyway. Besides, Helena was where Marquette and Joliet had set up their base camp; it was near here that De Soto first saw the river before he died and was buried in it; and most importantly, according to my calculations from reading Twain's AUTOBIOGRAPHY, this was almost to the mile as far as Huck and Jim got. There were other considerations too. Like Huck we had wanted merely to "put in the time," but could we any longer. Our summer was nearly over, and soon we'd have to go back. Then the weather turned on us, and suddenly the river was giving us a hard time—maybe somebody was trying to tell us something. In any event Bob took a bus back to Iowa City to get his car and return for the canoe, while I stayed behind.

One morning I went into town to get some nightcrawlers for catfish bait, and met Ted Meek. He was on the riverbank, leaning against his LandRover. Two small children were with him, and a couple of dogs. He had on a pair of big shiny Redwing boots, a slouch hat, tent-like ballooning levies; his shirttails were knotted around his gut. Beady-eyed, fat-assed, sweating in the hot sun—a real cracker. I would have gone around him, but I'd seen him too late and had to walk by. I asked him if he knew where I could get any worms, and he said hop in, he'd get me all the crawlers I wanted. "Shut up," he said to his kids as we drove off. "Quit poppin' that gum, you hear, or I'm gonna jar your heads." We left town and went bumping and lurching up a country road to his home. It was on a hillside back in the trees; it had a garden in front. His pack of hounds behind the house yelped and bayed as we pulled up. He got a coffee can and a shovel and we went out in the yard. He turned over the moldering dead leaves and topsoil, and nightcrawlers popped up all over the place.

After I had gotten all I wanted I happened to ask what kind of tree it was we were standing under. That was like opening the floodgates. Ted Meek led me around his yard pointing out this and pointing out that until my mind was reeling trying to keep up with all the names and shapes and colors of trees and bushes and vines that I was being shown. And for the first time I was seeing them, because they were being named: catalpa trees, bodoc trees, oaks, poplars, maples, mimosas, elderberry bushes and blackberry, dewberry and chinaberry, poke salad, wild current, muscadine.

He brought out his collection of Indian arrowheads for me to see, and filled up a sack with tomatoes and cucumbers from his garden for me to take along with the nightcrawlers. Driving back to town he was still naming trees. Seeing one he didn't know, in front of a house, he slammed to a stop, and we went knocking at the door to find out what it was—but nobody was home. We went up Reservoir Hill to the empty pit that was once the town's source of water, but that now resembled some ancient Mexican ruin. We looked down from the high bluff which is the end of Crowley's Ridge before it drops down into the river. The slopes of the bluff were buried under green carpets of kudzu. Kudzu, an exotic vine, introduced from Japan to prevent erosion. "Its roots run from forty to fifty feet deep," said Ted Meek. ". . . you must close your windows at night to keep it out of the house," James Dickey has said in a poem, the ". . . leaves rising to bury you alive inside . . ."

"Now we're goin' down into the swamp," said Ted Meek. Dense stands of trees along a narrow winding road, overhead a canopy of branches and vines. We had left the sun back on Crowley's Ridge, here it was dark, and clammy, and gloomy. We came to a lake; cypress trees rising out of it, the water covered with slime. I asked Ted Meek if he ever went gigging for frogs, or coon hunting. No, he didn't. He didn't "much go for stuff after dark." There were snakes; there were things of the night.

We stopped at a bubbling cold spring on the way back to the harbor. He pointed out a blue indigo bunting on a fencepost, and a Mississippi kite soaring high overhead. The next day he came back to give me some arrowheads and Civil War cartridges he wanted me to have.

That night I called Jennifer in San Francisco and learned that our house had been broken into twice within twenty-four hours. A camera, a pair of binoculars, records and speakers, rings and jewelry had been stolen. Eggs had been splattered against the walls, piles of shit left on the floor. She knew who had done it, a neighbor had seen them; young people we considered friends, they lived next door.

After the phone call I sat in a bar and got drunk and nursed—fed—a sick cold rage. I felt murderous, I wanted to kill somebody.

"Jesus Christ, why would I want to carry a gun,"

Bob had said that night in Caruthersville. "I know I'd never use it." Yes, and I should never carry one either, I realized that night in Helena, because I knew I would.

When Bob got back he told me what was happening in Iowa City. Women there had formed a group called WAR, or War Against Rape. If you were a woman in Iowa City last summer you didn't go out alone at night, and if you lived alone you were careful about how many people knew where. For there are monsters who stalk dark streets as well as those that dwell beneath deep waters. This one was faceless. He wore a nylon mask over his face, with slits for eyes. He had forced a friend of Bob's wife to submit to him with the threat that if she didn't he would kill her.

We sat in an all-night cafe, talking. Everything had been turned upside-down. We were in the heart of enemy country—or so we had been told, and we had been overwhelmed by the kindnesses of strangers. While back *there* . . . in the city of St. Francis, and in "The Athens of the Midlands" . . .

The next day we broke camp, loaded our canoe, and got back on the water. We wanted a few more days on the river. And one more river town. We came into the Greenville, Mississippi harbor on a bright and shining Sunday afternoon. The water in the harbor was green, the first green water we'd been on all summer. The beaches were crowded with swimmers and picnickers and fishermen. There were party-barges, houseboats, sailboats, johnboats, tugboats and cruisers. Outboards pulling water-skiers cut back and forth in front of us. We passed a party of men and women and children on the beach; a lovely blonde woman in a bathing suit hailed us over; we stopped for plates of fried chicken and cold drinks. Kids flocked around us, asking questions about our trip. The woman was also asking questions: "Weren't we planning to go on to New Orleans? What would you all need for provisions? How much do you think it would cost to go on? I hate to see you all so close to achieving the realization of your life's dream, and not doing it."

We made for the Greenville Yacht Club, once more overwhelmed. Talking to her, we had both suddenly realized what she was on the verge of offering, had we said we wanted to go on.

Two girls and a guy in an outboard came roaring up. The guy handed us a couple of beers. "A little redneck hospitality," he cried as they went roaring back off.

Willy Smith is 63 years old, black, the caretaker of the Greenville Yacht Club. He met us when we pulled up to the dock and took us in. We stored our gear in his office, drank his beer, joined him in the morning for coffee. We took showers at the Club, shaved, had access to all the facilities. We were his guests. Willy introduced us to the Mayor of Greenville, who gave us permission to pitch our tent in the city park, now we were his guests too.

What better way to close it out. After Greenville, there was no question of going on. Bob had to retrieve his car again, but the only bus connection was by way of Memphis and took ten hours. At the Yacht Club we got a piece of cardboard to make a sign so he could hitchhike. Willy stood watching. He was grinning but didn't say anything. Then he reached into his pocket and handed Bob a five dollar bill. Looking at us both, and still grinning, he said: "You don't take that, you'll make me feel bad. It's a small world, and you never know."

"If you would learn the secrets of nature," Thoreau once wrote, "you must practice more humanity than others." Huck Finn discovered what Thoreau was talking about when he wrote his note to Miss Watson to tell her where her runaway nigger was. Jim was property that belonged to somebody else, and he was doing the "right thing." Church, school and state had taught him as much. But he had learned something else on the river. It's been quoted before, but it bears repeating:

I felt good and all washed clean of sin for the first time I had ever felt so in my life, and I knowed I could pray now. But I didn't do it straight off, but laid the paper down and set there thinking—thinking how good it was all this happened so, and how near I come to being lost and going to hell. And I went on thinking. And got to thinking over our trip down the river; and I see Jim before me all the time: in the day and in the night-time, sometimes moonlight, sometimes storms, and we a-floating along, talking and singing and laughing. But somehow I couldn't seem to strike no places to harden me against him, but only the other kind. I'd see him standing my watch on top of his'n, 'stead of calling me, so I could go on sleeping; and see him how glad he was when I come back out of the fog; and when I come to him again in the swamp, up there where the feud was; and such-like times; and would always call me honey, and pet me, and do everything he could think of for me, and how good he always was; and at last I struck the time I saved him by telling the men we had smallpox aboard, and he was so grateful, and said I was the best friend old Jim ever had in the world, and the only one he's got now; and then I happened to look around and see that paper.

It was a close place. I took it up, and held it in my hand. I was a-trembling, because I'd got to decide forever, betwixt two things, and I knowed it. I studied a minute, sort of holding my breath, and then says to myself:

'All right, then, I'll go to hell'—and tore it up.

"You must practice more humanity." Elbert Woodruff in Hickman, Kentucky doesn't need to be told this, or reminded of it, but I know I do. And one of the things I value from this past summer is that I *was* reminded of it, again and again.

I would write this to Elbert Woodruff, but I would also write it to Howard and Carol Brent, and Porter Young, and Mark Kunsman, and George Owik, and Jim Ashley, and Harry K. Brown, and Joe Brunkhorst, and to a good many others whose names I never learned. I would write it to a woman who bought us a round of beers in a bar in Nauvoo, Illinois, because she had a daughter hitchhiking through Wisconsin and she hoped that strangers were treating her kindly. I would write it to a crippled old black man in Helena who insisted on showing us the shack where he lived because he had extra space, and it was ours if we ever needed a place to stay. And I would write it to a twelve year old boy in Caruthersville named John Mark Fowlkes, who made it a special point to ride his bicycle down to the river one morning to see us off. He too wanted to be going down that river, and I hope someday he does.

There's one person I didn't meet this summer, but I'd like to sometime. He's old and retired, and supposedly intends to spend the rest of his life going up and down the Mississippi in his houseboat. He has a theory, we were told, that the bad people are spreading all across the land and forcing the good people onto the river. I found myself thinking about that old man after we had gotten back to Iowa City and I was hitchhiking to Columbus, Nebraska to see my parents. I got picked up by a big green converted school bus full of hippies. The bus had been on the road for over a year, driving back and forth across the country. Only two had been on it when it left New York; the other ten or so, like myself, were picked up along the way. The bus was outfitted with speakers and cassettes. *It's a Beautiful Day* was playing when I got on. There was a couch, some big soft easy chairs, and double-decker bunks in the rear for anybody who wanted to crash. The walls were lined with shelves of provisions. There was a refrigerator, a gas stove to cook on, and a wood stove for heat.

"You're either on the Bus or you're not on the bus," Ken Kesey has said. Did that apply to rivers too? The river and the road. Huck on his raft, and Twain in his stagecoach going west. Now I too was going west in the modern day equivalent. A girl was curled up on the couch who looked to be about fourteen years old. She was on her way to join an Ashram she had heard about in Sparks, Nevada. Two guys just back from Vietnam rapped about shooting up smack. Two others got into an argument. One of them was very short, he looked like a tall dwarf. He was bare-footed and had on a Micky Mouse tee-shirt. He talked about how bad the cops were in New Jersey, how they had beat on him.

The other guy was a hulking shaggy longhair. He had majored in criminology and worked as a prison guard. He said Jersey cops weren't like that at all, he knew many of them personally.

I had been up late the night before, and I was hot and tired, and hungover. I didn't want to be where I was. I closed my eyes and tried to sleep; I wanted to dream myself back on water. I remembered sitting in a cafe on a high bluff in New Boston, Illinois. Dusk, the cafe about to close. A three-quarters moon rising in a deep blue sky. We watched a great blue heron flying over the river above the green forests on the Iowa side. We walked down the town's main street, went past the Abraham Lincoln Hotel, the New Boston Baptist Chapel, then a charred gutted-out old building that looked like the last picture show. I asked somebody and found out that it was. We stopped at Rudy's Place and had a beer. Ray Price was singing *For The Good Times* on the jukebox. A drunk asked if we wanted to shoot a game of pool. We said no, but he bought us beers anyway. The woman sitting next to us bawled at the bartender: "Give me a sloe gin and a squirt and piss on the rest of 'em." We bought a six-pack and walked back to the campground. We sat on top of a picnic table and drank beer and talked about girls and books. It was a quiet moonlit night. The river looked as still and wide as a lake. It was our first night on the river, and it had been a very special one. I wanted it back—I wanted the whole summer back. I thought of nights on sandbars and riverbanks, miles from any town, nobody in the world knowing where we were. I remembered swimming at night, and running naked on the sand to dry myself off. I remembered the sounds of crickets and locusts, of doves, owls, frogs, the flop of a fish, the foghorn blast and the laboring chug of a towboat, its light probing the darkness, sweeping back and forth across the water. I remembered nights in our tent. Lying with my back against my knapsack, a book in my lap, the hum of the lantern outside the tent, and the hum of the thousands of bugs beating and fluttering and battering themselves to death against the lantern and the tent like an incessant patter of rain. I'd try to read, but I always fell asleep . . .

The bus stopped at a filling station and everybody filed out. I bought a coke, but would one ever again taste as good? I remembered gliding along past a high steep bank, the sun blazing down, baking us browner than we had ever been in our lives, the river cutting the bank back, huge slices of sand and clay toppling, collapsing. Drenched with sweat, we broke out beaded cold cans . . . Sheer pure joy in a swig of coke, a guzzle of beer. I'd gasp, cry out, tears come to my eyes. So good it hurt. The sky a hazy, milky blur. The river dimpled, pitted, rippling. Small gentle swirls, a soft gurgle and lap. The play of light on the shimmering brown water. That sandbar seemingly suspended in mid-air, held up on a bed of fire. Being on water, in water, of water. Immersion. I would drink it, breathe it, dissolve in it, flow away. I am swimming in water, I am swimming in light. What is more holy than a river?

At night, outside of Omaha, we stopped in a parking lot, somebody cooked macaroni, and we all ate. One of the drivers announced that they planned to lay over in Denver for a few days. He said anybody planning to go ahead from there should know that Colorado was one of the worst states in the country for hitchhiking. What about Wyoming? somebody asked. In Rawlins, they still shaved heads, somebody had heard. In Rock Springs, it was ten dollars and ten days, somebody else claimed. Make up a sign and they'd leave you alone, said somebody else. Heed the warnings. On the road as well as the river.

A cop drove up. He asked where we were from, where we were going. The short guy in the Micky Mouse tee-shirt asked about hitchhiking in Nebraska. The cop said it was illegal. Since when? Since we've had so many rapes and killings, the cop replied. But is it a law that's *enforced*, the short guy persisted. The cop shrugged. It'd depend on who stopped you. You might get a warning or you might get run in.

After he left, the short guy said he was going to take his chances hitching south through Nebraska and around Colorado. He didn't want any more cops beating on him. He didn't have anything to carry, he didn't have any shoes. Swinging his stubby arms and taking short chopped-off strides, he left the bus and started back the way we had come.

"Man, that dude was really weird," said the ex-criminology major.

The two drivers were dead-tired and needed sleep, but I had said I wanted to reach Columbus that night, so they drove on. The bus rolled through the night. Fremont, Nebraska . . . Schuyler. The drivers switched. One of them came back and sat down. He had been busted for dealing in New York and had to stay away from there for awhile. He talked to somebody about Sam Peckinpah movies, and what he thought Peckinpah was trying to do with the subject of violence. The driver at the wheel played *Abbey Road*. It seemed a long time since I had heard that.

We got to Columbus about two thirty in the morning and pulled into an all-night truckstop. I introduced myself to the waitress, told her who my father was, and asked where the people on the bus might camp for the night. Most of the places I knew about as a boy have since been fenced-in and posted. But she knew of a campground outside of town, near a lake, with picnic tables and toilets.

Before I left the bus I gave the drivers my father's phone number. I told them that if there was anything they needed while they were here—if they wanted showers, if there was any kind of trouble—they were to call and let me know.

They never called or took me up on my offer of showers, but at least I had made it, and I felt rather good about it. I hadn't come off the river after all. The flow was still unbroken, and I was part of it.

---

it was a slipshod job.
the cows could have done it better.
they should have slept on it.
they should have laid their heads to rest on it.

I never could understand it.

even now, in the asylum,
I can't understand it.

pillows for cows.

, ...   carl wyant 1971

I was awakened by the sound of whales
outside my door.
why they came to my house
I'm not certain.
they were friendly enough
but when they asked to stay for dinner
I had to turn them down;
I was fresh out of plankton.

.   .   .   .   .   .   carl wyant 1972

carefree was the word,
he laughed his way.
as long as any sun burned, he moved
more like a rabbit
than a bay.

but he did move
and from ten trees I watched him laugh.
he laughed a clarinet.

then it all happened;
the spiders were upon him.
he had laughed his last clarinet.

.   .   .   .   .   .   carl wyant 1970

WIDOW MAKER
WIDOW MAKER
WERE THE WORDS
SO BRIGHT AND BIG

PAINTED CROSS
THE BUMPER
OF A SHINY RIG.

"WIDOW·MAKER"

WIDOW MAKER

AND CLIMBED
INTO HIS RIG.
SAID HE'D BE BACK
A' TUESDAY NIGHT
SO PLAN ON
SOMETHIN' BIG.

BILLIE MACK KISSED WANDA ANNE

JUST A FEW MORE MILES AND BILL WAS ON THAT MOUNTAIN RANGE

"WIDOW-MAKER"

WHERE DEAD AHEAD A PICKUP FULL OF KIDS BLOCKED BOTH THE LANES.

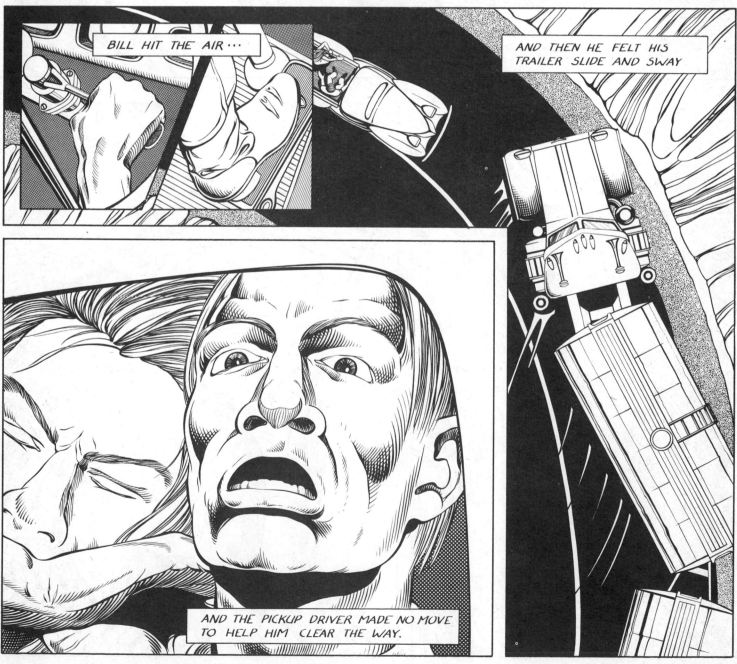

BILL HIT THE AIR···

AND THEN HE FELT HIS TRAILER SLIDE AND SWAY

AND THE PICKUP DRIVER MADE NO MOVE TO HELP HIM CLEAR THE WAY.

For quite a few years now, critics and reviewers who are prone to say such things have been calling Wright Morris "one of America's greatest/most gifted/talented writers." The surprise to a fellow like me, who is prone to sarcastic and suspicious remarks at the sight of such utterances, has been in finding this particular estimate to be true. Wright Morris long since turned out to be my favorite living writer.

Still, there's no reason why you should find one young fellow's idolatry impressive; more to the point is the fact that the man has written, from *My Uncle Dudley* in 1941 to *Fire Sermon* in 1971, nineteen books—fourteen of them novels, three photo-texts, and two books of essays. An output that large hints at the presence of abundant imaginative drawing power, or at least is indicative of one hell of a lot of energy. In point of fact, Morris has both, along with a fair share of raw material. He was born in Nebraska (Central City, to be exact, in 1910), and that state (of mind and on map), recreated and imaginatively possessed, forms setting and substance of many of the novels I like best. But he was a teenager in Chicago, there just in time to empty a wastebasket on Lindbergh's head and be so affected by the hero's feat as to begin a singlehanded series of travels that has not yet fully ended. Morris has spent years seeing America first and recording the vision. So the world of his books is just as likely to include suburban Philly as a jail in Mississippi, or for that matter, the wholly fictive town of Lone Tree, Nebraska.

Not that you could call what he writes travel books; you couldn't even say actually they are about place. A bunch of people watching a bullfight, for example, is what *The Field of Vision* (National Book Award Winner) is "about:" the simple astonishing fact that each one sees the bullfight as only each of them can. The point is something close to the heart of Morris' work: photography of consciousness, pictures of the act of sight. But the importance of place in any such picture is central, particularly in America where the land was the only building material around for the construction of souls, and spirit's been the most important (if least tended) crop. Morris, more than any other writer I've read, is sensitive to this fact, as well as savvy to the mythic distortions of Nostalgia and/or The Territory Ahead that blur its true dimensions in our lives. As far as I was concerned, he was the logical fellow to put questions to on the place of place; so though I was surprised when he consented to this interview, my true wonder only commenced when, after swapping stories of car trouble and being down and out, I turned the tape recorder on in the living room of his house in the hills behind Mill Valley, Ca., and he picked up a piece of paper, leaned back, started to talk—and this whole amazing thing began to roll. —F.P.

QUERENCIAS, and a lot else: an interview with Wright Morris

WRIGHT MORRIS: LET ME SEE NOW---the mystique of place: there is a place in the bullring where the bull feels at home. There is, you know. It's called the *querencia*, and in Americans, it's important to their self-esteem.

FRED PFEIL: A lot of us though, a lot of Americans, have traditionally had the idea that the *querencia* lies behind us somewhere, haven't we?

WRIGHT MORRIS: We've always had the idea of the good place as a reality. And for many it was, however limited. Especially a good place to be *from*. The richer the promise of conscious life in the city—that is, more conscious, instead of just the unconscious life in rural circumstances—the richer the promise, the more it involved complications and deceptions. The lack of an adequate concept of reality, free of excessive expectations, naturally led to disenchantment and the backward look that falsified the past. We begin to look back and say "Ah, the glorious life that once was." And an interesting point is

whatever the European experience, it is free of this particular nostalgia because it's free of that option.

FRED PFEIL: Well, my immediate question is, is this still a working dynamic, do you think, or has it changed?

WRIGHT MORRIS: No, I think that it has changed. I was reflecting on this, and it led me to ask—what do *we* mean by nostalgia? And I come up with something like this: nostalgia is an inbred psychic craving. In one guise or another it may be part of every culture. Let's say that it's part of human nature. And American style is great expectations followed by early disenchantment. The formula of the small-town dream to big town disillusion, and then, the backward look. That happens to be the American version. And probably we would be surprised to find that there is another type of nostalgia, but I'm sure there is. I'm inclined to feel that nostalgia is a hunger deeply rooted in millions of years of human experience, the backward look is redeeming; it makes the look of the present bearable. For nearly all people there was another time, back to the bliss and the prospect of the mother's arms, a secure environment, the threatening world of reality held at bay. Perhaps most creatures of any self-awareness, and any consciousness, have nostalgic ties. They look back.

F RED P FEIL: But is the point then about the American version that we've had the land to project those feelings on all these years, or felt that we had the land?

W RIGHT M ORRIS: Well, certainly it is indigenous to American experience, because the reality is that we had this new world. The constantly receding frontier *is* a reality. We've been able to recede along with it for almost a century and a half. There's always a corner we can go into. Escaping from the expectations that failed us using the excuse of even greater expectations to ignore the world we are involved in. Although destructive, this has also been creative. We might even find, to our embarassment, that if this nostalgic world should diminish or disappear from our lives, that we will have lost more than we will have gained, in terms of psychic energy; but we will be more—more adult human beings. We will not be haunted by essentially unrealistic traumas and impossible resolutions.

F RED P FEIL: What you're talking about is a sort of loss of innocence.

W RIGHT M ORRIS: I don't know as I'd say loss of innocence. I would say it is going to be different. Nostalgia is not going to be as destructive, as distorting, as falsifying. Simultaneously it may prove to have less energy; it may generate less of what so much creative life is made up of, that is, the projection of imaginative concepts, and so forth. This might prove to be an interesting loss, you see, since we will gain in terms of becoming more "adult" and adjusting ourselves to "life," but we may prove to be less creative in the sense of complaining about wherever we are.

F RED P FEIL: I put it that way, I guess, because I was thinking of people I know who've grown up in L.A. or some other urban area, and have decided to literally take to the woods. And it seems like they're more gimlet-eyed about it than the people of Brook Farm, maybe have more hard-nosed expectations that you don't just go back there and slip in, that you have to evolve some kind of life-style that takes your urbanity into account.

W RIGHT M ORRIS: Well, it does still resemble older American experience in that the present is inadequate, the circumstances are inadequate, so we're going to improve them. The way we improve them is go somewhere. So that go-somewhere instinct is still viable because the continent is still so open that even though we are constrained and feel that we're fenced in by cities and suburbs, the continent is really wide open, and largely empty. That instinct of "I'm gonna get the hell out of here," or, as the Beatles put it, "Step on the gas and wipe that tear away." That's it. Now that speaks to me with a kind of poignant nostalgia. But on the other hand, it is so profoundly American, it's Beatles singing it; so what is the connection? (Laughs) The Beatles talking about stepping on the gas and wiping that tear away! No I have guesses about that, and they're not really germane to our discussion, but I would say *they* have been shaped by American sentiment, even though they're in England, and their batteries charged with American sentiment. And I am interested because I would like to ask why do we not find equivalent achievement among Americans. Here they're using a media that is an American invention, really, this sense of improvisation in the use of lyrics and music, and I'll be goddamned, here these kids from Liverpool, or wherever the hell it is, out-achieving Americans at their own games. Now that to me is damned interesting, but it might, again, lie outside of our discussion.

F RED P FEIL: Well, I wonder. The whole sense of fun, the sense of goofing on the scene, might be just because they're outside it; and in that sense, place-related. We might find it a little more oppressive, or—they certainly don't have the whole-hearted depth of response, say, to a line like "Step on the gas and wipe that tear away." (Laughs) They don't hurt with that line like I hurt with it. And maybe they're more able to goof on Americana.

W RIGHT M ORRIS: You could easily be right. I would not be able to distinguish on the level of their art form, on the Pop art form, that area of commitment, of emotional commitment, along with technical and stylistic success; I can't tell, you see, whether they *feel* it more or less than an American performer in the same situation. They sound pretty convincing to me. It's only when I ask, realistically, On *what* gas? and Tear away from *what?*

F RED P FEIL: Yeah, what kind of cars are they driving?

W RIGHT M ORRIS: Exactly, and where are they going? But up to that point, they may indeed feel that they are stepping on that gas and wiping that tear away as much as Bob Dylan or anybody else. Even though we know that there is a difference, we cannot pinpoint that difference.

F RED P FEIL: Yeah. You think we might actually be exporting American culture at long last.

W RIGHT M ORRIS: I think so. I think we're exporting it all over the place. We are the inventors of the vernacular as a literature, and vernacular has really taken the world over wherever American literature is read. And that contagious and almost epidemic influence is the subtle way in which we have exported ourselves and our attitudes and our discomforts and our neuroses, the whole bit has gone along with this. It becomes an extremely subtle business involving life and literature simultaneously, the removal of barriers so that life and literature in Pop art forms are almost identical. This to me grows out of the gradual erosion of the vernacular on the concept of an art form.

F RED P FEIL: I'd like to talk about that, all right? I mean, I know we can't possibly exhaust it. But isn't there some kind of strange intermediary position that the vernacular occupies between the place you live and the mind you have, which is why the vernacular is so extraordinarily successful in America? You talk, for example, about being a Nebraska writer, and the way that means you write.

W RIGHT M ORRIS: You mean about where I'm *from*. About the fact that I do not ever really get away from where I'm from, I take it with me.

F RED P FEIL: But that makes a language for you too, doesn't it? I mean, that sets up a whole series of choices that you make because of where you're from. What I'm trying to get at is the vernacular is something entirely different from the grand style of the European novel, because it's much more hooked into the territory itself, isn't it?

W RIGHT M ORRIS: Yes, yes, I accept this distinction. This was not possible to literature until you have a new land. Whitman prophesied it when he said we are a *new* people, and we're going to have a *new* language, and everything's going to be *new*. Whitman was there, Whitman's language was a vernacular, and it's related to artifacts. Twain's the first one to stumble—or rather grope his way back—into the vernacular with Huck Finn. And from that point on, the notion of a distinction in language and literature, or in life and literature, is threatened. Gradually there is an inevitable approximation and a desire to approximate, that comes in; and whenever the vernacular makes its appearance, the notion of a separate style for literature recedes. It's inevitable. And this was James's predicament. That we should have figures like Henry James and Mark Twain alive at the same moment, you know, is incredible. One of the subtlest minds for three or four hundred years, and one of the most nuance-like in its perceptions, was simultaneously totally ignorant and blind to what was really happening in the American language. *His* language. And that is why he is out of phase and this cornpone frogjumper is *in* phase.

The vernacular appears at that point, and then, by a series of refinements reached the stage of acceptance that now leads us to question if literature has any alternatives. And the best talents have diverted all their energy to this particular resource of the vernacular. And the vernacular is constantly reinforced and fed by streams of new experience, and even the involvement that we had with European experience becomes vernacularized, because we interpret it into our own terms. And that enriches it. So that it is constantly being fed by the old and new.

Now what I feel to be the obstructive element becomes subtle. It comes with the notion that we gradually begin to feel that "life" exists in the language, and that if we're true to the language, we're true to the life, and that if we become involved, we become easily more involved in telling it like it is than in knowing how it is.

FRED PFEIL: Sort of substituting style for life, is that it?

WRIGHT MORRIS: The language becomes the crucial element in experience. The language is so rich, it is so inviting, it is so open to the widest possible gamuts of experience that the writer unconsciously finds himself more involved with the language than he is with the more complicated problems of what the language is supposed to do. For instance, I could show you five selections of prose, and you could never by any means choose between them on "style." One would come from a journalist's morning report about an accident, the other would come from a girl of sixteen who is writing a letter to Dr. Hippocrates, another from a letter that an older person is writing to a younger one, another from a professor who is writing a history of the youth rebellion. Because of our sense of a common experience, created by vernacular disciplines, and by the talent and intelligence we've applied to the vernacular, we finally have *one* language. There is only one language, spoken and written, that speaks for and to us. And purely because of this triumph we are in the danger that concerns me, that the language itself has taken precedence over the complexities of experience that the language is supposed to deal with. We're never going to get away from the vernacular, and this is not an attack on it. I am merely attempting to call attention to the fact that we are producing more and more writing in novels that resembles more and more writing in novels that resembles more and more writing in novels. That is, the language itself is the writer's subject and his inspiration— the language leads, and the writer follows where it leads. Why do so many remarkably diverse writers end up writing such similar novels?

FRED PFEIL: So that we all end up writing about the same thing.

WRIGHT MORRIS: Exactly! Because that's what the language *wants* to write about, that's what the language is *able* to write about. The vernacular, by its very nature, inclines downward. It goes to the bottom of the barrel. It does not take flight. Now this is in contradiction to that aspect of our nature which wants to fly, take wings, but the vernacular wants to dig and grub, because that's where it speaks with conviction. It wants to say *Shit, man,* and when it wants to say more, say something that is difficult and lyrical, it's embarrassed. So it doesn't say it. It says Aw man, aw come on off it, aw manmanman. It's all right for Huck Finn, or Holden Caulfield, for some kid who doesn't really know better, but it's not for grown-ups. It wants to simplify, keep the feet on the earth, take off the shoes and wiggle the toes in the mud. That is the vernacular inclination that now needs to be reversed, and confronted with the up-cline. Because of the cliche that "dirty" facts are real, and imaginative perceptions and truths are "unreal," the best fiction talents of our time are reporting on less than half of our life—the lower half. The vernacular can do anything. *Anything.* And it will take the up-cline with greater ease and to newer heights than at the time of James and Twain. Twain did not know how to lift the vernacular to that level, but he did very well within the range of Huck Finn. James could simply not touch the vernacular at all; he simply couldn't do it, as great as he was. Now we've so ordered it that the imagination is embarassed at the possibility of departing from the dictates of the language. This is what I mean. The imagination is now constrained in order to be true to the vernacular. It wants to tell it like it is, if the language is agreeable.

FRED PFEIL: But how do you get away from that? If people are all outside of the books talking like that, I assume we're all talking vernacular now, right?

WRIGHT MORRIS: Yes, we write, talk, breathe, live, dream, have our fantasies in vernacular. We have a medium here that everybody participates in on the level of their sensibilities; I don't believe there *is* a distinction any more. But no difficulty lies in the language *itself;* the difficulty lies in that the success, the triumph of the vernacular has for the moment so persuaded that writer and so influenced him as to feel that all he has to do is just use the language, not question it, fashion it, and run it once more through the process of his imagination. Now he feels that if he uses the language, he's writing; and that's enough.

FRED PFEIL: What about the image, the advertising image that you talk about in *Bill of Rites . . .*? Is the media part of, or does it help in, this vernacularization?

WRIGHT MORRIS: Everything has become media. Now, in the McLuhan sense, we are familiar with the possibilities. But forgetting that electronic imagery naturally excites McLuhan, I think that it's simply taking place on a language level also. We get it from every conceivable source; when we talk to each other, when we read a book, when we dream, we are constantly exposed. To me, the advertising aspect of it—I suppose it's simply that I'm weary of thinking about it, or I would think of it as a particular, localized type of irritant. Right at the moment, largely because it's simply something I'd rather not think about, it's such a tedious and tiresome subject, I would see it as simply another symptom of the triumph of vernacularization. Because it too does not make any effort to introduce a fresh element into our experience.

FRED PFEIL: It slides downwards, the image slides downward in the same way that the language slides downward.

WRIGHT MORRIS: Exactly, what we have is *illustrated* vernacularization. The girl stands there and combs her hair, or lets it hang before her face, and the housewife comes forward with a box of something. Now that is tiresome, but if we think about the language that comes along with this visualization, it is this familiar thing; this facsimile of life: I could take it, you could take it, any writer could take it *verbatim.* You see what I mean? You just take it—well, [shoves his hands forward with an imaginary mess of words cupped in them] you know, here it *is.* It's a question of just putting quotes around it, or picking it up and slipping it in somewhere. And it's the same if President Nixon wants to address the country. At a certain moment if he wants to say "damn" or "dang" or something of this sort, he really feels that he *has* to put quote marks about a term that doesn't fit the old-style language. And he'll say "As we say today," or "As the young people put it" or something of the sort. And the squares among them will think [puts on a high, nasal, old person's voice] "Well there's somebody at least, that really has a sense of style in this country." But basically he has simply admitted to being terribly out of phase, out of style, out of tone.

FRED PFEIL: His language is really an extreme narrowing, in the sense that we've been talking about. There's so little the man can say.

WRIGHT MORRIS: He can't say *anything*. He represents in both his virtues and his limitations that real notion of a human computer. [He points to the tape recorder]. Like the controls on your machine—they're all in, and they all have these fantastically limited responses. You know, just as we think of a very limited character on a farm who has three stories and one or two responses to the weather, and so forth. He represents this in great purity. And in his own nature, he is perhaps a complicated person, to himself. And of course, being a human being, he is. But in terms of the role and the experience that he is meant to mirror or reflect or comment on, we have what will perhaps increasingly be a grotesque malfunction of intent and the responsibilities at hand. We will go through this business of electing these very limited men to deal with very complicated situations. Like having a $75,000 taping outfit in here, and letting the cat meeow all afternoon; there'd be nothing on it but mewing.

FRED PFEIL: What we're talking about, then, is, with Nixon, a rather extreme stunting of the imagination, and which you point to as being done entirely by the language. Is that happening, in some sense, to all of us?

WRIGHT MORRIS: It is—and when you have a limited imagination, what we have is a means of keeping it stunted. There's nothing in the language that challenges the writer, or makes him aware that he's *using* a language. If we went into the writing or the reading that was done by very simple people fifty years ago, we'd see exactly what I mean. They *wrote* better, they *read* better, they understood more because this vernacularization had not taken place. They were either illiterate—and therefore subtle sensually—or they were literate, and used words with understanding and authority. They sought out, and used, unusual words. This has now become an undefined and indistinct mess of verbalization (in which individual words dissolve) and we just accept it, because it does look and sound very life-like. And also, when we get someone who is intelligent and informed, the vernacular may rise to the occasion. We have journalists now who are very definitely superior; you get a man with a good deal of intelligence and one paragraph is factual, one paragraph is speculation—it's all there. He is free; the vernacular, in short, has freed him of the limitations that once existed. At one time, he would say "I must not say that because it will go over into another sphere." Now we have blended the fiction, the fact, the speculation, and with a good writer it's beautiful, better than it's ever been.

FRED PFEIL Well, you sort of started to answer my next question which is, being an American, what I want to know is where do I *go* to get fresh language. And the place is obviously not—you don't have to go anywhere, you do it yourself, is that right?

WRIGHT MORRIS: That is right. Let's put it the other way around, Fred, let's say that our problem is that we are like people who've been exploited sensually, or sexually. They've lost a sensibility through abuse and lack of discrimination. We are so over-languaged, that is, we are so over-exposed to indiscriminate language, that we have lost the sense of how extremely subtle and delicate the language we know to be abused still is. Follow me? We don't need a fresh language, we have all the freshness we can conceivably use: it is too fresh, it needs to be reprocessed by the imagination. My own problem as a writer is how to restore to simple words something of the vigor, something of the feeling, that the words actually still contain, and will always contain. It's why I'm reacting against the ver-

nacular, and why I've become very sensitive about even skillfully felicitous writers who simply toss off the language. They're *very* skillful, like Philip Roth; you get into the vein and it just writes itself. And that's very entertaining, we like it, it's lively, it's revealing, but it has ceased to be imaginative writing on that level that nourishes the language and communicates real emotion and new imaginative experience. The writer doesn't *have* to do it, it seems to be done. You read something, you hear something, you watch a movie, and it's *all* there. We feel an exhaustion from this exposure. I don't know what we'd do if we all didn't have eight hours of total darkness; without these eight hours of the human system lying dormant, we would burn out within a few weeks. And it's that single biological fact that makes it possible for us to go our murderous way; we become worn out, and yet overnight we're back, and we're able to wear each other frazzled again the next day. Now the language—if we were to talk like union leaders *talk*, attempting to work out a contract, men of this sort who talk at each other don't work out *compromises,* they simply wear each other down. Because gradually we fatigue, it's impossible for us to bear up. And then somebody with a *slightly* fresh mind comes in and spells out something, and in a horrible state of fatigue, they say "Yes, we agree, all tables should have four legs," after ten days of wear and erosion they make "peace," they give up. Yet their *intentions* are good. We are frail; our abilities are frail; and so far as our talents have any subtlety, they wear out, they fray away. Think of Eliot's remark: "Words, crack, erode" etc. absolutely. And he wrote that at a time before this had really begun to take its toll, because he was a poet, and could intuit.

FRED PFEIL: This standard vernacularization certainly diminishes the richness that we traditionally associate with places in the country, diminishes the renewal we get, or think we get, on new ground.

WRIGHT MORRIS: It will—well, I think we can say it does. It does because there is no way whatsoever that we can both exploit an area and a sensation and an experience, and have it fresh. On the other hand, what I believe is possible, for at least a period of time, is the actual possession of things which we have very hastily gobbled and not really possessed imaginatively. Now I might use an example: simply my own struggle with Will Brady, with *The Works of Love*. Now that experience was simply a fictive creation of something that I really did not have, but felt I must have: a background.

FRED PFEIL: I don't know whether I understand.

WRIGHT MORRIS: Well, my Midwest is actually rather limited. The Midwest for me is fundamental but I left it as a boy of nine. I'm a little city boy by the time I'm ten years old; I'm in Omaha, and then I'm in Chicago at fifteen. And I had no particular feeling about the Midwest until after my college years, when I began to write, when I began to grasp all of the complex notions of rediscovery that are involved—involved actually in being a writer as much as being an American. We tend, again, to reduce all problems to their American constituents. But every writer is involved in the essential problem that Mann states in *Death in Venice* which is "Who will unriddle the puzzle of the artist's nature?" Now actually, this is what most American writers are doing, although they never think of putting it in such a pompous manner. But what a lot of us are apt to think of as simply the American rediscovering his past, is a natural process of the writer, of the artist, coming into his own. It isn't something peculiar to Americans, you see, it is something peculiar to the artistic sensibility. We see everything in such goddamn parochial terms, however, we want to reduce it and say . . .

FRED PFEIL: It's the country, it's the country.

WRIGHT MORRIS: That's right, when basically it's the person.

PHOTOGRAPHS BY WRIGHT MORRIS

FRED PFEIL: It's us trying to take possession of ourselves, then.

WRIGHT MORRIS: Exactly; and it just so happens that for the so-called writer, or artist, this *is* his raw material, such a past as he has; his real background is his nature. So he's attempting to fathom his own nature, not the goddamned country. But the country is naturally going to be there, because that is essential to his nature. In my particular case, I had to reconstruct and invent the Midwest that was adequate to my need of it. And my experience happened to be rich enough so that I didn't lack for raw material, the basis for my elaborate reconstruction. Take the character of Brady, who is fashioned out of nothing so much as my need of him. There's a scene in *The World in the Attic,* a little book that grew out of a fragment of *The Works of Love,* where an old man is up in a hotel room in a small town, and all he does is sit there and look up and down the tracks, and he becomes involved with looking east and west; and out of this—I wrote this scene about 1945—the town, its appearance, the hotel, the whole bit, just grew out of my need, so that I invented this place of Lone Tree. It's a complete fiction, it doesn't resemble my town at all, just one or two things. But out of it came this figure, and out of this figure, eventually— brooding on the possibilities of this Brady—I had a center for the whole reconstruction. And this was an excitement; for two or three years I was out of my mind!

FRED PFEIL: So the whole point is to create, according to one's needs—not to go back and explore the literal place that you come from, is that what the Nebraska books are about for you?

WRIGHT MORRIS: Right. Except for *The Home Place—* which is largely an act of salvage. Growing up in this small town, which is more like an Indiana town than a Nebraska town, because it was beautifully treed, and I had typical Penrod and Sam adventures as a boy;—I don't think I knew what the plains were like till I *read* about them. Even today this small town is like one in Indiana or Illinois because of all the trees that were planted when my father was a boy. There wasn't a tree out there, previously. And at one time this was called Lone Tree; I won't go into that, but I never knew it. It was never mentioned. They changed the name of the town thirty-five years before I was born.

FRED PFEIL: Did you find out about it after you had invented the Lone Tree of your books?

WRIGHT MORRIS: *I did. I did.* Now of course it's arguable that at some point I had heard it—subconsciously—but no one could have been more overwhelmed when I found that out.

FRED PFEIL: It's sort of a beautiful little example of what we've been talking about, about making the place where you really come from. What is it—the dream of Adam, or something; he dreamt of the garden, and woke up and found that it was true?

WRIGHT MORRIS: Yes, yes, that's the idea. I invent this whole thing then I find out it's true! So I would not invent another place, I still have to invent *that place.* I don't have to; but for me it's suitable. Another writer might invent just the opposite place because he'd had *too* much of the plains. But I *hadn't* suffered the plains. I did not see the plains, I grew up in a town of great elms, cottonwoods. And I left the place at nine, and gave it no thought until I returned from Europe determined to be a writer. Then the missing ingredients were added, which I recall even as I speak; it was on my way back to California that I crossed the plains for the first time in almost fifteen years! and it came to me! I *missed* the plains! So I had to think my way back. And it freed my imagination to really reconstruct it, to invent it—not to simply remember, but to recreate it. That's the whole thing. The two have to have a certain kind of parallel; there needs to be, between the need to create and what it is you are, some kind of rapport. Otherwise there is simply some kind of obstruction, and then perhaps the writer gets off into fantasy. English writers and European writers have seldom had this particular privilege, or problem— they have to do things very differently because they never have these options. They begin as writers on a more adult level because they're never quite caught in this dilemma. Towns have *always* been there, houses have always been there, everybody's *been* there—

FRED PFEIL: And the style's always been there, the style of writing, too.

WRIGHT MORRIS: Exactly, it was even the *high* German, until very recently—how you were going to write, it was all given to you, the whole bit.

FRED PFEIL: But anyway, at this point, you began to, more or less, make the place where you were most comfortable.

WRIGHT MORRIS: Manufacture my own *querencia,* absolutely. First scribbling: I begin to take pictures of alleys, fences, doorways. This goes on for five years. It was through this effort that I create the nostalgia that gets me back, in 1947, to *The Home Place* and, a year later, to *The World in the Attic,* which speaks of hometown nausea. In *The World in the Attic,* I am already slightly schizoid; because that same character [as in *The Home Place*], Will Muncy, he experiences hometown nausea. Then I'm away from it for several years, until I come back to it in *The Field of Vision.* But that's quite another country. By the time I'm actually back into *place,* I've had a tremendous, an exalted sense of rediscovery. That was brought about with an essay about the plains that was printed in *Holiday.* And it grew from that landscape—grew absolutely from my recapturing of the landscape. And I worked myself into such a lather, like a man inventing his own new-found land, that I was obliged to work it out in *Ceremony in Lone Tree.* The first scene in *Ceremony* is very, very close to that essay; I think you'll remember it: "Come to the window . . ."

FRED PFEIL: But apparently this imagining, the creation of this landscape, and all your work in Nebraska, has come to a rather decisive end for you—or at least your friend the critic Granville Hicks implies that.

WRIGHT MORRIS: Well now, there is an obvious sense of a closure about some of these things. And I think he's right to have had this feeling about *God's Country and My People.* That is a kind of casting back, the salvage of familiar objects, or the effort to see them as they are, combined with fresh reappraisals.

FRED PFEIL: Was the motive of that book that you were to do this and have done with it?

WRIGHT MORRIS: Perhaps—a self-conscious "look at these things for the last time," and a last visit to the attic, sort of. And then a surprise—when I got into it, how freshly reanimated I became. The text in that book is not long; I forget at this moment just what got me into it, but I felt dissatisfied that I had not said all I wanted to say in regard to the subject. Or perhaps my dissatisfaction was with *how* I had previously said it. Too much nostalgia—or inadequate writing. I did have that feeling, and when I finished it—well, that's that. But who knows? Take *Fire Sermon,* for example, and then the book that I've just finished—it's the same character, the same old man. And if anything, he's profoundly Midwest. So I continue with this experience on another plane, I carry this old man through the last day of his life.

FRED PFEIL: So it doesn't really end. I wanted to ask you whether you felt some kind of decisive break, like "Now, I must leave this place."

WRIGHT MORRIS: Well, I feel a break of a certain kind, a willful break. Let's say the break that I feel in the sense of a

THE MAN WHO LIVES his own life, and wears it out, can dispense with the need of taking it with him. He dies his own death or he goes on living, and where the life has worn in the death will come out. Skin and bones, jacket and shoes, tools, sheds and machines wear out; even the land wears out and the seat wears off the cane-bottom chair. The palms wear off the gloves, the cuffs off the sleeves, the nickel off the doorknobs, the plate off the silver, the flowers off the plates, the shine off the stovepipe, the label off the flour sacks, the enamel off the dipper, the varnish off the checkers, and the gold off the Christmas jewelry, but every day the nap wears off the carpet the figure wears in. A pattern for living, the blueprint of it, can be seen in the white stitches of the denim, the timepiece stamped like a medallion in the bib of the overalls. Between wearing something in and wearing it out the line is as vague as the receding horizon, and as hard to account for as the missing hairs of a brush. The figure that began on the front of the carpet has moved around to the back.

—*From* **GOD'S COUNTRY AND MY PEOPLE** *by Wright Morris, Harper & Row, Publishers, 1968.*

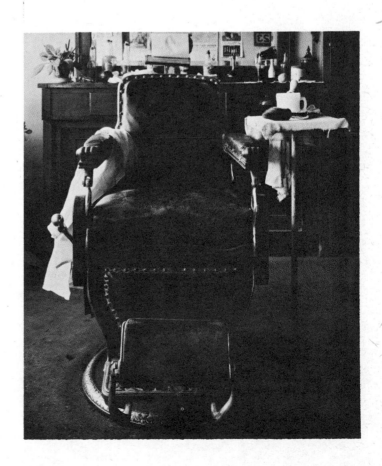

closure, very definitely, is the idea of carrying on the same personality, like a third volume dealing with Boyd [hero of *The Field of Vision* and *Ceremony in Lone Tree*]. No. *Finito.* But otherwise it would be like saying I'm finished with my own life. I don't know what's going to come up. I have a lot of strings to my imagination. I have a novel that's largely set abroad . . .

FRED PFEIL: *What a Way to Go?*

WRIGHT MORRIS: That's right, then there's *Love Among the Cannibals* [set in Southern California]. And then *One Day* is a kind of composite, of all sorts of elements. And that in itself is instructive, perhaps that shows a sort of gathering of loose ends. But I have no idea of what next—although I'm always preoccupied with it. I could never say to what extent it would depart from what we might think of as echoes of the Midwest material. I would suspect they'll be constant. Yes, I'm almost certain. It wouldn't matter if I was writing about space, they'd still be there. In the main, these elements will remain; the closure is in a certain type of experience that was introduced in *The World in the Attic* and closed itself off with *Ceremony:* and that's essentially an imaginative re-examination and rediscovery that has strong nostalgic overtones, and is largely invented. You see, I really am inventing my own raw material, not abandoning it, and now I see it from a different, from a longer perspective. Now I just accept it. Something like that.

FRED PFEIL: Right. Getting back to *God's Country*—what excites me particularly about it is that it seems to do what Agee says a photograph can do. You know how he talks about the way a photograph can make you see things clean. And in the same way, in the writing, you can see the fictive constructions you've made: you see that building, you see that whole place, very clearly and without illusion, without any mythic barriers or nostalgic tints, you know, like Here it is.

WRIGHT MORRIS: Yes. *Let Us Now Priase Famous Men:* marvelous, marvelous book. Also in Henry James, of all people: the commonplace artifact becomes an icon. You asked about the absence of people from my photos: the people are in the fiction, not in the flesh. Only in their absence from the photo will the observer intuit their presence in the object.

FRED PFEIL: The icon itself is almost more visibly holy . . .

WRIGHT MORRIS: That's right.

FRED PFEIL: Did you find the photographs helpful? You know, as a way of drawing back from all of that, a way of insuring that distance.

WRIGHT MORRIS: I probably did; yes, I think so. The good fortune was that when I got around to it again, I still had the prints. It was an act of salvage and closure at once. I wouldn't go back, you see; now I have no desire to, that's the main thing. I could easily work myself into it, but I no longer feel impelled to make that kind of record, which I once felt absolutely *compelled* to, I just couldn't let something so beautiful get away. There again is that sense of the disappearing, of the vanishing American scene. I can remember a letter, from somewhere in Tennessee, I sat down and wrote to Henry Allan Moe, of the Guggenheim Foundation, when the hell was it—either '46 or '47. I was wandering about on some other purpose; and it dawned on me that about half of the things I saw were not going to be there ten years later. Suddenly I saw the whole country bereft of these expressive things: old houses and barns, the icons of our experience. And I worked myself into a state of mind where American culture would be absolutely barren without these things; I saw myself as salvaging the remnants of a civilization for future generations. So I sat down and wrote him, I said Henry, this is ridiculous, I'm one of the few people alive who realizes that something of value is disappearing, I've got to do something about this, and I will willingly give two years of my time, I will go up and down the alleys and the byways of the country and I will, IwillIwillIwill . . . an hysterical letter. But that's the way I felt, and there it was. I *knew* what I was feeling, none of this was really ridiculous. I *knew* I could do these things, I knew how they should be done, I had a prescient notion of where they would be. It was just a question of—oh, all I wanted from him was simply money to buy film, gas, and food. It added up to nothing, but it wasn't a ridiculous project, it was a good project;—sometimes I regret I didn't do it.

FRED PFEIL: Still, the point still obtains.

WRIGHT MORRIS: Sure.

FRED PFEIL: But you no longer feel the impulse to do that?

WRIGHT MORRIS: Let's say that the impulse is felt, but it is not compulsive. It's—I don't *have* to do it. Sometimes I am sorry that I don't *have* to do it, I feel that I should. But the problem is simplified for me: it's simply too damn much work. I carried around a lot of equipment: my camera—there's a heavy tripod—I looked like Matthew Brady in the Civil War, and it was physically exhauting. That alone simplified it. The sheer physical work: first on the road, then in the darkroom. That has proved impractical for years. The darkroom work alone is physically exhausting. My sentiments are still there—I *indulge* in them, but I don't get carried away by them.

FRED PFEIL: It's no longer an irresistible impulse.

WRIGHT MORRIS: Right! That's been for quite a while. I stopped taking the pictures in 1954, and maybe for six or seven years, I really missed it. But then you grow out of it. I trained myself not to do that, that is, not to get involved that way. My recent photo-text book, *Love Affair:* a Venetian Journal—were color-slides and the "work" was done by the engravers and printers.

FRED PFEIL: We have just a few minutes of tape left. Do you have anything you want to add?

WRIGHT MORRIS: Let me see. I wonder if there's something that I haven't got around to. Ways out for example: the young have a grip on them. A reduction of self-interest, self-exploitation, ego-tripping. I feel that the most destructive thing in American life is its self-interest. The feeling that anything *we* do is *important,* anything about us is *important.* Witness that ghastly TV serial, *An American Family.* A collection of innocent, decent boobs; but they all *feel* themselves important, and we all watch them because we feel they *have* to be important, it's an *American* family, isn't it? See what I mean?

FRED PFEIL: [laughing] Yeah, so it must count.

WRIGHT MORRIS: Yeah; it has to be. I mean, what else is there? *An awareness of more than people.* This is what I feel to be absolutely crucial to the future of the novel—or anything else. "What else is there?" Amazing question: while it is askable, the trap is set. From a few miles in space, it is impossible to detect evidence of man and his works on this planet. Even his abuses are not apparent. The meaning of this perspective, not its shock value, must be incorporated into man's psyche; only this will inhibit his rampant egotism. Note, also, in this egotism, how it sees in man's smallness a confirmation of his greatness. That's a typical reversal.

FRED PFEIL: Like Pascal's big line, "Man is only a reed, but he is a thinking reed."

WRIGHT MORRIS: Exactly; "It is only man that conceives of himself as being small;" you know that one? All of this ends up in this egotism. An end to "man the measure" is what I want. Man the measure: this, I think, is now an outworn creed. We've taken it from the Greeks, and we've absolutely worn it out. These are the veils that conceal man from man and man from nature. This I believe.

Getting away from it is a question of talent that will look around and see what is *there,* but in our self-interest, we can't see it. Self-interest blinds us just the way the vernacular blinds us, because it's so perfectly obvious. We know there *are* other cultures which see other things when they look out the window than we see; but we are determined that there's nothing else out there but what *we* see. Well, somehow, sophisticated human beings have to learn that they can see *more* than themselves, without giving up their self-centeredness. It's a level of human culture that we're at; for four or five hundred years now, we've been making the most out of our*selves.* And it comes in with Montaigne when he exclaims that he's going to talk about himself because there's nothing else that he knows so well. And then we get it again from Thoreau, saying the same thing. And we get it again from Whitman; we're endlessly, endlessly exploring that fascinating creature, *ourselves.* Well, that's the bottom of the barrel that we're now scraping. And it's just pathetic because we *are* aware, and young people are especially aware, that there's another world out there; but historically and culturally, we're trapped in the sense that it's got to be brought back to the world of the ego. Think of how every scientific research program is invariably based on the conceit that whatever is going to be done to an animal will be to the advantage of man. We look at apes to see if we can't see how men grow better. We look, we kill, we dissect, we do everything on the basis that if what is being done proves to be an advantage

to *man,* it is justified. That is the most poisonous creed conceivable. That is the *end of man,* right in that man. And every time I watch one of these nature programs, I see it, every goddamn time. A young woman who knows better, this Jane Goodall, she goes to Africa in order to study the apes, and to drum up a TV program they trap a bunch of these poor goddamn wild African dogs out there, and they put these dogs through their paces, and at the end of it she makes the pitiful observation that in the study of these creatures, *perhaps* some light will be shown on the origins of man. You see, we go on and on, it's bottomless; so long as anything we do can be related to some vantage point of ourselves, we will without question let this planet float into disorbit, we will allow anything. And the folly of that can be seen by any person; even the most foolish can grasp it. Young people, I think, are very open to this knowing, but until we all grasp it we're going to go on with the notion that there's nothing to exploit but ourselves. Even when we're abusing other creatures, we think of ourselves. And this is part of fiction, Fred; fiction insofar as it is a means to expand man's consciousness. So it may come from fiction. I don't know; but it *is* part of fiction's future—if it is to have one—to divert man away from himself. I don't know how he's going to do it, or when, but I'm convinced that he must.

Snakepit Highway

or A Tale of Two Highways

After driving along a number of our country's highways, I have noticed a curious dichotomy: most of the roads are either four-lane interstates with Howard Johnson's every so often, or tourist highways lined with funky billboards, neat old motels or truckstops, and, most distinctly, snakepits and dinosaurs.

The HoJos are almost all identical, fitting an achitectural style that is the visual equivalent of Muzak. The food is dished out in computer measured amounts, tastes awful and, worse, the coffee is 25¢ *and* undrinkable. The interstate traffic served by the HoJos is bent on one thing, getting to where it's going with as little sensation and experience as possible.

The snakepit and dinosaur lined highways, on the other hand, are a child's paradise. Bordered by rock shops, teepee motels, Regal Reptile Ranches, dinosaurs, and other crazy raiments, these two-lane roads are a veritable smorgasbord of adventures. In Jensen, Utah lies a gas station with a twelve foot high plaster dinosaur built in front and called "Dinosaur Service;" in Oklahoma along Highway 66 stands a snakepit with a twenty foot cobra made from old stovepipes lunging towards the highway; and in Oregon there is a peculiar spot called a Thunderbeast Park that contains a collection of huge, shiny, enamel painted, cement dinosaurs and places billboards along the highways as far as 140 miles away! Then there is Rapid City, South Dakota with its huge Brontasauras visible for forty miles, or the snakepit in the state of Washington that is operated by a woman who looks as much a part of the place as the snakes do.

Now, I listed all of these sights to point out the curious dialectic of America's roadways. On the one hand, there are the gray, streamlined, totally unexciting interstates and freeways and, on the other, the highways with the plethora of folk art and reptillian delights that I have photographed.

My only question is: Which will survive? Will the reptiles eventually replace the HoJos and dominate our roads or are the dinosaurs doomed for extinction once again?

Steve Fitch

Truckstop sign; Benson, Arizona   Highway 10   1972

Thunderbeast; near Chiloquin, Oregon   Highway 97   1972

Tourist lady; Giant Meteor Crater, Arizona   Highway 66   1971

Snakepit billboard, La Place, Louisiana   Highway 61   1971

Truckstop waitress; Gallup, New Mexico   Highway 66   1972

Snakepit, Sayre, Oklahoma   Highway 66   1972

Snakepit operator; Sayre, Oklahoma   Highway 66   1972

Big Chief Motel; Gila Bend, Arizona   Highway 80   1972

Maybe *The Foxfire Book* and its successor, *Foxfire 2*, from which excerpts are preprinted here, represent only a clever teacher's way of turning his students on: Eliot Wigginton, who is responsible for the *Foxfire* activities calls them an educational experiment. And maybe the obvious enthusiasm with which his students have carried out their investigations is basically sentimental, a rural high school's version of Marie Antoinette playing shepherdess or milkmaid. Maybe the thing that hooks Wigginton's students is mere quaintness, the picturesque; several confess their astonishment at finding a whole unknown, faded, but persistent world back in the hills of Rabun County. Maybe the careful studies they produce are no more than a how-to manual of cottage crafts, recipes, games, ceremonials, and simple witchcrafts, an embalming-place for extinct folkways, a rural waxwork museum of gaffers and eccentrics. Maybe this is all just local color.

But let us be careful. Maybe it is more.

I don't personally believe that our dissatisfaction with our technological and plastic culture is to be fully cured by a return to pre-industrial patterns of living. I don't suppose our high-energy civilization is going to revert to a low-energy level until it has to, and that implies something close to Armageddon or Apocalypse. But assuming that a cure or a partial cure is to be found, I am sure it is going to have to give us some of the things that Eliot Wigginton's students discovered while lugging their tape recorders up and down Rabun Gap—some of the satisfactions whose absence, like a vitamin or hormone deficiency, threatens to make spiritual invalids or monsters of us.

These students discovered over and over, for instance, the joy of work, especially work done in common with others, with family or community or neighborhood, work that is more fun than play, and that often, as in quiltings and raisings, turns into play. A man who knows work in that way is saved from the contemporary hunger to be entertained, and therefore from many of the most vulgarizing pressures of our times. Maybe it is not the work ethic, so much maligned, that the Rabun Gap students re-discovered. Let us say that it is at least a healthier version of the pleasure principle than the one plugged on the media, or in Las Vegas, or in the teachings of St. Leary.

Related to the joy of work are the joys of making and using, pleasures reverentially recorded in *Foxfire 2*, and inadvertently demonstrated as well. In making *Foxfire 2*, the students came to know people who knew the dignity and worth of things made with the hands out of honest materials, by a process in which hand and material help shape one another. That kind of dignity is rarely, perhaps never, achieved by the machine-made or the mass-made. A little of the maker's life has gone into the making, as a little of the user's life goes into the using. By 1973 the American Way, which means mass production with interchangeable parts, has all but deprived us of both those enjoyments.

But Wigginton's students did more than learn what making and using can mean. They submitted to the process themselves. *Foxfire 2* has that handmade look. The pleasure it gave its makers, as well as the care and skill it enforced from them, shines off the pages. The makers of *Foxfire 2* were not dominated by their tape recorders, they were not taken over by their tools. In time I expect them to discover Stegner's Law, which says that any tool more than twice the length of its user's arm, or with more than twice the energy of its user's muscles, or with more than twice the range of its user's senses, is dehumanizing.

There are other discoveries, hinted or expressed, in *Foxfire 2*. How to be a person, for instance. It is a problem that obsesses many young people in 1973, and the cues given them by our times lead many to hunt the answer the way a biological researcher might hunt the operative enzyme in a phase of digestion. We do our damndest to live experimentally; we talk a lot about "life style," as if it were something we could elect, like bell bottomed pants as against slim jims; and there is a fairly wide-spread feeling, at least among the literary young, that all sorts of behavior ought to be sampled, in the spirit of research. We ought to commit experience so we can write about it, or so we can choose among alternatives with a clear notion of what they are.

The results I would describe as lamentable. Vast studies, funded by the great foundations or the government or the Council of Learned Societies, examine into how we should deal with leisure, how we should "relate," whatever that means, to others, or how we should "interact" with others, or how we should or do handle our "interpersonal relations." We are up to our hips in jargon; we wander over the garbage dump of psychological experimentation, pawing around among group sex, open marriage, freeform marriage, Esalen, encounter techniques, group therapy, couch therapy and what not, in search of ourselves and our lost contentment. What experimental living means for the poor soul who embraces it is that he is condemned to wander outside all truly human contacts like a space ship that has lost touch with Houston.

I would guess that some, perhaps many, of the *Foxfire* students will be spared a lot of that anxiety. They won't have to worry about their interpersonal relations, not if they use their heads; they won't have to endure an identity crisis. For they have seen the example of some people whose way of life obviously spared them all those questionings. They were themselves—and never in any doubt—not because they tried to be but because they never even had to question. They were themselves because they had lived deeply in a place, and their place was known to them in their skin, their hands, the

FOXFIRE 2

Excerpts on the following pages are from FOXFIRE 2, edited by Elliot Wigginton. To be published in June by Doubleday-Anchor.

soles of their feet, under their fingernails. They were themselves because they lived and worked with others in traditional, not experimental ways.

Traditionalism, which looks like simplicity, turns out to be the profoundest wisdom. And it does not (though I don't recall any student's commenting on this) inhibit personal freedom. It is only by living together in groups and communities (exactly what many young people feel compelled to drop out from) that people become individuals. Who they are is moulded by the language they learn to speak, the songs they sing, the games they play, the houses they build, the things they grow and make, the ways they marry and die and are buried, and also the faiths and the fears they share. You do not become human by experimentation. That is the way to become a modern zombie or an unhappy wanderer in inter-human space.

Some of the *Foxfire 2* students, if I read them right, got more than a glimmer of how a *community* is created and perpetuated, and how essential it is to the individual—how it first shapes and then supports him. A community is the flowering of x number of people in a given place, and it grows more by accident, accomodation, and habit than by conscious experimentation. And it implies a continuity among the generations. Not the least important thing the *Foxfire 2* students found was their elders, who it turned out knew something the young might learn, and who among them could draw upon a coherent past. Every anthropologist from Margaret Meade up or down has told us we must find ways to revise our social life, our communities, our domestic architecture, so that the generations may be brought back together. In Rabun Gap they have already made some of those moves.

Whether there is a way by which that past whose charm and strength the students felt can be channeled through the present and into the future, that is another matter. The world is very crowded, also it is obsessed with its high-energy goals, also it is more often than not quite mad. To ask a bunch of high school students to solve its excruciating problems is asking too much. But they are headed in the right direction—back into the past to find what the species-and-community wisdom says, back to a reconciliation among the generations, back to the sense of place and community.

WALLACE STEGNER

---

from Eliot Wiggington's
INTRODUCTION

I believe we have become a nation of nomads with no sense of that security or serenity that comes from being able to say, "Here is where I belong. Here is my place, my time, my home, my birthright, my community. Here I am loved and known, and here I love in turn."

It happens all around us. *Foxfire* has had four different editors at Doubleday. The first three have left. And it happened to me personally. My mother was from Poughkeepsie, New York; my father from Marietta, Ohio; my stepmother from Washington, Pennsylvania. I was born in Wheeling, West Virginia; raised in Athens, Georgia; educated in Pottstown, Pennsylvania, Ithaca, New York, and Baltimore Maryland; and I now work in Rabun Gap, Georgia. I have no more idea of where I fit in space and time and community than if I had just landed inside a meteor from Pluto. I make my home where I can.

And it happens to my students. Over half our kids in Rabun Gap move away never to return. They are giving this county away. Our three tax assessors are all land developers from outside our area. The destiny of this county is in foreign hands.

The only way we are going to get our kids committed to our neighborhoods and our communities is to get them so involved in their surroundings that they become determined that the destiny of their communities will be in *their* hands—not in the hands of land developers and commercial rapists. They must feel that they are essential to the future of their homes.

Otherwise, we are doomed to watch them leave, creating a vacuum filled, in our county's case, by ten thousand summer homes.

Until we put together the article on shuckin's and house raisin's, none of us realized the extent to which people used to be involved with each other's lives in a true community. We knew that once there *were* shuckin's, but these sounded somehow remote—isolated incidents—curiosities of a bygone day. Now that they've done some real work on the subject, I suddenly realize how widespread and pervasive and varied and common these practices were. They were a part of everyone's existence here—and they were a constant part, not a once-a-month rarity.

Somewhere along the way, we've lost something fine. Perhaps in our search for *personal* satisfaction and pleasure, we've dug so deep into ourselves that we've forgotten each other. The extent to which neighbors are strangers is frightening, and the extent to which we've blocked out and structured and programmed most of our time for our own self-gain may be tragic. It may mean that we truly *have* lost our sense of community, and in the process killed these activities for good.

It's a mad cycle. We get jobs to support our families. The jobs take five days a week. They also take our time. Our time gone, we do less together with our neighbors. We see them less and less frequently and a certain gulf is formed. With the loss of contact comes loss of friendship, and with the loss of friendship/dependence comes hesitance at reopening the contact (you have to work at being friends), and with the hesitance comes suspicion. We read about crime and dope and . . . I wonder if . . . ?

Soon we are a community of isolated islands, and the damage is done.

"Who are those people who just moved in?"

"I don't know. I heard they had two kids but I'm not sure."

"Well, I hope they're decent people."

"Why don't we go find out?"

"Yeah. We really ought to one of these days."

And that's as far as it goes. And what a loss. We need only look at a friendship quilt to see how great a loss it is.

Don't get me wrong. I'm not suggesting that everyone should suddenly get together and have a pea thrashin'. A barn raisin' in the middle of suburbia is likewise far-fetched. But as our leisure time increases, and as we search for new ways to fill it, surely we are inventive enough to be able to find ways to work/play/create together as communities.

There are a few hopeful, tentative signs. Community-wide trash cleanups, for example. Or community "street theater" projects. Or neighborhood parks and recreation areas built and designed by the community for the community. But they are often tentative, groping, short-lived.

Too often we fail to see any common bond between ourselves. Maybe if we set about creating some fertile ground for those bonds, we'll find how close our interests and our instincts and our needs as human beings really are.

Until that time, we may have to resign ourselves to a world where our kids flee "home" to join communes, leaving their parents behind: lonely, embittered, bewildered islands on a whole wide street full of people.

As I said, I am far from having all the answers. But those things I believe. Those things I hold true. I am convinced that we, as adults, must constantly cling to, affirm, and then celebrate with our kids those things we love: sunsets, the taste of a good meal, the warmth of a hickory fire shared by real friends, the joy of discovery and accomplishment, the constant surprises of life, laughter, empathy with the Aunt Aries and their triumphs and sorrows; and we must hope that in the process of that celebration and that empathy, we will build in our students' souls such a reservoir of warmth and hope and generosity and energy and self-assurance that it would carry them through hell. That is surely what those who do not have that reservoir will face.

Foxfire is one means I have stumbled upon to help with that building. It is not enough by itself. There are hundreds of other ways. I don't advocate for a moment that anyone else copy our scheme exactly—though they are welcome to if they wish. The struggle must be to find a means that both we (as teachers and parents) and our students are most comfortable with and most responsive to—and then use it to build a race of kids that are not against us as adults, but with us in a great shared struggle to save this land.

Those of us who are in public schools know where our front lines are. The buzzards may, indeed, win in the end; but God, we ought to give them a hell of a run for their money.

BEW

KENNY RUNION

"Put these riddles 'fore th' school and see if there's anyone in there can answer 'em!"

> Round as a ball
> And sharp as an awl;
> Lives all summer
> And dies in th' fall.
>
> It goes all over th' field,
> Through th' creek;
> It has a long tongue
> But it never drinks.
>
> Big at the bottom,
> Little at the top,
> Little thing inside
> Goes flippity-flop.
>
> Black up and black down,
> Black and brown
> Three legs up and
> Six legs down.

"Next time y' come back, tell me if anyone can answer 'em. I don't know. I don't believe they'll ever get that first 'un." (For answers, see Appendix, *Foxfire 2*, when it comes out.)

Kenny Runion is a craftsman. He makes everything from laurel wood rocking chairs to belts to wooden necklaces bespangled with dime store jewels. He loves his work, he loves people, and he loves to talk.

Kenny has always lived in the mountains and sometimes spends hours each day tramping through them for his own enjoyment and in search of old wood, rocks, and relics to use in his craft work. We asked him how he learned to make such a variety of things: "Well, I just studied it out. I'm about a third Indian and it just comes to me. That belt there was hard to figger out. See, I'd never seen nary'un. I'd never seed anything like that." He just uses his imagination.

Kenny lives alone in a tiny frame house. We interviewed him a number of times, and he was always ready and willing to talk—even if he was in the middle of carving a chair leg. He'd pop up his hand in a friendly wave and, grinning, say, "I'uz wonderin' when you were goin' t'come see me again." Then he'd begin to talk about anything from witchcraft to "whuppin's." Kenny's conversation is as well spiced with wit and serious philosophy as his carving is with ingenuity and imagination.

JAN BROWN

People now's a'havin' a good time. Now whether it'll last . . . I'm a'feared it ain't. They'll be somethin' happen. People ain't thankful no more. They don't 'preciate what they got.

And ever'body's in a hurry. Where they goin'? Where they goin'? Back then you could meet an ol' feller with an ol'ox wagon and he'd stand there a half day if you wanted t'talk. Stand as long as you'd talk. You meet a feller now, he'd run over y'. Where's he goin'? Just ain't got no patience.

Yeah. Back then he'd just stop his two oxen in th' road and git off. Talk as long as y'wanted t'talk. Maybe he'd give y'a drink a'liquor. But now people's a' gittin' there fast, ain't they? People now, they go more in a week then they went in a year back then. They go more places now then they did in a year. They go more'n'more ever' week. They's people raised around here—*old* people—never seed a train. And now they're ever'where, ain't they? If they'd seed a airplane, they'd run in th' house and shet th'door.

People made their livin' back there. They had a woods fulla hogs, sheep, and cattle. Chestnut trees bent with chestnuts. All they had t'do was go out in th'fall and go t'killin' hogs. Bring 'em in just as fat as they got'em. They seen a good time, but they didn't have th'cars and money. You'd see fellers goin' up and down th'road 'fore tax-payin' time tryin' t'sell three bushel a'corn for a dollar.

I learnt how t'build fences, split wood, hoe corn. Worked just as hard then as I do now. I was raised poor and still poor. Me and my daddy'd work just anywhere we'd get a job. And we had fun. You had people meet up, y'know, and drink and dance and have all kinda fun. No fights much. You could go down th'road in broad daylight with five gallon a' liquor on your back and not be bothered. Shore you could. You could go down with a five-gallon jug on your back and never be bothered. It was twelve mile t'th'sheriff and there wadn't no phone. Had t'walk it, and wadn't nobody goin' t'do that, y'know. They'd just let y'go on.

[We asked Kenny to tell us the best advice his father ever gave him.]

Stay out of meanness. He raised me right. I've never been arrested in my life. Never been in jail except goin' t'see my folks. Never been locked up. Yeah. He raised me right. My mother, of course, was tight on me too. I don't drink. Don't cuss. Don't do none a'that. If I see I'm goin' t'meet bad company, why, if I have t'go by, I just say, "Howdy," and go by. I don't fool with 'em. Bad company'll get you in trouble. 'Course, I ain't feared when I get mad. I ain't scared of'em. But I'd rather stay out of trouble.

Kids today do as they please. You know that? Mother'll tell'em t'bring her a bucket a'water. Says, "Ain't goin' do it. You go get it yourself." Boys,

when I'uz raised up, my daddy told me t'do somethin' and I done'er. I done'er. I tell'em now that a hickory don't hurt like it used to. It don't hurt now.

I used t'get more whuppin's than anybody. Boys, I'm tellin' you th'truth. Back then, people had their children under control. One word and you'uz gone. My daddy used t'whup me and Gus fer fightin' back when we was six, seven'r'eight year old. He didn't whup me with a second handed hick'ry. He'd go out and get two. Now when he got through with us, we'uz dressed out. And it wouldn't be long till we'd get'er again.

I had a teacher in school. He'uz a fine feller. He sat in a new cane-bottom chair sort'a in th'corner a'th' house. Guess he had twenty-five hick'rys there. He'uz blame lazy when he whupped y'. He wouldn't even get up. No, he wouldn't get up. But now you'uz dry cleaned when he got through with y'. Boy, that'uz a mean teacher. About six foot high and stout t'go with it. I couldn't whup nobody in a chair, could you? He'd bring 'at hick'ry around 'at a'way. Mankind! He'd whup girls. It didn't make no difference. Anybody 'at'ud come up there and disobey or didn't have their lessons.

But in a way, hit'uz worth somethin'. It'uz worth somethin'. Mankind, you had t'have 'at lesson. Ever' time you'd have—examination, I call it—we all get in them seats plumb across. Not a dadgone book. Nothin' but a tablet. And when they'd get askin' y'somethin', you had t'put'er down. You had t'put'er down. You didn't have no book t'go by and you couldn't ask nobody, either.

[Kenny has much longer hair than many of the people we interview, so we asked him what he thought of young people wearing long hair.]

I think it's nice. Other words, it's hippie-like, ain't it? I believe we ought t'be good to'em, don't you? I shore do. I like t'see'em with long hair. My folks is all again' me wearin' it. I'm th'only one that wears it. I've got a brother—he shaves ever' mornin'; has his hair cut ever' week. 'at's his pride. Want t'look good, y'know. Look pretty. Well now, 'at's what it's for.

You ought t'seed me. I cut my beard off. 'at beard was *way down.* You wouldn't a'knowed me if I'd a'come in th'street. It got t'botherin' me—people a'laughin' at me, y'know—and I just cut it off. Yeah. I really ought t'have some beard with m'hair t'look good. Long mustache. Back when I was a boy, you never seed a man but what he didn't have a beard way down t'here, or a mustache one. And long hair like mine. Ever' one of'em. I don't believe it's wrong t'wear it. I've got pictures down there at home of Jesus and his hair's way *down* here hangin', fallin' 'round on his shoulders. That's what I told my folks. Said, "Look 'at picture. You believe that?" I said, "It's not wrong. Christ wore it, didn't he?" And Samson wore it till he cut it off, and what'd he get into when he had his hair cut off? Makes y'stouter. It does!

I don't think it makes much difference what y'wear. If y'want t'wear shorts, mini-skirts, or wear your hair long I don't think that bothers y'. Do you? I ain't again' none of it. I've had big arguments. People said, "Runion, you'll just argue anything."

I said, "I think it's nice."

I don't think it makes much difference what y'wear ner nothin' 'bout it. It's how yer heart is.

Yeah. Why, I ain't again' a hippie. Why he's just a man just wearin' his beard. I ain't again' him. But now, people'll talk. Sometimes when I go through Clayton I can hear'em back behind say, "There goes another ol'hippie." They don't know me hardly.

Yeah. I ain't goin' have mine cut no more. I can't marry nohow, and I'm just goin' t'let my hair grow.

[The Bible is one of Kenny's favorite topics of discussion. He has his own colorful version of many stories, such as this one of Samson.]

Now a preacher argued me that Samson just had one wife. He argued me down, but he *had* two. They burnt.

After his first wife, he decided he wanted another one a'them ol'Philistines, and he went down and got 'im another'n. And that's th' one that had his hair cut. She kept on and on and they cut them seven locks off and he wasn't more'n just a boy in strength then.

Then he went t'work pullin' a syrup mill. You ever see how they grind cane? All kind'a jobs like that.

But it passed on and he got revenge. He didn't ask fer revenge in only one thing: said he waned revenge fer his two eyes. They gorged'em out. It's a side a'rich people, I guess, t'have big times; and ol'Samson, I'm satisfied he'uz up there in prison chained. "Come on around! Go up and git Samson! Go up and git'im!"

'Course th'lad, he went and got'im. I'm satisfied he led 'im with a chain; brought 'im back down. Sit around awhile and said, "Let's walk out around th' buildin'."

Walked out there and Samson said, "Would you mind me a'stoopin' down?"

'Course that lad, I reckon, told him yes. But when he reached down he got aholt of each one a'them pillars and over she went. Killed him and thousands. Five thousand on top of it.

Now you know it took strength and power t'do that. But he got revenge fer his two eyes. That's all. This whuppin' and beatin' and dealin', he didn't rest w'that. He just revenged his two eyes. Them ol'Philistines—they'uz rough.

Bible's a good thing t'read.

[Knowing Kenny to be a religious man, we got on the subject of religion and what proof there was for him of a God.]

Well, it's right here a'fore your eyes. You can see things a'happenin' ever'day. Different things. I was sittin' here th'other day and a ol'hen was comin'

through here that had chicks. She'd go a little piece. Then she'd cluck. Now what cause her t'do that? I studied about that. Just sat here and watched. She'd go a little piece; then she'd cluck again. Now what makes her do that? 'At's Nature. 'At's Mother Nature.

And they'll sit there on those eggs three weeks, and 'at's Mother Nature. Three long weeks. And they'll stay there, too. Well, there's somethin' behind that some'ers, or she'd get off and leave. There's somethin'r'other keepin' her there.

Why, you *know* that there's a power if y'just look out. Now they talk about goin' t'th'moon, and they may of went. I don't know. But that moon. Is it standin' still, or movin', or what about it? Rises here [he points], and th'next mornin', it's here. Plumb across th'world. What d'y'think about that now? And when it goes, it's dark nights. And when it starts up, it's a bright light thing. It's little and gets bigger and bigger. What changes that? They's somebody—somethin'—behind it. It'll change. Then it'll get fuller and fuller till it's a full moon.

There's a whole lot to study about in this world, boy, when y'get right on t'th'business. Shore is. Some says when y'die, if you're a sinner, you'll go t'Hell and burn forever. Some says you won't do it. You'll just burn up like paper. So that's another question. Well, I kindly believe you'll suffer. You just got t'take all 'em old things and figger'em out. Figger'em out.

MAUDE SHOPE

Maude Shope is one of our newest contacts. She was born in North Carolina within seven miles of where she lives now, and she steps right out of an age that is long gone. She's been to corn shuckings ("Oh, that was a big thing, y'know; goin' to shuck out a man's corn"), log rollings, has spun wool, sewed clothing, raised twelve children, done midwife work, walked to church and school—and a thousand other things; but even at the age of seventy-six, she hasn't slowed down much. And neither has her thirty-two-year-old mule, Frank. When she claimed she still rode him, we looked at her in disbelief, I guess. So she proved it, as the photographs show.

When she's not being visited by family, or visiting with her grand-daughter (who attends Western Carolina University) and her son-in-law who live just up the dirt road, she stays alone in a tiny frame house.

The grass hasn't grown greener up at Maude's, and she has never won any world titles or medals, but if there were ever one to be recognized for just plain, simple, old-fashioned ways, Maude would surely be a prime candidate. She lives rough, but she has pride, dignity, warmth, a joy and enthusiasm for life that is boundless; and she has our respect and affection.

BARBARA TAYLOR AND SHEILA VINSO

Maude began by telling us about her childhood: We didn't have th'things that children's got now, but we didn't have'em and we didn't look fer'em. When we'uz children, we'd all get out'n'play, y'know. Instead of a horse, we used t'have a stick and ride that around. As fer dolls, oh, had one doll apiece in our life. And we thought we'd got somethin'. We saved eggs and bought our dolls—give a quarter apiece fer 'em. And Mama made us a dress th'next mornin'. Well, that'uz worth more than a ten dollar doll would be now.

We thought Santa Claus, up t'when we was great big young'uns, brought all this stuff. I know one Christmas, we couldn't wait, hardly. And they wouldn't let us get into things, and we felt of th'stockin's we'd hung up. Oh, we didn't know what was in'em, and we *couldn't* get into'em till just before daylight.

And we used t'walk t'school. Now, y'know, grown-ups and children don't have t'walk as fer as from here t'th'creek hardly. Now we used t'go and stay all night with our neighbor's boys and girls when we'uz children. Mama'd let us go, and we thought it was th'greatest thing there was, y'know—git t'go t'somebody's house and stay all night. And us and them children'd play—oh, we thought we had th'biggest time. We'd git into this sandy place—old gray sand. If we could git into that sandy place, we was havin' our fun!

And I did farmwork and housework. Went t'th' field and worked in th'field all m'life since I was a child. I always fed th'cattle an'stock. T'tell th'truth, I'd rather work in th'field than t'work in th'house. I like t'see a purty, clean house, but I'm not too good a housekeeper.

[The subject of children led us naturally into a discussion of how children should be raised now, and what advice she would give them, if she had the chance, to help them deal with today's world.]

Well, I don't know. The first thing is to be honest and truthful. That's about th'best thing I could think of. Live their life; be honest and truthful and not steal. That's honesty, y'know. If you're honest and truthful, you're not a'gonna' steal.

Now I've heard, and you have too, heard people say, "I'd starve before I'd steal." Well, I don't think I would. I think if I couldn't do no other way, I'd

slip me a bite a'somethin'. What I mean is, they's not many people has t'steal anything. You can get somethin' t'eat without stealin'. That's one thing, young'uns, you can take down. I'm not a'gonna'steal if I can get by it. I won't steal a thing. I won't lie t'you, and I won't steal. I say bad words sometimes—I don't deny it. I say nasty words sometimes, and cuss sometimes. I've done that. But stealin'r'lyin' to y', I'm not a'gonna' do it. I think that is a dirty thing t'do. I believe in bein' honest—tellin' th'truth. That's th'way I feel.

I don't live like I should. I one time belonged to th'church and prayed in public. I don't no more. I try t'live right, but still I don't live like I should, not as good as I should live. At one time, I was counted as good as anybody in th'church. But th'feelin' is just as important [as praying in public]. I don't git down on m'knees and pray, but in my mind I pray, and I do believe that there's a higher power than us. I do believe that. I can't say that there's not. [God shows himself.] He's got control of—like this mornin'. It'uz as cloudy as it could be, and we all said it'uz gonna' rain; and God done it, I suppose. We didn't. And it cleared off, and now it's a purty day. He's got his ways.

I don't read th'Bible a lot. I don't read it like I should. It's very important, though. I'd be afraid t'give th'Bible a lie or somethin'; I certainly would. I'll tell y'one thing I don't like—th'way they drag it

around. I like th'old Bible better than I do this new style they've got now. I don't know if that's contradictin' th'Bible or not, but I don't think so. They change and try t'tell different things, but I'd be afraid t'try t'contradict some a'God's things in th' Bible.

I feel like I'm a Christian, and all that; but still, I'll break over and say nasty words, and I think it's a habit more'n anything. Just shore as somethin' goes wrong, I'll say, "Well, dammit." And I don't mean a bit more than—it's just habit. Just like you'll say little ol'—like, "dadburnit," or somethin'r'nother. I think it's just as dirty as sayin' th'other. So I don't think that a body's doin' th'wrong thing. Well, of course they're doin' th'wrong thing in one way, but show me one that don't do somethin' wrong. There's nobody but what does somethin' wrong. They might think they was doin' it right, but I might see it [another way]. It's just your way a'seein'. I might see that they was doin' awful dirty, and they might think they was bein' honest with ever'thin' they done.

[That's why] I feel like I can't tell you [young people what to do]. You're gonna' do as you please. But I could tell you what I thought was best. I'll tell you one thing I don't believe in. All right: if you was courtin' a boy, maybe I'd just hate him. Well, and I wouldn't have that boy if it was me. But it's *you* talkin' to'im, and you've got your feelin's, haven't you? You're gonna' do what you think is right, either way. It might be somebody I just hated. You've seen people thataway. But I don't believe in tellin' you what t'do. You do th'best you can, and do what you think is right. People say, "Well, if I'uz her, I wouldn't marry him." Well, they're not a'gonna have t'live with'im. It's *you* that's a'marryin'im. I believe in tendin' to your own business and leavin' other people alone. If you tend to your own business, you've got plenty t'do without a'tendin' t'mine and hers. Not t'say I'm perfect'r'anything.

My parents was good about lettin' us make up our own minds. They was good t'us. They was strict about makin' us mind, but they was good. Had a Christian mother and father all my life. We worked. Didn't work like slaves—I don't mean that. But we had t'work for our livin'. And they didn't 'strict us t'havin' t'belong t'th'church that they b'longed to ner nothin'. We had our privilege. They was Methodist—both of'em—and I'm a Methodist. But if a'wanted t'been Baptists, they wouldn't've objected. Same way with politics. They were all Democrats, but it we'd a'wanted t'be somethin' else, they wouldn't've fussed on us.

[But they *were* too restrictive in one way, she felt.] But grown people wouldn't've talked about havin' babies'n'such as'at a bit more'n you'd go out here and shoot somebody. My gosh, we'uz taught up till we'uz great big kids [that] th'doctor brought th' little babies all th'time. We didn't know. When I'uz a great big girl, I didn't know no more about sex than a dog does. And little calves—we thought cows scratched 'em out from under a stump or log out there till we was great big children. That's th'way I'uz brought up. Now you know [about sex] from th'time you're born, nearly. I believe it's better t'let children know. If y'know somethin', you're not as apt t'do somethin' wrong as you would if you didn't know it was th'wrong thing t'do. Years ago, y'know, if somethin' happened then, it was awful. But now it ain't so awful. Well, th'girls know how to behave theirselves. I think girls ought t'know what t'do and what not t'do.

And like it is by dressin'. Years back, well, if a woman had her dress up and somebody seen her knee, awfullest thing ever was. But now they don't pay no more attention for their knee than they do for their hands. And so I don't know. It's just human nature.

Now when I first come to this creek, we broke up our land with a mule and a single-footed plow. We made plenty of corn t'do us all year long—never bought no corn when I first come t'this creek. Take what we called a single-footed plow, break up th' ground and then go and lay it off, cover it with a singlefoot plow, drop it by hand. Now it's changed so that my grandchildren couldn't build a fire in that wood stove 'cause they don't know how. Well, I don't

know how t'drive a car, so I guess their way of doin' is just as good as mine. But I like my way of doin' th' best.

When I come t'this creek, didn't know what buyin' meat and lard was. They made their own meat and killed their hogs in th'fall of th'year. You can remember your parents killin' hogs, and maybe they still yet, but they don't like they used to. Kill three or four big hogs, or whatever you had, and take care of your meat and render out th'lard, and have it and have lard t'do y'. But nowadays, th'younger generation—they don't know how t'go and make it, and so all they know t'do is go and buy. Well, it's like fixin' a meal. I can put me on a pot a'green beans or shelled beans or whatever I got, and cook'em here on th'fire. Nine times out of ten, nearly, they [the younger people] stop at th'store and get some canned stuff and then come in and fix their supper in a few minutes where it takes me all day t'cook a half a pot a'beans.

I don't know which is th'best. I guess a wood stove's better for *me.* It's old-fashioned, and I like it. With a 'lectric stove, you can heat one of them, y'know, and have your meal ready before y'get your first fire t'burnin' in that'n. But just for th'old-fashioned of it, I like it. And then, it heats th'house. I like it for that. It's best for *me* t'do it th'old-fashioned way, but then, I've got my way and they've got theirs.

But I think they oughta know how t'do this too. A person don't know what might happen. They might get t'where they needed t'do it and didn't know how. Like milkin' cows. They's not none of th'younger generation knows how. Wouldn't know which side of th' cow t'go to t'milk. Lots of y'don't. Well, I do. And I think because I know it, some of th'young'uns quarrel at me. I know how t'do somethin', and I just think it's better t'know how t'do that work; and they think it's better, a'course, t'do other work.

I just think ever'body's got his way of feelin'. You've got your way, and if you think you're right a'doin' somethin', well, you're just as honest as I am because you're doin' what you think is right.

Maybe there's somethin' I like t'eat, and you don't like it fer a thing in this world. I'd say, "Oh, eat this. This is good. Eat it. Eat it. Eat." Well, now, if you don't like it, you don't want t'eat it. I think that's right in lettin' th'other man have his privilege.

Some people have superstitions, for example; and that's their business too. You've heard these old tales where if you dream a dream and tell it before breakfast, it'll come t'pass? Or th'old sayin' on New Year's mornin' that if a man comes t'your house first, you'll have good luck. If a woman comes t'your house first, throw th'broom in front a'her 'fore she comes in th' door or you'll have bad luck. That's an old sayin', y'know. And not t'take th'ashes out between Christmas and New Year. If you do, you'll have bad luck. Or eat black-eyed peas for New Year's day? I seen a piece in th'paper where someone was eatin' cabbage for New Year. If I had cabbage *any* time through th'year, I'uz proud of it.

And some believe if th'smoke's a'goin' t'th'ground, it's a'gonna' rain. Or if it's clear fogs [fog without clouds accompanying it] through th'month of January, then there'll be frost in May. Lots a people believe them, and that's their privilege. But I never pay no 'tention to'em.

[Changing the subject, we asked Maude what else she considered her most valuable possession to be.] Water. That's important. But that comes by th'Almighty. But it's our place t'get it.

I guess cattle and stock is actually th'most important t'me. They're company. You take stock and them blamed old dogs—well, they're company to a body. A dog usually comes ahead of anything else, don't it? You know yourself that you'll hold up for your dog. If somebody was t'come in and kick that dog just t'get t'kick him, I'd fly all mad in spite of myself, I guess.

[As the interview ended, we asked her if anything really worried her.] I'll tell you what I'm afraid of. You may live t'see it. I guess I'll not. And that's that th'government will come and cut up our land—[take it from] all that's got more than a certain amount. There's s'many more people bein' born into th'world, y'know. Ain't no tellin' how many more people they is now than they was forty and fifty years ago. Well, they've got t'have a place t'live. We've got land here. In a few years they'll cut it up and they'll take off so much and sell it. That worries me. There's so many new houses put up down th'road in just th'last little while.

I don't want no city life. I like country life better. I've never lived in a city, but I don't want to. For one thing, if you're in th'city, it's a noise all th'time. Back in th'country, you got your free runnin' water and all such as that.

Why, I wouldn't swap this little shack here for th' finest house in New York. I wouldn't do it. That's just th'way I feel.

MRS. ARDILLA GRANT'S HAINT STORY
from Boogers, Witches, and Haints

Well, one night we went out there, on th'end of th' porch, and th'lights was shinin' out th'windas, y'know; and they'uz a barn out yonder. Great big ol'barn they had.

We'uz out there on th'porch, an' this ol'lady, she come out from under that barn now. I'm tellin' y'th' truth exactly th'way we seen it.

Well, I didn't say a word, nor she didn't either. We watched her till she just came up close t'us, an' she had her hands out like that [Mrs. Grant puts her arms out like a sleepwalker in front of her], and she'uz just as quiet an'th'purtiest thing. She was old, y'know, and she had her hands out like that, an' she came up close. And this woman that was with me, she said, "Lord, child, do you see that?"

And we run back in th'house an' we told th'men— it was a boardin' house then—an' we told th'men what we saw, an' they got up and went out on th'porch. They thought maybe someone had stopped out at that barn t'camp out'r'somethin'. But they didn't find nobody. Not a sign of anybody. No tracks nor nothin'. Now that did scare us!

And then down below there—what they call th'Mud Cut—there's a curve in th'road, and a railroad went aroun' down there. An' down below there you could see a man—his legs and a lantern. Y'could see th'lantern an' his legs; an' he'd come up on that railroad an' he'd walk down that railroad t'th'top of th'grade they called it; an' he'd just get out'a'sight till he'd pop up right in th'same place.

That starts about nine o'clock, and I'll bet you go right up there tonight at nine o'clock an' see th'*very* sight. He'd go along and disappear an' start right back where he started from. He'd just keep a'goin', y'know You could see th'lantern swingin', and his legs, and right back down th'railroad he'd go.

Now lots'a'people seen that. Now it must a'been in time—some time'r'nother—they'd been somebody murdered there.

[At this point Mr. Grant said that he had heard that a Bill McCathey had killed his brother there by mistake, thinking he was a groundhog.]

Then on up th'road they was a second house that th' railroad men boarded at, y'know. Now I didn't hear that. This is what they told me; but now they told it, an' I think it was true: somebody—just went like somebody'd come in an' thrown down a load a' lumber an' got t'hammerin'. Just like he was makin' a coffin.

Well, it just worried somebody that lived there. It was that way continually. An' it sounded like it was in th' wall, y'know, at times.

An' he went an' tore th' ceiling off and he found a little baby skeleton in there!

DANIEL MANOUS' HAINT STORY
from Boogers, Witches, and Haints

No, I don't think there's anything like that. Do you? I don't think so. I think that's th'imagination. You think on a thing till you think it's real.

I used to hear my grandfather tell one about when he'uz a boy. They'uz a cemetery right close to where he lived, and he could hear a baby cryin' every night over at th'cemetery.

He'uz scared and didn't know what t'think about it and told one of th'neighbors. Said, "I heard a baby cry over yonder at th'cemetery every night. I didn't go about it." Said, "I'm afraid to. Are you afraid to go over there?"

He said, "No, I'm not afraid to go over there."

Grandpa says, "You come over t'my house tonight. If that baby cries, if you'll go over there and see what it is, I'll give you ten dollars."

So he came over then that night, y'know, and waited till seven o'clock. Said, "All right. If you're not 'fraid t'go, now's th'time t'go."

That man just took off and went over there, and they'uz a big basket sittin' on top a'th'tombstone, and they'uz a baby in it. Little baby boy. He just went and picked up th'basket, went on back and took it to him and said, "It's a baby."

He'd been a'hearin' th'baby for several nights he claimed. He kept that baby and raised it, and it went by th'name a' Billy Tombs—after th'tombstone. That was actually th'truth. I've heard my grandpa say that he'd seen th'boy a many a time. Billy Tombs.

The Bible preaches that th'dead don't know anything at all. After any person dies, why they don't know anything. They don't have any thoughts, don't know a thing in th' world.

Well, they *couldn't* come back here. They couldn't come back and cause trouble and bother th'livin' because they can't *get* back. They're dead. They don't know anything.

If you don't believe th'Bible, you just as well not believe nothin'. If it didn't teach that, y'might have somethin' t'base it on, y'see. But since they don't know anything, how could they come back? 'Cause they'd have t'be doin' a little thinkin'r'somethin'r'nother before they could get back and trouble anybody'r'anything.

They's mediums that say they could talk t'th'dead and all that. I don't believe that. That's just a evil spirit. Really, I don't believe in 'em. They's nothin' t'base it on. They's no foundation. Cain't build a house without no foundation. Th'Bible destroys all th'foundation. If somethin' dies, it's gone—don't know a thing in th'world. You kin find th'stories, but there ain't no foundation for'em. That's what I call a myth. Just not reality.

RAISING SHEEP
from From Raising Sheep to Woven Cloth

The sheep which were grown years ago for wool were a smaller and hardier strain than the sheep of today. They weighed only about thirty to forty pounds and were no bigger than an average size dog; yet they were stout little creatures that withstood cold, hunger, and disease in the Blue Ridge and Great Smoky Mountains. But they were also shy, timid animals whose only source of protection from wild animals was to flee in fear. If they were attacked by an animal, they would give up and let the attacker kill them. Once they were caught and scared, they just gave up without a fight.

For the most part these sheep were white, but a few black sheep were born. George Grist, a sheep producer in Rabun County, said, "They were white. They didn't hardly have any black on'em. Back yonder most of'em had a black sheep or two crop out. They wanted that 'cause they'd weave socks and sweaters out of'em and they wouldn't have to dye it." This is a classic example of utilizing what is available. The farmers like to have a black sheep born every now and then, but sometimes superstitions grow around black sheep. Not according to George Grist, who, when asked if he knew of any superstitions, replied, "I don't know of any superstitions, but you always heard of black sheep in the family."

When the contacts were asked where the first sheep came from, no one knew for sure, but George Grist stated, "I guess if there'd been sheep here, they'd brought'em where they came from. I'd imagine they brought'em here from England. I got some shears from Sheffield, England. I believe that's where the first sheep came from."

It was hard to obtain sheep if you wanted to buy more to increase your flock. Here's what Minnie Buchanan said on obtaining sheep: "Well, you couldn't hardly find'em then. Most folks just kept what they wanted. Then in later years they got to where they kept th'sheep for th'lambs to sell in th'spring. But most everybody back when I was growing up just kept what sheep they had of their own. If they got a bigger flock, they jest had to raise'em. 'Course the sheep didn't cost nothing a head then—about two, two an'a half dollars. They jest didn't have no market sale."

Years ago almost everyone raised sheep. If some family didn't have any sheep, some of their relatives would and they usually shared the surplus wool.

Sheep were relatively easy to raise as they could forage for themselves. Since it was open range here years ago, farmers simply fenced in their gardens, and then turned their cattle, hogs, and sheep loose in the hills to graze. The animals would stay together, and were branded with some identifiable marking; then rounded up when they were needed. As Minnie

Buchanan said, "We'd turn our sheep out in the spring and they'd go to the mountains. Maybe they'd come back in the field onst in a while, but not very often in the summer. In the fall, we'd git out and hunt'em up and bring'em through the winter."

When sheep roamed free in the mountains, the sheep producers needed a way to identify their sheep. Minnie Buchanan told us, "We notched their ears and that mark was registered at Franklin, North Carolina, and I guess it's right there yet." When asked if she could remember her father's mark, she wasn't sure, but she thinks it could have been an "overbit." She explained what an overbit looked like: "It's a notch on the top of the ear; if it's on the underside, it's an 'underbit.' A 'crop' is just the end of the ear clipped off."

George Grist said about ear markings, "They'd cut the ears to tell everyone's sheep apart. Lots of time they would split their ears—what they call a 'swallow fork.' They'd split the ear, either the right or the left one, and then cut off the end of the ears and call it a 'swallow fork with a clip;' or they'd notch under the ears, two or three notches. Everybody around had their own mark and they could tell'em apart that way. Then they turned'em loose in the woods. All summer they'd go a long ways off and stay. They'd come home about once a month for salt. We wouldn't take salt to'em on account of we were afraid they wouldn't come back."

When we asked George how they could be sure the sheep would come home, he replied, "Well, they gotta come home, just like we do. When they want something, they come home. You see, they won't hardly come home unless they feel a need for something. You don't need a fence for'em. If anything gets after 'em, they know to come home. They wanna have a place at night to stay—about the same place usually. I heard my daddy say that they'd come back; one morning he'd wake up and they'd all be back. They'd give'em salt and look about'em and in two, three days they'd be gone."

If the sheep weren't home when the owner needed them for some reason, they'd have to be hunted up. When Minnie's father wanted his sheep, he sent his children to hunt them out of the woods: "Us kids'd get out an' sheep hunt in the fall. Sometimes we'd find'em maybe five miles from home. Well, there'd probably be somebody else's sheep with'em, but we'd jest bring'em all in together an' then let them come and get theirs. An' they'd always put a bell on one an' they knowed that there bell."

Of course, not everyone let their sheep run loose in the mountains. Some people, like Belle Dryman's father, kept their sheep fenced in pastures. This eliminated the problems of hunting for the sheep and notching the ears to identify his sheep from the other

men's; but then again, fences had to be built and pastures had to be kept in grazing condition. When the sheep were fenced, the best pasture grasses were blue grasses and various types of rye grass for winter grazing. The sheep preferred this softer, more tender grass to the coarse hays or fescue.

To continue the existence of their herds, rams were needed. To keep from interbreeding the sheep year after year with the same ram, the neighboring farmers would swap their rams with one another. In

doing so, deformed sheep and undesirable characteristics and traits were not common. George Grist said that his father kept one ram for every twenty ewes, and when they had a surplus of rams, he said: "They killed an'ate'em. That's about all you could do with'em,

except maybe for wethers. [Wethers were castrated rams which were slaughtered for mutton when they grew into a desired size. The size depended on how much meat you could use before it spoiled. There was one problem concerning mutton: there was no feasible way to preserve it. Therefore, whenever you needed meat to eat, you had to go out and butcher a lamb. After a lamb or small ram was killed, it had to be eaten right away, unless it was killed during the winter, due to spoilage. Several of the contacts stated that salt would spoil the meat and there was no way to cure or preserve it.] They'd castrate'em and let'em grow until they needed'em. Maybe it'd get two, three, or four years old. Maybe if they wanted one when the sheep came in, in the summer, they'd get one. They'd get an old one. They'd never get a young one 'cause he wouldn't weigh much. You see, they only weighed thirty to forty pounds full grown. It took'em a year or two to get big. They'd let one get big and fat. Maybe they'd weigh sixty or seventy pounds."

At times the rams would fight but usually they would get along. The old mountain rams had large curved horns and sometimes they would lock their horns together and starve to death in the woods before they could unlock their horns.

In the spring along about March the sheep begin to have their off-spring. This is what George Grist had to say about lambs and their mothers: "The old type would nurse their young. Now anything that you improve, you run into problems. They take those old mountain sheep and improve'em so they have more wool and mutton, and now they're not as good mothers. Sometimes they don't wanna claim'em and they you gotta make'em nurse. Those old sheep would hold their jug up for'em and push the baby to it and just tell'em, 'you either get it or you die.' And some of these others [improved sheep] just look at their babies and smell'em and paw at'em. And the older type, no matter how cold it gets, they'd clean that

baby up and dry it with her mouth. They'd hold their breath right next to'em and keep her baby warm, and some of the newer ones won't do it."

Gertrude Keener, when asked about raising lambs, said, "Sometimes they'd have twins, an' I've heard of 'em havin' triplets, but usually when they had triplets one was kinda weak and the mother'd discard it. You'd have t'take it in an' raise it on a bottle. I raised two little lambs on bottles."

Sometimes the ewe would disown her lamb and if she did, it would have to be bottle fed in order to survive. If a mother ewe died, the lamb would be shut up with another ewe and the ewe would be forced to nurse the orphan lamb. The majority of the contacts at one time or another have raised orphan sheep with a bottle and a lot of loving care. Claude Darnell said, "I raised one all the way one time till it was grown. Then I took it out to the barn. It lived. That beat anything I ever seen. It'd follow me through the house and if I'd get away he'd just bleat."

The men and women who raised sheep many years ago were a sturdy, independent type of people. They raised sheep because they had to. They couldn't run out to the nearest store and buy clothing or material. This emphasized how important sheep raising was. Without wool, clothing, blankets, and woven goods could not be made. This type of independence is what made the people in this region so unique.

DYEING WITH WILD PLANTS
from *From Raising Sheep to Woven Cloth*

Back many years ago when store-bought dyes were scarce, often only the natural shades of wool were used for material. However, when people did start dyeing wool different colors, usually their only source for dyes was plants, which were boiled down in iron pots. Today, copper vats serve this purpose although none of our contacts used them. When the plants were boiled down, the material or thread was added to be dyed.

People often mixed mordants with the dye to set or fix colors and keep them from fading. Vinegar and salt were used quite frequently as mordants when dyeing with plants. Copperas, a green sulfate of iron; and alum, a white mineral salt, were also successful mordants for dyeing cloth. Acetic acid was used as a mordant to color red and potassium bichromate to color yellow. Most of our contacts didn't use a mordant when dyeing with walnut hulls, however, as the brown produced by the hulls rarely faded.

To keep the wool from getting full of roots and stems, some of our contacts boiled the plants to produce the dye, strained the foreign matter out of the liquid, and then boiled the wool in the dye. Other contacts boiled the plants in a bag together with the wool to prevent them getting entangled with the wool. Still, many of our contacts boiled both plants and materials together.

When the cloth is boiled, it should be dyed a shade darker than the color you want, as the shade will lighten as the wool dries.

If you're really interested in dyeing with natural plant dyes, try it. There are plenty of books that explain the detailed procedures for dyeing with plants. A fascinating book on this is *Natural Dyes in the United States* (Rita J. Adrosko, Associate Curator, Division of Textiles, Museum of History and Technology, Smithsonian Institution Press, available at $3.25 from Superintendent of Documents, U.S. Government Printing Office, Washington, D.C. 20402). But it's almost more fun to experiment and surprise yourself. Minnie Buchanan described a woman who experimented with different dyes:

"Now there's a woman been aworkin' here a little with me for th' last month. She worked up t'last Friday just learnin' t'weave. She'd been studyin' dyein', too. She found a recipe somewhere t'dye with coffee an' tea leaves. She got her some white wool an'dyed it an' got a nice gold color. She got it spun right up here an' wove her a mat out of it last Friday. Then she tol' me she'd tried some with dandelion blooms an' she said it didn't turn out as well as she thought it ought to. She did get a pale yeller out of it. Then she tried some with clover leaves an'said she got just a pale pink with it. She set it with vinegar."

From eleven contacts, we were able to amass a collection of recipes they used for dyeing cloth. Again, however, the real fun is in experimenting and surprising yourself with the colors you get. Good luck!

KAREN COX

BROWN-BLACK

Walnut hulls, roots, and bark were commonly used as a natural dye to produce shades of brown and black. The hulls were used for dye when the walnuts fell off the trees in the fall of the year. Darker shades of brown or even black were obtained by leaving the hulls, roots, or bark in the boiling water a longer period of time.

Edith Darnell: Use the outside hull of black walnuts. Add hulls with the material to boiling water. "They're damp an' when they get wet, that makes th'prettiest brown. Now they might put th'hulls in some kind of a bag in th'bottom while it boiled. 'Cause I know Mommy used t'dye quilt linin's an'all with it. I don't guess it'd take too long. I guess she'd boil'em till th' dyes got in 'em."

Mrs. Darnell said you'd need approximately a peck of walnut hulls to dye a quilt lining. The hulls can only be used once as a dye. Her mother added salt as a mordant to set the dye, just before the material got through boiling.

She also said you could dye with the walnut tree roots. First, you heat the roots and then peel off the bark. Next, add salt or vinegar to the dye as the mordant. Then boil the roots with the cloth. It colors a dark brown.

Belle Dryman's mother only dyed with the brown dye from walnut hulls—she used plain wool and then dark wool from the black sheep. Belle told us people usually used white wool for blankets and colored wool for clothes. These are the directions she gave for dyeing: Wash the wool directly from the sheep. Do not card or spin before dyeing. Fill a large iron pot with a layer of wool (about two inches in height) and then a layer of walnut hulls. Continue in this fashion until pot is full. Fill pot with water and boil it until desired color is reached. No mordant is necessary.

To make a dark brown, Aunt Arie said to use the walnut bark off the roots as soon as you dig them. Alternate a lyaer of wool and a layer of bark to fill up the pot. Then fill the pot with water and boil. She said a mordant is unnecessary to make the walnut dye set—the dye will not fade. For a darker brown, add extra bark.

Mary Carpenter's procedure for a brown dye: gather walnut hulls in the fall, when the hull starts drying up. Boil the hulls in an iron pot; then remove hulls and strain the juice. Add mordant (one pint of vinegar or one pint of salt) and stir until fully blended. Add material and let it boil. Lift material out of the water regularly. Rinse wool out until water is clear.

Mrs. Norton's method was to boil walnut hulls until mushy. No mordant is required. Strain the dye and put material in and let it simmer. The colors are shades from tan to brown. To color a rose beige, add madder root (a plant that grows around the mountains).

ORANGE-YELLOW

Gertrude Keener: Use the gray moss from an oak or apple tree. Add water to the moss in a kettle and boil for one hour. Use more moss for a stronger dye. Sift out the foreign matter. Put thread or material in. Add five cupfuls of salt as a mordant per two gallons of moss. Color varies from an orange or yellow to a light brown. Mrs. Keener commented, "It would be nice t'keep yer moss in a bag. Th'lady that taught me t'do all these dyes had us t'put th'wool right down in th'moss, all in with th'roots."

Mrs. Keener also told us that wild broomstraw would make an orange or yellow dye. Fill a ten-gallon pot with broomstraw. Boil the broomstraw and cloth together. Add salt as a mordant. Broomstraw colors both wool and cotton.

Margaret Norton: Use dye flower (dye weed)—blooms in late summer in untended fields. Gather the flowers when in full bloom. Boil in water from ten to fifteen minutes, long enough to make it a shade darker than your desired color. Strain it. It makes a yellow color.

Mrs. Norton also used coreopsis flower (plant of the same family as the aster with yellow, red-and-yellow, or reddish flowers shaped like daisies) for a yellow color. She boiled the blossoms.

She also gave us this information on black bark making a yellow dye: "Th'outside of black hickory bark was made for yellows. Just go out and beat it off th'trees. Boil it up and it makes beautiful yellows." For mordants, alum for one shade of yellow and potassium bichromate for another. "We put th'bark in flour bags. They hold quite a bit." By putting the bark in a bag, the solution doesn't have to be strained before dyeing the material. When asked the length of time to boil the bark: "There's no way of measuring your time. The bark has to be boiled until you get the desired color. People used t'do a lot of things by th' moon. They thought by getting it on a certain time of the moon, they made more coloring or juice."

Yellow root can be boiled down to make a yellow and then it fades out to a soft green.

Get hickory bark when the sap is up so it will peel out better. Boil it down to make beautiful shades of yellow.

Oak bark also makes a yellow. Boil it until you acquire a thick "ooze" and then add material.

BLUE

Mrs. Norton: Use indigo root (colors a blue). "I know that when my grandmother was making her indigo, she had what they called a 'dye pot.' They had to let this indigo set so long. I used a kind of lye to make my indigo. They used some kind of a 'brand' and mixed it up and let it ferment several days before they used it. [The brand is used to make it ferment.]

"I've understood that they had to put it in barrels of water and let it sit so long and ferment. The settling to the bottom of the barrel was what they used for the dye [a clay-like substance]. Now I bought it in the powdered form. I had a chemical to go with a powder. You don't boil it; you just dip it in the hot dye until you get the indigo."

Mr. and Mrs. Tom McDowell: Use maple bark. The color is obtained mainly from the inside bark, but both inside and outside bark are used. Boil it in a kettle. Remove bark from the dye; add copperas to set the dye and let it boil about a day. This colors a blue.

Blue can also be obtained from galls (insects form these on the stems of a ragweed plant, or any other plant). Boil the galls and add material.

RED

Mrs. Norton: Use madder. Grind the root up into powder and boil it with material. Colors from shades of rose pink to red are obtained from madder. "When I was at Berea, Kentucky once, I heard of a girl who had inherited her grandmother's madder bed."

Gertrude Keener: Use poke berries (one gallon of berries to a ten-gallon pot). Boil them and add your material. This colors from a red to a maroon. Blackberries, grapes, or any other berries will yield various other shades of red.

Use red clay (one gallon of clay to a ten-gallon pot). Put clay in a cloth bag and let it boil. Remove clay and add material. Possibly use a cup of salt as a mordant. Clay colors a deep orangeish-red.

PURPLE

Use pokeberry roots. Chop up the roots and boil them. Add material to get a deep purple color.

GREEN

Use green oak leaves. Boil leaves with material for one to one and one-half hours. Add salt as a mordant.

HOW TO WASH CLOTHES
IN AN IRON POT

"Th'place of th'washin' is by a branch. That's where most ever'body washes. Now, my great uncle lived up away from a branch, and they built what they call a wood pump. In other words, they took a little log and they took an auger and bored a hole all th'way through that, and then they joined'em together. And they made a line for th'water t'come down to th'house from th' branch."

Even as he said this, Mr. Dickerson led us over to the pile of wood he planned to use.

Mr. Dickerson then made the paddles that we would use that afternoon. Both were of pine, as it is light, soft, and easy to work.

First he shaped the handles using his hatchet, and then he smoothed up the handles and paddle blades with a drawing knife. "When you're cuttin' a straight line like this [the handle], you use your drawin' knife like this [with the beveled edge of the blade up]. When you're comin' into a curve, you turn your drawin' knife over. See, this edge is beveled. If it was straight, you'd dig in."

While he worked with the drawing knife, the paddle was clamped in a vise. A shaving horse could also have been used, though.

Additional smoothing was accomplished with the edge of a small piece of glass.

Then, using a large black iron pot and two pairs of bluejeans, we began the actual washing.

"Well, let's get our water started then. Get our bucket and we'll put some water in there and we'll build a fire. That water'ud run all th'time at th' old-fashioned wash places. People usually kept a bucket settin' under there so if y'happened to want some water right quick, you'd always have a bucket full when y'went t'th'spout.

"Now, y'have t'put a little water in [the iron pot] before y'start th'fire so th'heat won't crack it. Here th'wind's kindly wrong, but I guess we can make it, maybe. Y'need t'stack your wood under your tub kindly, and y'have t'keep it a'goin' all th'time. If you'll put some a'those chips up in under there, she'll come."

Mrs. Dickerson, carrying out the process from there, began to fill the pot with water as the fire caught. While she was waiting for the water to boil, she took the clothes and rinsed them out in cold water at the end of the battling bench. Then she took each piece separately, lifted it sopping wet onto the bench, and battled it with the short paddle, turning it over and over continuously as she worked. Then each piece was rinsed, battled again, and then rinsed again. Had there been any heavy stains, they would have been scrubbed out.

When the water was boiling, soap was added and the battled clothes were put in to boil.

"It helps to keep'em stirred so th'soap can go through'em and get th'dirt out of'em. Workin'em down with th'paddle helps it come out better. Now we just rench'em and hang'em out."

The clothes were then lifted, steaming, out of the pot and carried over to the tub at the end of the battling bench, which had been refilled with fresh, cold water. After being rinsed there, they were carried over to the second tub, under the spout, and rinsed well a second time. Then they were shaken out well and hung up to dry while still completely wet.

"We used t'rench our clothes three times, and then hang'em out wet.

"Y'usually turn'em after y'rench'em so th'insides of'em can dry better. it's better t'hang'em out a'fore they start dryin' cause they won't be so wrinkled and they're softer."

On each side of the pot is an eye. Two poles are run through these to empty the water out of the pot without getting burned.

"Th'pot has little eyes on th'side. Th'reason for those eyes: Y'can set th'pot off and on your fire. When y'go t'set it down, you're out here where y'can see when you're hittin' your rocks. When y'get through your washin', turn your water out. Then turn your pot upside down on these pillars here t'keep your pot clean. It won't rust then, and y'don't have t'scrub it out ever'time y'wash.

"It's a job washin' for a whole family. All your bed clothes, all your towels, and if y'live on th'farm y'have extra overhauls, shirts. If th'weather's fit, you wash once a week. Y'try t'pick a day when it's not rainin'r' somethin', but if there's snow on th'ground, y'just have t'go on and do it anyway. I'll tell y'what I did: bought me a boiler and put it on my kitchen stove and boiled mine in there.

"I *have* washed about all day. Used to wash till dinner time and go fix dinner and then come back and finish washin'. It didn't take too long t'wash a load. We'd boil th'clothes say maybe thirty minutes' r'so, and sometimes not quite that long dependin' on how much dirt they was in'em. But y'see, you rubbed'em some before you put'em in th'pot, and got th'worst out. Now if you'uz gonna boil a pair of real dirty overhauls, you'd have t'boil'em a little longer than you'd boil a sheet.

"We had flat irons then. We'd set'em down in front a'th'fireplace, or on th'stove, and heat'em and then iron. They'd weigh, about five pounds—six pounds—and some seven. You could iron five'r' six pillow cases—maybe a little more'n that—and then you'd have t'heat your iron again. Y'kept *one* heatin' all th'time though.

"Now that's th'whole bit!"

The MOUNTAIN EAGLE

IT SCREAMS!

WHITESBURG, LETCHER COUNTY, KENTUCKY

Words about the Mountain Eagle are necessarily words of praise. I've been reading it for over sixteen years now, and what I know, what all Eagle readers know, is that it is one of the best weekly newspapers published in the United States, that it is *the* best periodical of any kind published in and concerned with the life and problems of the coal-producing regions of the Southern Appalachian Mountains.

The Mountain Eagle was founded some sixty years ago, and because the mountain country it serves is unique, the Eagle has always been a unique community newspaper. But it is these last sixteen years—years in which Tom Gish has been the owner and editor—that have seen the Eagle grow in excellence, until today it comes exceedingly close to being a model weekly newspaper.

Most weekly newspapers are bland, one-dimensional affairs, vehicles for advertising mostly, filled with canned views and non-news about the superficial doings of the local "polite society." Impolite society gets scant attention, and impolite views, especially political views, get no attention at all. Weeklies that purport to serve rural counties are usually dominated by the interests of the county-seat town in which they are published. That is where the courthouse is. That is where the lawyers live, and the doctors and the insurance brokers, the bankers, the merchants, the bureaucrats, the golfers, and their wives. The town is where the *power* is concentrated and most small newspapers (or large ones, for that matter) are little more than instruments, consciously or unconsciously, of that power.

But as many a Kentucky politician, strip-miner, coal company executive and federal bureaucrat has discovered to his frustration and chagrin, the Mountain Eagle is the instrument solely of its editor, Tom Gish.

Tom's beat, the Eagle's domain, is Letcher County, Kentucky, population about 20,000. Tom was born and raised there, and after his University education and early experience as a reporter of state government in Frankfort, he returned to his native county in the middle 1950's as the new owner and editor of the weekly Eagle. With him came his wife Pat, herself a newswoman, University trained, a first-rate reporter

for a Lexington, Kentucky daily. Together the husband-wife team took over the Eagle and applied to it their intelligence, their keen political and social awareness, and their high standards of professional journalism. The Gishes did their job so well the Mountain Eagle in time acquired an audience beyond its native county, particularly in northern cities among transplanted mountain people, and in Washington where people in government who want to understand Appalachia consider the paper indispensable, even if they hate it for the truth that it contains.

By extension, the Eagle's beat has been enlarged to include the whole of Southern Appalachia. The problems, the issues, the details of the daily life in Letcher County are to a large extent the same problems, issues and details of a much larger mountain universe, which spreads across parts of five states. The modern experience of that mountain region is the experience of being colonized, of economic and social subjugation by large, monolithic outside forces like the coal and oil industries, and the federal government.

In the Southern Appalachian Highlands, the Mountain Eagle has over the years of the Gishes' ownership established itself as the most courageous, consistent voice against those colonial forces, whose brute presence works constantly to destroy the native mountain culture.

Week after week, year after year, the Mountain Eagle has reported upon and editorialized against strip-miners who destroy whole mountain ranges in their lust for coal; giant energy corporations who extract the mineral wealth from beneath the mountain soil without benefit to or regard for the people who own and live on that soil; the federal government, which promotes a multitude of schemes to uproot the people and re-settle them in cities, and then to dam the deserted mountain valleys to make reservoirs for the use of people far away; and a host of local, petty politicians who aid and abet the colonization in all its forms.

But the real miracle of the Eagle is the fact that while it may be the *instrument* of its independent owners, it is the *medium* of many people, hundreds of them, local average citizens mostly, who not only read the paper religiously, but who write for it as well. As the excerpts on the following pages show, the paper is to a large extent reader-written. The frequency and the volume of letters to the editor, and the amount of space given over to the neighborhood columnists, is a measure of the sense of kinship the people of the country feel for the Eagle. They regard the paper as their own. They speak to each other through its columns, and in doing so, they strengthen the fabric of their local life against all of the powerful outside forces arrayed against it.

TOM AND PAT GISH

The essence of the Mountain Eagle is that it gives voice to people who otherwise would have none. That comes as close as anything I can think of to stating the basic function of a true community newspaper.

It is perhaps unnecessary to say that the struggle of the Gishes to keep the Eagle alive, and independent, has not been an easy one. There have been lean financial years (Tom and Pat will get a laugh out of that one). The energy-drain in all weekly newspapering is constant. Tom had a serious heart-attack two years ago, and he is only just now able to do any substantial work on the paper.

Had it not been for the help of some talented young friends it is hard to see how the Eagle could have survived the crisis brought on by Tom's collapse.

But there they were, a whole staff of young writers who had been gathering around the Eagle for some years, working part-time, working as volunteers, contributing free-lance articles. The writers were drawn to the Eagle because it was one of the very few publi-

cations in all of Appalachia that was wholly committed to saying the truth about how it really is in the mountains. By now the by-lines of Tom Bethell, Phil Primack, Lauran Emerson, Sally Bright, Mike Clark, Jim Branscome, and photographer Jean Martin, are familiar ones to Eagle readers. Their news stories, features and photographs of mountain life in all its variety have kept the Eagle strong and vital during Tom's convalescence. The Eagle is indebted to these writers, but hardly more than they are indebted to the Eagle, for it is hard to imagine a better place for a young journalist to find his personal, professional voice than with the Mountain Eagle.

Voice. That one word seems to sum it up. The Eagle is a voice that is heard all over the Southern Highlands, and beyond. The eloquence of the voice is manifest in the excerpts on the following pages. I have chosen the material to be reprinted in PLACE from my own collection of back issues of the Eagle. I have tried to select material that would provide a sense of what a "typical" issue of the paper is like. I have only partly succeeded. The only way to really get at the heart of the Eagle is to subscribe and read it every week for a while. But at least the outline is here, a beginning sense. I have reprinted some news stories, some editorials, some of the columns by neighborhood correspondents, and two pieces, by Hawk Littlejohn and Jim Branscome, that talk specifically about the problem of colonization in Appalachia. Because this theme is such a constant, on-going fact of daily life in the mountains, it is an on-going theme in the Eagle as well. Look closely and you will notice all the Eagle writers touching upon it one way or another.

The central thing that the writers and the readers of the Eagle have in common is love for the place, and the way they live. That place and that way is threatened by an aggressive, dominant national culture that hates all things native, all things local, all things individual. The Mountain Eagle is a kind of cement that binds together a community of people determined to fight for its life, and its identity.

—GURNEY NORMAN

To subscribe:
The Mountain Eagle. Box 808, Whitesburg, Ky 41858
$7/1 year outside Letcher County
$5/1 year in Letcher County

89

Mudslide Threatens Mill Branch Home

By LAURAN EMERSON

An orphan strip mine holding "a great big lake" of water gave way last week on the Mill Branch, bringing huge boulders and trees and acres of mud down the mountain.

At the mouth of the Mill Fork, Andy Bates and his wife woke on Monday morning to find a wall of mud oozing toward their house. By noon, the muck had advanced another 50 feet, covering the Bates' garden and inching to a stop about 100 feet above the house.

The Bateses and other residents of the area fear that the mudslide will move again when the next heavy rain hits Letcher County. Kentucky Commissioner of Natural Resources Thomas O. Harris, who has sent engineers to the site, said, "At this point, I don't think there's any danger, but we can't underestimate the possibility it'll continue to slide."

"The danger will be if it rains, and the water builds up above the slide," Harris said.

Andy Bates owns the land surface. The mountain was strip-mined four years ago by Don Nicewonder's Maxietta Coal Co., which was sold out to McCulloch Coal Co. two years later. Mineral rights to the land are owned by the Kentucky River Coal Corp., which leased stripping rights to the company. The State Bureau of Reclamation inspected the site during the stripping operation, and made Maxietta halt operation twice "because they were going so deep into the hill."

Who is responsible? Don Nicewonder is no longer in business. McCulloch Coal didn't do the stripping. Kentucky River Coal is merely the mineral owner. The Bureau of Reclamation told Maxietta not to exceed strip-mine regulations. The land was stripped before today's reclamation requirements were law.

The courts have never detailed the legal responsibilities of the mineral owner, the stripper, or the company that buys up someone else's abandoned mines. The Bateses are caught in the middle. They don't know what will happen. What they do know is that, "We'd do anything to move out of here. We love this place. We always did. But it looks bad tonight, and we just need a place to go."

Andy Bates is 73. His wife is 68. They have lived in their house on the Mill Fork of the Mill Branch for more than 25 years. Six of their nine children were raised here.

"Four years ago," Bates recalls, "the company came in here trying to buy the land off of us. They paid us $3500 for a right-of-way for one seam of coal, but they got two. They called the second seam a 'rider' but in some places it was 36" thick. Now that doesn't seem like a rider to me."

"I don't own the mineral," Bates said. "It's Kentucky River that owns it, or at least they say they do. The company mined for about a year and a half here. Our agreement was the dirt wasn't going to come over 80 feet from the highwall. Now it's 400 or 500 feet from their highwall."

"They gave me a paper back then," Bates said, "but we can't find it. It must be in their records."

Mr. and Mrs. Bates and their nine children moved into the house on the last day of 1945. "When we moved in, the house wasn't much at all," Mrs. Bates said. "But Andy had been hurt in the mines on Thornton and couldn't work, and we had nine children to raise. So we came down here, and had a little money for a down payment on this place."

"To pay for the house," the Bateses recall, "we used to go to the hills and cut little pieces of kindling to sell for stove wood. We'd sell that for ten cents a block. Then we used to cut props. Just anything that we could do for a little money, and we did it."

As a new rain began drumming the roof, the Bateses were brought back to the present. "For two or three years, we paid for this house. Every time we got as much as $5.00 that we didn't need for food, we'd pay it for the house. We did all that, and now, with that mud, it looks like we'll have to start again."

"We had potatoes, beans, just anything we could raise, in the garden above the house. It's all covered up now. The rock wall up there was torn up a year ago last August by another mud slide. That was from a slip about a quarter mile above this other one. There was three feet of mud in the house that time, and water coming through the yard."

"We had to get shovels to dig ourselves out that time," Mr. Bates said. "The bridge got washed out that time. too. The county had to fix it. The company wouldn't even fix that bridge. Maxietta finally paid us sixty dollars to hire a boy to help us fix that rock wall. Sixty dollars."

This time it is more than a rock wall and a bridge that are endangered. A representative of Crawford Engineering Co. sent to the site by McCulloch, told the couple that, "No doubt it won't be safe to live here." "You've been damaged," he said. "Damaged is

MR. AND MRS. ANDY BATES were forced to leave their home on Mill Branch when tons of mud, rock and trees slid down upon their farm from an orphan strip mine. The Bateses had invested a lifetime in their small mountain farm.

(Eagle photo)

right. We've been ruined," Bates said. The Crawford representative said later that he had been informed that McCulloch Coal Co. had no responsibility for the mudslide, and there was nothing the company could do for the Bates family unless Don Nicewonder asks for our advice." He said the case is being turned over to Nicewonder's lawyer.

Resource Commissioner Harris said that Maxietta had put up bond on the stripping operation in July 1968, and had been given a hundred-percent release on Dec. 30, 1970. McCulloch bought out Maxietta in 1971, and Harris said, "I'm sure they (McCulloch) are not responsible in any way for what Maxietta did." "It's difficult for me, as a layman, to pinpoint whose responsibility this would be," Harris said.

"We may have to relieve the impoundment of water up there, and we don't know who's going to pay for that," the commissioner added.

Where does that leave Mr. and Mrs. Bates? Unless they are successful in bringing suit against the company or the state, it leaves them without a home to live in, or for their children to come back to for the holidays. It leaves them without a garden which has been their main food supply for almost 28 years.

"We don't even have a place to move

our things that we canned or put in the freezer. All that food, we couldn't live without it," Mrs. Bates said. The couple lives on a minimal payment from Social Security and Aid for the Aged. "By the time we pay our coal and light bills, there's hardly anything left, and sure not enough to buy a place."

Since last week's mudslide, Mrs. Bates has been spending the nights with her son's family, who live further up the Mill Branch. Her husband joins her if it's raining. "But they're so crowded themselves, they just don't have much room for anyone else," Mrs. Bates said. "But I don't guess we'll stay here tonight with this rain. The rain just keeps us on the road," she added, "and I'm just not able to get around that much."

The Reclamation officials and engineers, and representative of McCulloch Coal Co. who visited the site, "didn't say too much," Bates said. "I think somebody's responsible," he added. "I don't know who it is, but it must be somebody."

"I've done my best to get along with the company," Bates said, "But I don't think they want to do us half-way right. We'd be satisfied if they found us anything—move this house or find another. If only we could have water, we'd be satisfied. We're just scared to stay in this holler now. We'd do anything to move out of here."

Blackey confronts the monster

By GAYNELL BEGLEY

One of the largest gas and oil companies in Kentucky and West Virginia has begun moving D-6 and D-9 bulldozers into Blackey in preparation for drilling for gas and oil in the hill behind the homes in lower Blackey.

Among the benefits of this arrival of big industry have been 3-4 inches of clay mud in the streets, on our school children's playground, and on the street of lower Blackey. The road to our burned-out school location has been rutted by large, medium, and small gas trucks. The school grounds have been criss-crossed by 3 bulldozers, destroying a proposed nature trail and basketball courts. When contacted about this destruction, the Letcher County School Superintendent, Mr. Kendall Boggs, said that he had not given permission for the company to go on school road or property. Mr. Harry Caudill, Whitesburg attorney for the Letcher County Board of Education, said that he is contacting the company.

There are other property owners in lower Blackey who were visited by company officials only after the bulldozers had cut wide roads through their land. One elderly, sick lady was alarmed to hear the dozer only a few feet above her house. She had not even known there was any work in the area

like this. Most of the other homeowners in this part of town are increasingly concerned about their water supplies as the mud, trees, and rubble slides toward springs which have been their source of water for 30-40 years.

The uneasy situation with this company came to a head when their employees began to haul heavy equipment over the only bridge into Blackey. This bridge has a posted limit of 12 tons. Three drivers hauling dozers have been arrested and fined by Magistrate Monroe Hogg. The fines were assessed with warning that jail sentences would be meted out upon second offense.

On Monday, Nov. 27, just at dark, the company attempted to move a drilling rig across the bridge. This rig weighs 44 tons. The truck hauling it weighs at least 15 tons. A company official, showing a permit from someone in Pike County, which he claimed gave them "permission" to cross the bridge, said that he would be escorted across the bridge by the Sheriff and state police. A large group of Blackey citizens gathered on the bridge and when Sheriff Lewis Hall came to assess the situation, he denied the right of the monster rig to cross. A driver turned the loaded truck around and took it to Perry County where it remained until Tuesday.

Massive layoffs have hit the underground mines of Eastern Kentucky and more than 500 miners have lost their jobs in developments the past few days.

The largest layoffs came at Wheelwright, Ky., where Island Creek Coal Corp. announced it was closing the big Wheelright mine and a sister operation, the Spurlock mine. The Island Creek closings took the jobs of 340 miners.

In Letcher County, SouthEast Coal Co., announced it had reduced its work force by 100 miners.

At David, in Floyd County, 90 miners were dismissed in the closing of the Turner-Elkhorn Coal Co.

A company spokesman for Island Creek Coal Corp., in Cleveland, O., blamed the shutdown on the high cost of production and low return on coal.

Harry Laviers, Jr., vice president, South-East Coal Co., said his firm decided to reduce its work force so that the remaining miners could work a full five-day work week. He explained the company had been selling enough coal to work only two or three days a week with the larger work forces, but now everyone is working a five-day week. The cutback was from about 310 to 210 miners.

Heavy inroads into the traditional electric utilities market for coal by the oil industry was cited as perhaps the chief reason for the current layoffs. Electric utilities, faced with air pollution control requirements for cleaner air, are turning increasingly to oil and away from coal.

The eastern Kentucky coal fields also are beginning to get competition from mining developments in the west. The Tennessee Valley Authority has contracted for large amounts of coal from Wyoming. The Wyoming coal, although delivered to TVA at a considerably higher cost, has only one-half of one percent sulphur content.

The David mine closing was blamed by company officials chiefly on the high sulphur content of Kentucky mountain coal. A company official said he believes much coal remaining in the mountains no longer can be mined and sold in view of present air pollution control requirements.

Generally, the coal marketing situation remains confused. During the past two years there have been nation-wide cries of a fuel shortage and during that time, and largely as a result of the claimed shortage, there have been substantial increases in the nation's mining capacity with numerous new mines, both underground and strip, being opened. Also, fearing possible fuel shortages from a threatened miners' strike, many large users stockpiled large quantities of coal.

Grand jury indicts 28, suggests aids

The January Letcher County grand jury has returned 26 indictments, including eight for felonies and eight for misdemeanors.

Jury Foreman Mrs. Mary Newell said the jury also made a suggestion that county make an effort to modernize the record keeping practices of the circuit and county court clerks, through up-to-date equipment, possibly "by means of a grant through the Appalachian Regional Development or other agencies involved."

The jury also suggested that the sheriff's office be painted, and that filing cabinets be made available in the county clerk's office. The jury also reported it had found the courthouse to be in a clean and sanitary condition.

Officials of the Appalachian Regional Hospital chain were named in one indictment. It charges T.P. Hipkins, president of the hospitals; the members of the hospital board of trustees, and the administrator of the Whitesburg hospital, Bernard Wysocki, with obstructing a public road.

At issue is access to the farm of Robert Fields, behind the hospital. Fields argues that the road to the farm is a public road, that he has no other access, but that the road has been blocked since Wysocki took over as hospital administrator.

Other indictments included:

Troy Adams, petit larceny; Jerry Richard Ball and Silas Frazier Holbrook, grand larceny.

Harold D. Bates, murder; Johnny Wayne Collier, negligent homicide.

Morgan P. Day, trespass on enclosed premises; Larry Miller, storehouse breaking;

William Hermit Sizemore, bigamy; Danny Pease, improper registration; Durand Cantrell, robbery.

Ann Breeding, use of obscene language on telephone;

William Grant, Woodrow Phillips Jr., and James Bentley, one count of grand larceny, and another count of dwelling house breaking and feloniously taking therefrom wares and other things of value.

Arlie Ray Adkins, wilfully and maliciously displacing a TV cable and tapping thereon; Freddy Bryant, wilfully and maliciously displacing a TV cable and tapping thereon.

Harmie Melton, forgery.

TAMMY GREEN AND FELLOW MEMBERS of the Whitesburg High School Band play for "Pancake Day."   (Photo by Lauran Emerson)

Ministers oppose local option

The question of whether Letcher County should continue its ban on the sale of alcoholic beverages is up for discussion and possibly a local option election.

A temperance meeting was held Jan. 20 at the Mayking Regular Baptist Church, with several Letcher County ministers and laymen attending.

They formed an organization, the Citizens For A Dry Letcher County, to act as a steering committee. The Rev. Bill Mackey, pastor of the First Baptist Church, Whitesburg, was named committee chairman.

Others serving on the committee are Bro. Manus Ison, Bro. Kirby Ison, Bro. Buford Dunavent, Herbert Banks and Donald Cassidy. Cassidy was named secretary.

"The purpose of this initial meeting is to alert Letcher County citizens concerning the local option petition that is being circulated requesting the sale of alcoholic beverages in Letcher County," the committee said.

"Citizens should know what they are signing. The petition is asking for an election to allow the sale of alcoholic beverages in Letcher County. If you are against the sale of alcoholic beverages in Letcher County the citizens for a Dry Letcher County urge you not to sign the petition," the group said.

Rev. Delbert Butts, executive director of the Temperance League of Kentucky, said it is a common "misconception" that legal sale of alcoholic beverages will stop bootlegging.

"The wettest states have the most illegal sales," he said.

Others attending the meeting included Bill Adams, Jake King Sr., and Jake King, R., Hunter Heltsley, George L. Abel, N. Webb, Leon Wesley, Doc Beale, George Spangler, Robert Wagner, Dave Wagner, Harry Fegan, Crit Eldridge, Delmer Kincer and Rev. Leon Wesley.

The office of Letcher County Clerk Charlie Wright said no petition for a local option election in the county has yet been filed. Some residents of the Jenkins area brought in such a petition several months ago, but did not have the required number of voters' signatures on it so it could not be filed, the clerk's office said. The petition has not been resubmitted.

City wins development honors

Whitesburg was one of 16 Kentucky communities to receive the title of "All-Kentucky City" at the annual awards luncheon given by the Kentucky Chamber of Commerce in Louisville Friday.

About 50 Whitesburg officials and residents attended the luncheon and heard this citation concerning the city read:

"This small community in Eastern Kentucky is small in size only. The citizens are big in heart and have a great deal of pride for their city.

"In April, 1972, the construction of the outdoor drama theater for the showing of "The Little Shepherd of Kingdom Come" was undertaken. By opening night June 30, the drama theater was completed without need for any state or federal funds. The actors were all local residents who worked without pay. Approximately 2000 people were involved in the drama, which drew visitors from 47 states and 10 foreign countries.

"In other areas of recreational activity, the city park has been expanded. A swimming pool, tennis courts and small museum have been added.

"Additional opportunities in education have been offered with the completion of a new elementary school, and expansion took place at the Whitesburg Vocational School.

"Numerous projects have been initiated by the local Chamber (of Commerce) to clean up the city. City streets have been resurfaced—curbs and sidewalks painted. A new whiteway lighting system will soon be in operation. Two new parking lots were built to relieve parking congestion on the streets.

"Vast improvements have been made on the city's water system. New pumps have been installed, along with new lines, and new fire hydrants.

Local share

Letcher County will get a total of $255,946 under the new federal revenue-sharing plan approved by Congress. Of that total, $107,333 would go to cities in the county and the rest to the county government.

Allocations are based on a complicated formula which is supposed to take into consideration the population, tax effort and a 'poverty factor.'

The plan has not received final congressional approval but is in conference and is expected to be passed finally and sent to the President before the present session of Congress adjourns.

Perry County would get $407,170 under the program. Leslie County would get $71,632 and Knott County would get $82,786.

"A new sewer plant has just been completed at a cost of a half million dollars. It was a federally and locally funded project, and a sanitary landfill has been constructed. An industrial site is in the process of being developed.

"An urban renewal residential development was begun three years ago. Twenty-two homes have been built, leaving room for seven others.

"Last summer 168 homes were inspected and vast improvements have resulted due to the repairs that have been made.

"The citizens of Whitesburg are proud of the improvements that are taking place in their community, and well they should be."

The city's exhibit was prepared by Jimmy Brown, who serves as city administrator under the Emergency Employment Act, and other interested citizens and officials.

Eagles feel Yellowjackets' sting 45—49

Steve Banks continues to be the big gun for the Whitesburg High School Yellowjackets.

Banks scored 16 points and hauled down 14 rebounds to lead the Jackets to a 49-45 victory over the Letcher Eagles in an overtime Tuesday night.

Letcher drew first blood by taking a 1-0 lead on a foul committed by junior forward Frank Hollan. But the Yellowjackets were not to be denied as they pulled the lead out to 18-12. Whitesburg got into trouble after Banks committed his foul midway through the second period and fell behind by two points at halftime.

In the second half Letcher came out playing showdown ball to control the lead most of the way through the second half. The Eagles led by two points with about 30 seconds left on the clock when the Yellowjackets tied the score at 43 apiece. Then, Letcher brought the ball down the floor and with 11 seconds left in regulation play were called for traveling. Thus, the score was tied at the end of the half, and the game went into overtime. The Yellowjackets then showed their ability to come from behind to win ball games as the overtime period was all theirs. Rounding out the scoring for the Jackets:

Frank Hollan scored 10 points and took 6 rebounds; Mike Polly added 9

points and grabbed 9 rebounds; Eddie Stallard scored 7 pounts and was credited with 5 assists.

Friday night the Yellowjackets traveled to Hindman to romp over the Carr Creek Indians by a score of 71 to 52. High point man for the Jackets was Senior guard Mike Polly, with 29 points.

Prayer set

Letcher County churches will take part in a continent-wide Noon Prayer Call beginning the day after Christmas and lasting for two weeks. The program is known as the "Key 73" movement and will involve the establishment of noon-time prayer groups in churches, hospitals and schools, a local minister said.

A television show, "Faith in Action" will mark the end of the noon prayer call and the beginning of the "Key 73" project. It will be shown on Jan. 6 and 7 and will be followed by simultaneous services in 100,000 churches in the country.

Graduated

Army Private Henry D. Spears, 19, son of Mrs. Eula F. Spears of Worthington, Ohio, and Fred H. Spears of Jenkins, Ky., recently graduated from the clerical school at the U.S. Army Armor Center, Ft. Knox.

Pvt. Spears entered the Army last April and received basic training at Ft. Knox. His wife, Elizabeth, lives in Powell, O.

Girl Scouts need leader

The Junior Girl Scouts of Whitesburg need a leader for their troop. These Girl Scouts did not have a leader last year, and desperately need one for the coming year.

Anyone interested in this volunteer job, call 633-2313 or come to the meeting of the Girl Scouts' mothers Monday, Oct. 2 at 11:00 a.m. at the Letcher County Library in Whitesburg.

Revival services

The First Baptist in Jenkins will hold revival services beginning Sunday morning, Oct. 1 at the regular services, through Oct. 6. Services will be held at 7:30 each night.

Tuesday night will be family night; Thursday night youth night.

Special music will be provided every night.

The public is cordially invited to attend.

Floyd Warrix is pastor.

Another lesson

If you drive out Sandlick Road and down the mountain a few hundred feet toward Camp Branch, you will see a sight that makes all the argument in Washington about all the virtues of strip mining seem pretty silly.

There, three modest hillside homes occupied by four generations of Letcher Countians are about to be crushed by tons and tons of mud and rock washing down from a strip mine road. Mrs. Eliza Jane Hall, who has attained the fine age of 95 or 96 years old, was carried from her home to safety by neighbors who fear her home may be crushed at any moment.

It all is the handiwork of Victor Hurley and the Valley Coal Co. And it is one of those continuing messes that causes just about everyone who knows of the situation to doubt the good faith of state officials when they say they are controlling the worse abuses of the strip mining industry.

Kentucky law says coal can't be stripped or augered on slopes of 27 degrees or more. We don't know the degrees of the mountain side along the road going past the three endangered homes and on down into the valley. But beyond question, it is one of the steepest of all mountain hillsides and the slope must be somewhere in the neighborhood of 50 per cent. It is straight up and down, to all practical purposes. And there's scarcely a tree or bush left on it to hold the soil.

But despite the dangers of stripping in such a spot so obvious that even a child could see, Hurley succeeded a few years ago in getting state permission to strip mine in the area. Loud protests came from Columbus Sexton and other Camp Branch residents, who filed charges with the state over and over. Every now and then, the state would levy a small fine on Valley and its owner; it even revoked the company's license at one point.

But the efforts of the Camp Branch residents and the highly-acclaimed law enforcement efforts of the state never interfered much. Valley continues strip mining in the Camp Branch-Isom area, full speed ahead.

All of which, as we said, makes the talking and the arguing in Washington about whether there should be federal or state control of strip mining, or indeed whether there should be any kind of control, seem just plain ridiculous.

Any senator or congressman who has not sold his soul to the coal company dole knows, if he takes a look at Eastern Kentucky and the Appalachian area, that prohibition of further stripping in the mountains is absolutely essential to survival of the area and to the future of the nation itself. And anyone who sees the mess on Camp Branch must acknowledge to himself that state regulation of strip mining has failed, and is failing more day by day. To talk about federal strip mine laws that would require regulations, with the regulating to be done by the states, is to talk absolute nonsense.

Freedom costs job

How much is your freedom worth? Well, it's worth your job, Willard Gilliam learned this week. To be more accurate, Gilliam learned that you can't be a state employee, apparently, and excercise your constitutional right of free speech—not if in so doing you are critical of land use plans and planners, development districts and the Appalachian Regional Commission, and particularly the Kentucky River Development District and its director, Malcolm Holiday.

Gilliam, a 16-year career employee with the Kentucky Department of Economic Security, became something of a mountain hero a few weeks ago when he single-handedly challenged a proposed land use plan for Letcher County. The plan, drafted with money provided through the Kentucky River Development District, would have ended traditional mountain ways by prohibiting people from living on the hills and in the hollows. The plan was regarded as a model for other mountain counties to follow.

Gilliam, who likes hill and holler living, sounded a warning. The result was that hundreds and hundreds of Letcher Countians poured out to the courthouse for public meetings, demanding the scalp of the planners and politicians who were responsible.

The Letcher County Fiscal Court responded to the showing of force on the part of the people, and both rejected the plan and disbanded the planning commission.

And now Gilliam has been scalped.

Gilliam announced today in a letter to the The Mountain Eagle that he has been harrassed in his state job to the point that he has been forced to resign. He said he was "fed up" with the "feeling that if a state employee stands up for his rights, he is a second-class citizen."

Gilliam said he had had to defend himself against telephone calls to his bosses from the Kentucky River Development District and the Letcher County Judge's office. The pressure, he said, caused him to resign from the state post. With 16 years toward retirement, this represents a major sacrifice and punishment for Gilliam.

In his letter to the editor, on Page 3, Gilliam says that "Eternal vigilance is the price of liberty." He might have said "Eternal vigilance and your job is the price of liberty." But Gilliam obviously is not the type of man who places job above personal honor and integrity.

The way I want

To the Editor:

In reference to the statement made by Mr. Bill Morton, Mayor of the City of Hazard, in your September 7 issue of The Mountain Eagle:

It was reported that Mr. Morton stated that he did not want to live next to a house trailer and referred to them as instant slums.

I presently live in a house trailer which meets code standards in every way.

Mr. Morton, did it ever occur to you that people may not want to live by your standards? That they would prefer to build and live the way they wish? Should any man or agency such as KRADD be placed on a pedestal to dictate the manner in which others must spend their lives?

I do not advocate living in filth or in deplorable housing, Mr. Morton, but I do feel that I have the right and freedom to design and live on my property the way I want.

Mr. Morton, I can guarantee you that my trailer shall never be next to your home. I would prefer a neighbor with respect for people and their ideas than a fine home conforming to zoning standards.

FRED BACK
Mayking

Cumberland mountaineers won't be forced

To the Editor:

They have tried to move us off of the hills and the hollows and take our homes. I request that you intercede for their sakes and being the last recourse for their right as Americans to call to, beg your looking into the Development Association and their practices in these regards.

In traditional beliefs, the people of the Cumberland Mountains wish to be left to themselves and not be subjugated to the ideas of progress as envisioned by organizations such as EDA and others who have almost destroyed life here as cherished before.

In this last stronghold of a fierce, free spirit of independent life styles and the people's right to be this way, we extend this letter to you.

I, Aaron Adams, have been put under so much pressure that it looks as if I will have to leave Letcher County after 40 years of hard work of building it, i.e., coal mines, construction work to put it up and all.

Hats off to Willard Gilliam, to run for the office of County Judge of Letcher County next.

AARON ADAMS
Whitesburg, Ky.

THE MINER: Unique and sometimes a little hard to understand

To the Editor:

There is a type of man who is quite unique and sometimes a little hard to understand. This man is the underground coal miner.

You can usually tell a man who has spent many long and hard days in the mines by his stooped shoulders and labored breathing.

He is a brave man, because it takes guts to go back in those dark and damp holes and make a living. He is always mindful that his very life depends upon a lot of roof bolts and timbers; also, how careful his buddy is. The threat of death is every present in a coal mine. It can come at any moment, anyplace. A timber could splinter beneath a massive rock fall. A rock fall could break out above the roof bolts and half leaders. A spark could touch off an accumulation of dust or a seepage of gas, which no one was aware of. A machine could bump a high voltage line. A dynamite charge could go off prematurely while being tamped into a hole. A drill could become a death trap, and there is the every present coal dust to turn lungs black. Death takes no holidays.

When a miner leaves his family when he starts to work, he doesn't know if he will ever see them again. Maybe he will make it home safely and maybe they will carry him back, with only a brief stay with his family before being returned to the ground, perhaps not far from where he had worked only a few days before. Only this time, it is not for a single or a double shift, it's forever.

But he tries to push these thoughts from his mind and goes to work as usual. He lives with Black Death constantly. He sees it, feels it, breathes it, and even eats it. He takes a sandwich out of his bucket and can't see to tell what kind it is, so he just shruggs his shoulders and eats it anyway. He will blow his breath across the water in his bucket to blow the coal dust to the other side so he can get a drink. As he sits eating his meal out of a dinner bucket, all is quiet. No one is talking and he hears the steady drip, drip, drip as the water drips from overhead. He wishes there was a better way to feed his family, but knows that this is all he will ever do. There's just not much work these days, and besides, this is all he ever learned to do.

Sometimes the dust is so thick he can hardly breathe and sometimes his arms feel like dead weights. His shovel feels like it's got a ton of coal on it, but it is still empty. He wonders if the fan is still running or if the bradishes are where they ought to be. Maybe because not enough air is getting to the face of the coal. And since the lungs have to distribute the life-giving oxygen into the blood steam, maybe they are so full of coal dust, there is not too much room left for air.

When he comes out of the mine at the end of his shift, about the only clean part about him is his eyes. If not for a little help from nature, they would be black, too. But his soul may be clean, too, which no mortal man can tell.

He often wonders what would happen if he became unable to work because he has inhaled so much coal dust. He has heard a lot of talk about Black Lung benefits. But will he live to enjoy any of the benefits, or will his widow have to try to collect after he is gone.

A miner sheds blood, sweat, and a lot of times, tears. But when payday comes, he knows he has earned every dime which he receives.

So I salute you, coal miners, one and all. And may God work with you during every shift.

RELON HAMPTON
Jeremiah

$5 TO WHIP THE EDITOR

To the Editor:

I got home last month to see my sick father. I have been gone since 1967, and the jailer and the police judge said if I would leave Letcher County they would let me out of jail. I have been picked up 16 times since I got home.

Well, I was born here 42 years ago, and I am going to stay here if I have to stay in jail.

I asked for a trial and never got one. They keep me five days and let me go. I never get to stay out of jail over two days at a time. I can work every day if they would let me alone.

I want the people of Letcher County to know what kind of city law we have in Whitesburg. Even the jailer tried to get me to whip the editor. He said he would give me $5.00 Then he came back in the jail and said he would give anyone $5.00 to whip that long-haired son-of-a-bitch. There were five men standing there.

And I want people to know they will keep me in this jail as long as I am here. But I am ready to stay. I have been on the road for 20 years. I am sick now and I am not going anywhere anymore. And I want everyone to know if anything happens to me or Aaron Adams it won't be an accident.

JACK SEXTON
Whitesburg

HONOR ROLL

Troy Randall Breeding of Isom was named to the honor roll at Transylvania University for the recently completed Fall Quarter. Breeding, the son of Mr. and Mrs. Van Breeding, made a 3.25 standing.

COAL TIPPLE IN LETCHER COUNTY (Eagle photo)

Abolishing the coal industry in Letcher?

To the Editor:

Like the proverbial West Point 90 day Wonders of World War II, a tobacco farmer from the Ohio River Flatlands has suddenly envisioned himself as the saviour of the beautiful upland Appalachia. His front is that of an expert coal operator who deems all others as cold, senseless beings who rape and pillage. He boasts that he may destroy the economy of Eastern Kentucky with a broad gesture of his kindness and sympathy. Commissioner Harris is a fast learner. He spent over thirty days learning all there is to know about Eastern Kentucky and the Coal Industry. He is a wonder ready to go to battle.

Like Bob Schulman and Ex-Governor Nunn, I find it highly ridiculous that Public Serpent Ford has taken so long to develop an attitude on strip mining. Perhaps he feels that the office of Lieutenant Governor has no responsibility to public trust. He is right in a small way. I very personally, never trusted him while he was in that office. I trust him even less since he has taken over the throne.

Through his severance tax and the new commissioner of natural resources he is very ignorantly though assuredly, bringing Letcher County to its knees. He is going to abolish the mining industry in our part of the state through political destruction and miscalculation.

Abolishing the coal industry in Letcher County will virtually wipe out the working man. He will have to go on welfare or leave this area for a new job. That seems to be the road this county is on. Coal production is down over fifty per cent here since last year. Business is likewise, off about fifty per cent. Unemployment has more than doubled. I have no difficulty in establishing a relationship between those three situations. Our economy depends on the coal dollar.

Mr. Ford has insulted the intelligence of every Eastern Kentuckian by choosing to hire as natural resources commissioner a man who hardly knows what a mountain is and who knows nothing of the coal industry. He either lied point blank, or displayed his own ignorance, when he disavowed any knowledge of the strip mining situation until a few weeks ago. Our taxes have paid him for over four years to know what's going on "up in these hills" as well as in the rest of the state.

IKE ADAMS
Jeremiah

MARION ISON LOADS HAY WAGON at his farm at Kingdom Come. (photo by Jean Martin)

Gilliam calls land-use plan Un-American

To the Editor:
I have written the following letter to Congressman Perkins:

Letcher County recently narrowly escaped being saddled with an un-American land use program and housing plan. This plan was engineered by the Kentucky River Area Development District located in Hazard, Kentucky.

A HUD grant was used to cook up this deal and the utmost secrecy was used to keep the plan from coming to the attention of the citizens of the county.

We learned of this plan in time to organize mass meetings all over the county. When the (fiscal) court met hundreds of people were there to oppose the plan and it was voted down.

Now, however, the Kentucky River Area Development District is trying to force this un-American land use plan on an eight-county basis (Letcher, Knott, Leslie, Perry, Breathitt, Owsley, Lee and Wolfe Counties.) This organization can manipulate Federal grants to gain their objectives.

We feel this whole set-up is bad. It seems any Federal monies, to which the counties may be entitled could go from the state to the counties concerned without being forced into an eight county unit, and lose the county's powers over its affairs in whatever the area may be that the grant covers.

If this KRADD is not changed, our citizens will have no other alternative to combat their activities except to go to each of the individual counties and explain the dangers facing them. We may need to call an eight county mass meeting to get some kind of changes made.

As presently set up, any Federal money is a disadvantage to the counties receiving it. If they have to lose any control over their affairs.

Any help you can give us in this matter will be greatly appreciated.

WILLARD M. GILLIAM, Chairman
COMMITTEE TO SAVE LETCHER COUNTY

Collins chosen as first termer

Sgt. Terry M. Collins, 22, recently was chosen the 26th Air Division Headquarters first termer of the month.

An announcement said he earned the honor by displaying superior performance on the job. He is an aerospace warning and control operator in the division's surveillance section.

Sergeant Collins, a native of O. Fallon, Ill., is the son of Mr. and Mrs. Jack Wise Collins, formerly of Millstone, Ky. He joined the air force in July, 1969, and served in Japan before going to Lake Air Base, where he won his latest honors.

He is the grandson of Mr. and Mrs. Claude Collins, Millstone.

Awarded

Kris Bentley, Mina Leigh Breeding and William Welch, of Letcher County, have been awarded graduate assistantships for the 1972-73 school year at Morehead State University.

Poke in wintertime

To the editor:

To have all the good nutritious greens a large family could use all winter, take an old tub or large wooden box, fill with richest soil you can find, set in dark corner of basement or cellar, fertilize well, after first freeze dig up 8 or 10 good size Poke roots, set one inch deep in water and keep well watered. In two or three weeks you will have the surprise of your life.

Poke like asparagus must be eaten, canned or frozen when it's 6"–8" high or it's bitter and tough.

Cook like spinach or asparagus or slice stalk and fry like okra or eggplant. You can buy poke greens canned in all modern food markets.

In spring pull up plants, reset in a rich sunny spot and recharge for next winter. Anyone who does not have poke available and will send me a stamp, I will send free seeds and information to grow and use.

Plant poke seeds at gardening time ¼ inch deep. Frost kills seedlings first spring. Plant around garden or backyard fence. Once started, cultivation not necessary. Seeds, when ripe, make fine tonics, wine, jellies and finest attraction for all seed-eating birds. Don't use for food first year, so it will make a good root crown. As long as stalk snaps like green beans, chop stalk, roll in flour and meal and fry. Freeze leaf and stalk for winter. The leaf is fine greens, canned and sold in most food stores. Roots are sliced, soaked in whisky, and a couple sips daily will cure rheumatism, arthritis etc. No more than two sips daily, roots are toxic. Poke is perennial, a plant lives 40 years or more, transplant any time by removing all new growth.

P.S. Green onions grow well as above.

GRAYDON B. CUMMINS
Mt. Vernon, Ky. 40456
Phone 256-2261

(Editor's Note: The Mountain Eagle will welcome hints from its readers on gardening, farming, canning, cooking and other aspects of mountain life. For the time being, they will be carried as letters to the editor; if enough arrive, they will be segregated into a separate column.)

and get run out

To the Editor:

To the citizens of Letcher County:
It's time for a change in our county government, especially with our county judge and commissioners.

When we go to a public meeting and just about get run off over speaking up about what we believe in.

Twenty years ago I was proud of our county judge. He was his own man then and I really believe it.

But today I honestly believe he is owned by the coal company. And is no longer his own man.

So I say to all voters, let's vote him and all county officials out.

At our special meeting, the county judge did turn his head and did not listen to what the people were saying as they begged the commissioners to pass a resolution to give the property owner a right to have his land stripped or refuse to have it stripped.

So people, I am calling on you to be ready to defend what is rightly yours. I will be willing to stand up and fight any way that we may choose and my friends, we will have to choose.

Let me say thanks to all the people who did stand up.

My thanks to Mrs. Billy Joe Caudill, Mrs. Gaynelle Begley, Mr. Tilden Crase, Mr. Columbus Sexton, and our great friend and attorney, Mr. J. T. Begley, and myself. And all whom I did not know.

So citizens, whom will you choose to fight with, our local courts or the strippers? You have a choice as of the present time.

LUTRELL HAMPTON
Jeremiah, Ky.

Good Eating

Bread from Pine Mountain

By JOSEPHINE RICHARDSON

The Pine Mountain Settlement School is known for many things—one, which I recently discovered is their whole wheat bread. Alice Westover, who resides at Pine Mountain gave me the recipe.

The school usually has a supply of baked loaves on hand, so stop by to pick-up one if you're in the area, or try the recipe below in your own kitchen.

Pine Mountain Whole Wheat Bread

1 cake yeast	½ cup dried milk
2 cups warm water	¼ cup hot water
2 tbsp. sugar	¼ cup brown sugar
3 cups white flour	3 tbsp. shortening
2 tsp. salt	3 cups whole wheat flour

Soften yeast in lukewarm water. Add sugar, salt, white flour and dried milk. Beat smooth. Set in warm place (82 degrees) until light and bubbly. Combine hot water with brown sugar and shortening. Cool to lukewarm and add to the sponge. Add whole wheat flour and mix smooth. Let rise. Place in greased loaf pans and let rise until double.
Bake in moderate oven (350 degrees) for 40 minutes.
Makes 3 one pound loaves.

MEMBERS OF "THE HIGHWAYMEN," a Detroit motorcycle club, attend the funeral of a fellow member at Blair Branch Church in Letcher County.   (Eagle photo)

A CHEROKEE ASKS:
How much does the white man want?

by HAWK LITTLEJOHN

When the Cherokee Indians were herded up at their last Council Grounds in the East—at Red Clay Council Grounds near Cleveland, Tenn., in 1836—they were gathered by the U.S. Army to be moved to the West and to be separated from the land they had called Home for thousands of years.

Over 13,000 Cherokees were displaced by the move and over 25 per cent died from starvation, mistreatment and cold. Their walk was called the "Trail of Tears."

Before moving to the West most Cherokees learned to read and write through the help of one of their great educators, Sequoyah, who had taken the Cherokee language and created an alphabet and taught the people. Overnight the Cherokee people progressed from a prehistoric society to a lettered society.

When the Cherokee people reached Oklahoma these same people who had advanced so far on their own had had enough of the white man. They had suffered so much abuse and grief because of the families who died on the "Trail of Tears." Many went back into the mountains and hid. They had seen so much bad in the white man's society that they reverted to the old ways. Some, today, still live very primitively back in the mountains.

In 1836 when the white soldiers were trying to round up all Cherokee a few hundred escaped into the Great Smoky Mountains to hide in the caves, grass and forest and to live in wood huts, for this land was theirs and they did not want to leave their home. Today their descendants are known as the Eastern Band of the Cherokee and number about 8,000 living on the Qualla Boundary in Western North Carolina.

When the Cherokee people moved up into Tennessee a couple of thousand years ago they settled along the Little Tennessee River. They built numerous homes and villages. The bulk of the whole Cherokee society started there. Along the Little Tennessee River were their great towns and villages, including the sacred town and capitol, Echota. Along this river, Sequoyah was born and grew up and started the Cherokee Alphabet and taught it. This is where the Cherokee people became one of the most civilized tribes of Indians in the country.

Today, there are very few Cherokee sites or old village sites left. They have all been flooded or destroyed. The only area which holds any history to the Cherokee that remains is along the Little Tennessee. Now it is being threatened to be flooded, too. The TVA has plans for a dam.

The Cherokee people have been run off their land, have been herded together like cattle, and have been shipped to a foreign land and have been raped of their identity. This country screams at atrocities which happen in other countries but the United States hides the fact that the atrocity of the Trail of Tears is no less than any other atrocity created by any other country or done by any other country. Now the government is going to finish the job that they started by the Trail of Tears.

They took and destroyed the Indian people when they moved them from their land, stole it, and said Indians weren't citizens of this country so therefore they weren't entitled to the land. Now the government is going to complete the job by coming back and saying these same Indian people do not have any right to have any history; these people do not have any right to have a place where they can come and say to their grandchildren: "This is where our great village sites were. This is where our culture started. This is where we cultivated our language. This is where Sequoyah was born. This is where we started from."

The white man is taking this from us. This is where the white man is committing total genocide on a people. How barbaric and cruel could any one people be to another people?

This is supposed to be a free country; people are supposed to be able to practice their own heritage and their own culture. The white man would not flood Valley Forge. The white man would not flood his great monuments. Doesn't the white man realize that the Cherokee or any other Indians' history is just as important, just as significant, to us? We ask the white man to have the same consideration for our history and our past that he expects us to have for his.

The governmental agency which is planning on flooding our land is called the TVA, Tennessee Valley Authority. They have already constructed 35 dams in this eastern part of Tennessee. The reason they give for building this dam and flooding our history is that they would like to build a model community by constructing a dam for a recreation area and building this area up and taking this land and reselling it for a profit. There seems no danger of flood control of this river. One mile from the proposed dam is Ft. Loudoun Dam. If the Tellico dam is completed, its waters will back up to the base of another dam up-

VIEW OF THE CUMBERLAND PLATEAU at early morning, looking north from Pine Mountain.
(photo by Dean Cadle)

stream on the Little Tennessee.

There is no great need for genociding a people's history when the whole eastern part of Tennessee is dotted with lakes. Responsibility for this project rests with the TVA Board of Directors, led by Abrey "Red" Wagner, a man already known to East Kentuckians for his policies of buying strip mined coal from the mountains. When the power for stopping this dam is in one man's hands all he has to do is say, "Stop!," and it will stop. But he has closed his eyes and ears to the plea of the Cherokee.

White leaders refusing to oppose this project are as guilty of genocide as Wagner is. White people should stop and examine their leaders.

The Cherokee people ask for support, not only from the white leaders but from Indian leaders. We ask for support from all groups, and especially those who know what it is like to be flooded out, to please, openly, help us in this fight.

How much more payment does the white man want for us being here first?

AUNT POLLY CAUDILL'S House on Sandlick
(Photo by Jean Martin)

Linefork

We should hold on to our land in these mountains

By THELMA CORNETT

Monday, January 15, brings us almost half through the longest, coldest, month of the year. I think one reason we always find January especially hard is because it comes after the Christmas and New Year's holidays which are usually filled with families, visiting, friends, exchanging gifts and greetings, and then we find ourselves in the humdrum everyday-way of life, and with many people trying to catch up from having overspent as well as losing days of work.

It looks like now from the last report on the rising cost of living that young men with families are going to need two jobs or the mothers in the homes will be forced to find jobs to help keep the necessities of life, with very few or no luxuries.

The warm temperature we had here at Linefork Sunday really brought back the ugly spots here. They look just as bad as ever when the snow melts.

The thing that really concerns me is that most of the very best homes that we had on Linefork when my parents and grandparents first moved to Letcher County have been abandoned and allowed to fall to ruin because of the immediate families moving away to find work elsewhere. Some have burned, and never rebuilt.

I think an old chimney and hearthstone left standing after the old home has been destroyed is about as desolate a scene as can be found, for the hearthstone in the early days of our country was the family gathering place where in winter evenings the corn popping was done and mountain ballads sung, also some religious songs. I am sure that many people can remember hours of pleasure spent around an open fire and hearthstone.

I wish there could be a way of preserving what few old homes we have left, for there will never be such lumber again as in our old houses. They were first built of fine poplar logs and covered outside with hand-planed weather boarding and inside with six-inch, hand-planed ceiling. Such homes were built with care and patience and great pride in the work of their own hands. I really hate to see this kind of home fall into decay, for they meant so much to their builders at the time.

If the severe earthquakes really happen in California and other places as predicted, people will be buying homesites all over the mountains before the close of this century. It may be wise for our people to hold on to what acreage they own in these mountains.

I am planning on going to Michigan soon to visit my son and his family, and Della will visit her daughters there too and we will go by bus. One reason is because Della refuses to fly, and other is I don't want my luggage inspected at the airport for I plan to have some shucky beans and salt bacon in one of my suitcases and I don't want anyone fooling around with part of my luggage, for I plan to cook them for my son and family while I am there.

Mr. and Mrs. Hiram Caudill visited her parents, Dave and Cinda Cornett of Gordon Ky., during the week end and Dave remains in poor health. He has been sick a long time and his friends and family would be so happy if he could be well again.

Elizabeth Sue Roark, daughter of Roy and Ruby Jean Roark, of Gordon, has been in Valley View Hospital for a few days, but is now home on medication for ear and throat infection and is expected to have to be out of school for three or four weeks. She is a student here at Kingdome Come and is hating to miss school. So her schoolmates could send her notes and get well cards.

Alan Cornett and his wife of Ashland visited his parents, Chester and Mary Cornett, of Gordon, last week. Alan is quite lame from a broken ankle or foot, sometime ago, which makes it very difficult for him to travel. We are very happy he is well enough to visit his parents, for it has been some time since his accident.

Mrs. Boggs succumbs

Funeral services were held Friday, August 18 for Pearlie Boggs in the Big Cowan Regular Baptist Church, Dongola Kentucky. She died on Wednesday, August 16 in the Whitesburg Appalachian Regional Hospital, Whitesburg, Kentucky.

Items from Ice

Hopes for peace and prosperity in new year

By SILLER BROWN

We close the book for 1972 which has come and gone and left behind many memories to be locked and sealed in the hearts of loved ones. Only God and the one that holds the key knows they are there.

As we say goodby to the old year with much sorrow and many regrets, we'll try to smile and say good morning to the sun as she comes smiling up over the mountain on New Year's morning. Yet we'll wonder what the new year has in store for the people of our nation. Peace and prosperity, we hope.

The holidays are about over now. But still are little bits of ribbon and some bits of tinsel here and there, and the smell of cedar left by the tree, and empty candy boxes to be put in the garbage, along with some extra wrapping paper and other things left behind to remind us that our friends had come and gone for the last holiday in the year.

There are many sick people about over our neighborhood, but some are better.

Mrs. Ann B Hughes says she received many nice gifts from friends and relatives, which pleased her very much. As the good book says, once a man and twice a child and as we get older we are pleased with many things, even the littliest things that may not be noticed by some are my greatest gifts.

I want to thank all my friends who sent me cards and letters, and gifts. All were greatly appreciated. We had no snow on Christmas, but a few flakes the day after.

We are having too much rain and dark days for the people to feel good. We ought to have gathered more herbs for our aches and pains, but we forgot until they are all dried up.

But there's still plenty of sassafras for tea and plenty mullen for colds and cucumber roots for women of all ages, and there's nothing that can compare with its value. Spicewood is also good, and birch scapped and put in sweetened water makes a wonderful drink and it's plentiful. To make cucumber tea, cut up some roots, put them in a kettle and boil down from one half gallon to one quart and let cool. But don't sweeten. Put in a jar, set in the refrigerator, and drink one cup before going to bed.

Mrs. Hade Caudill still is in the hospital, a very sick person. She has lived to be in her nineties, and very few ever reach that age anymore. Mary Caudill is 90 and seems to be in good health, but we never know we are here today, and gone tomorrow. Life is so uncertain anymore at all ages that it pays to be ready when Jesus calls, and make sure we have our ticket.

It's strange how Mary Caudill never could read. She had no schooling in her time. But for the past few years she can read good. She loves to read the church minutes, most of all.

It's a pity our older people had no chance to get an education. They were only taught to work to earn their own food, but it was good and pure and tasty to the last bite. We don't have fresh food anymore. It's all skiked with some kind of seasoning or the other.

Mr. and Mrs. Lawrence Brown had their children home for Christmas.— Mr. and Mrs. Larry Brown and their two little boys from Ashland, Mr. and Mrs. Jerry Nantz and little daughter from Lexington.

Mrs. Flora Standifer passed away Jan. 1, 1973. She was buried Wednesday, Jan. 3, in the Maggard Cemetery on Cumberland. She was staying with her daughter, Mrs. Lorain Adams in Indiana, at the time of her death. She had been staying with her daughter for some time. Lorain loved and cared for her mother with tender care.

She leaves a large family and a great many friends. She will be missed in the home and by her neighbors and her church. She had been in poor health for some time. But when God calls we have to go.

Most of the folks on Little Cowan had a wonderful Christmas.

Mr. and Mrs. Cassel Caudill had most of their family home to enjoy the holiday.—George Sigrest and family, Mr. and Mrs. Glennon Ison and family; Mr. and Mrs. Walda Stamper and family; Varon Campbell and family; Mr. and Mrs. Robert Caudill and family and Mr. and Mrs. Irvin Ison and family.

Mr. and Mrs. Edison Caudill were pleased to have all their family home for the Christmas holiday celebration.

Mr. and Mrs. Myrel Brown were pleased to have their children all home for the holiday—Mr. and Mrs. Steven Brown and family from Bristol, Va., Joe Brown from Arkansas and Randy Brown, at home. They all enjoyed being together at home.

They had watch service at Little Cowan church, with visiting preachers and singers from other churches, and a great crowd attended.

Mr. and Mrs. Chester Rayburn from Ohio and children were visiting with Mr. and Mrs. Bernard Banks during the holidays.

The Cowan singing group met at the home of Louama and Doris Banks while Robert Gatton was here. They all enjoyed singing with Bob again.

Boyd Banks at Ice is doing fair, just holding his own.

They had seven of their children home for the Christmas holiday. Three others could not come but their hearts were there with the family.

SILLER BROWN, author of the popular column, "Items From Ice." (photo by Tom Bethell)

Outdoors, the greatest symphonies

By MABEL KISER

I have just come in from the back porch, where I was listening to one of the greatest symphonies on earth. The perfect harmony of nature's creatures, the fall insects that always come out between sundown and night fall. I wonder what they sing and why they are so happy. Do they know that soon there will be cold and snow? But then like the "roots of the bright red roses" that are kept alive in the snow, God makes a way for the creeping things on the earth to live through the hard winter. But I really love to listen to them sing in the autumn, and feel the gentle breezes blow on my face. We have good neighbors, too, and as we listen to the insects sing we can hear the laughter of happy children in the background.

We need rain water here in many wells, which are getting low. Earnest Reynolds is having one drilled at his home. Now is a good time for well drilling, for the water level is low and plenty water now will mean plenty later.

The Edd Halls are lonesome this week for their youngest child, Robert, has gone to Detroit to find work. Robert is a graduate of Fleming-Neon High School. They have two other children— David of Dayton, and Janice (Mrs. Billy Stamper) of Detroit, and two grandchildren.

Week end guests of the Dave Colliers were their children, Mr. and Mrs. Fred Collier (Jo Ella) and their son, Steve, of Pikeville.

Mr. and Mrs. Wilson Cornett have returned to their home in Hindman after spending the week end with their son, Dewain, and his family (Lydia Duty) and children.

A stork shower was given at the home of Mrs. Dewain Cornett for her niece, Mrs. Jeffrey Everidge.

The infant son of Mrs. Connie Sexton is very ill in the community hospital at Norton.

Elder and Mrs. Alex Collier have returned to their home in Cleveland after spending several days here with her mother, Mrs. Dortha Hall, and his mother, Mrs. Louisa Collier. Elder Collier made a well box over the well at the late Enoch McCray home place. This place is now owned by a daughter, Mrs. Charlie Hall, (Dortha) and she did not want the good hand-dug well filled up, so she had the wall built around it. Mr. Collier also attended the New Salem Association meeting Saturday and Sunday.

Mrs. Hall and her daughter made a lot of good old time applebutter while she was here.

Our children called their father on his birthday—the Bob Bentleys, Ronald, Jeanie, Jessica and Robert, and the William Harold Kisers, Pamela, Michael and Timmy, all of Louisville. It made his day, for her had felt very bad when he got up Monday morning. Friends came to call—Elder and Mrs. Ballard Meade and their son, Junior, and Mr. and Mrs. Dave Collier, and he felt much better. Many friends called during the day to ask how he was, and this made

him feel better.

Mr. and Mrs. Edsel Lewis of North Dakota Air Force Base and their four children, Eddie. Randay, Rebecca and Claudette, were here over the week end visiting his parents, the Tom Lewises of Kona.

The Ballard Meades of Fleming tell us they have a new grandson, James Allen. The parents are Mr. and Mrs. Charles (Delinda) Spoon of Michigan. Grandmother is Mrs. Norma Lakes of Michigan. James Allen is the first child of the Spoons, the second grandchild of Mrs. Lakes and the 10th great grandchild of the Meades.

Mrs. Dortha Hall, Blaine and I and the Ballard Meades drove to the North Fork of the Pound, Virginia, to attend the Indian Creek Church. There was a good crowd at the church and they had some good preaching. After church we all went home with the Dee Bakers for dinner. Others from this area to attend church were Mrs. Elsie Hall, Hemphill; Alfred Adams and his daughter, Mrs. Flo Galloway and her two sons; (Flo lives in Appalachia, Va., and her father had spent the night in her home) Mr. and Mrs. Ralph Kiser and their children, Reno, Michael and Anthony. The Kisers took a picnic lunch and ate at the dam at the North Fork of the Pound.

Mr. and Mrs. Kelley Ballou and children drove to Winchester over the week end and visited their son, Ronnie, and his family.

I am grieving for my Weeping Willow tree that stands beside the road and is a friend to man. The lovely tree stands near the Mayking Pottery and the road makers are coming dangerously close.

Mr. and Mrs. Hansford Chester have a new, white, Toyota car. They have been visiting their children in faraway places.

Many attend Carcassonne day; park progressing

By CHARLES ANNE MULLIS

Some of the folks who enjoyed the special day at Carcassonne on Sunday were Aunt Mag Back Brown's complete family, who all attended school there at one time or another: Watson and Minerva Craft from Florence, Ky.; Jim and Jeanie Back from Alexandria, Ky.; Reed Back and family from Morehead; and John Back and family from Lexington.

Austin and Berdie Miller, Grace Caudill and Vivian Branson were there. Also there were Mrs. Tessie Cornett Caudill, Mr. and Mrs. Curt Cornett, Raymond Cornett, Clyde and Mabel Back, and Bill Bates.

The fellowship, the weather and especially the food were all good.

Aunt Artie Cornett held a memorial service for her late husband, Uncle Arch Cornett, at the Cornett Cemetery on Sunday. Mrs. Bill Bates, Mrs. Billy

Jo Caudill, Miss Artie Anne Bates, Jack Bates, Denice Bates and Amy Caudill attended.

One of our older friends on Bull Creek is very ill. Granville Halcomb is in the hospital in Whitesburg.

Aunt Mary Dixon, who has been very ill, is much improved. She will be staying with her son, Mr. and Mrs. R. B. Dixon, until she is well.

Loye and Brenda Caudill and little son Eddie have moved their trailer back home to Elk Creek from Indianapolis, Ind.

Mr. and Mrs. Wayne Blair and Little Joe visited Mrs. Blair's father, Joe Back, in Prestonsburg, on Sunday.

We had a few fishermen out over the weekend, but no fish were caught. Curt Blair and Darrell Hampton went to Tennessee on Saturday, and Bill Caudill went with a few friends to Tennessee on Friday. The way I heard it, you will have to wait until the weather is cooler.

Miss Artie Anne Bates was home from U.K. for the weekend.

Dave Dixon, who is very ill, has his daughter Irene visiting him this week. Mr. Dixon was taken to the hospital on Tuesday.

On Sunday, Mr. and Mrs. Joe Begley, Mrs. Tessie Mae Caudill, Mr. and Mrs. Cramer Mullis, Jimmy Begley, Alan Caudill Mullis, Beth Reasoner and Johnny Vanfchoren drove to Lexington to help J.T. Begley celebrate his 29th birthday. They also helped celebrate Owen Caudill's 20th birthday. We visited with the J.T. Begley family and Joannie Mullis.

The park in Blackey is progressing very nicely. Come by and see it if you can stop and talk a bit.

Don't forget the Chili Supper on Friday evening, from 6:00 to 7:00 p.m. at the Blackey School lunch room. $1.00 and 50 cents, and proceeds to the P.T.O.

Appalachia must have land reform

By *JIM BRANSCOME*

No one has done more to hold Appalachian life up for national ridicule than the producers of the "Beverly Hillbillies," "Green Acres," and "Hee Haw." It is no surprise, therefore, to find this brochure being handed out to tourists flocking into the Great Smokies through the Asheville, North Carolina, airport:

"Hello! I'm Eddie Albert . . . and I want to personally invite you to see my new film about the 'un-City' . . . Connestee Falls. As you may know, I have been involved in the fight for the preservation of our environment for many years. I am proud to be associated with Realtec Incorporated, the developers of Connestee Falls, because here in the Blue Ridge Mountains of North Carolina, Realtec is creating an Un-City: uncrowded, unhurried, unpolluted.

"I sincerely want you to see my film about this remarkable environmental achievement.

Signed: Eddie Albert
Star of "Green Acres"

Connestee Falls, and dozens of new developments like it in the North Carolina Blue Ridge, may be an eerie "Un-City" to farmer Eddie Albert, but to the farmers of the mountains, it is an intrusion, the kind of intrusion that has driven the price of marginal farm and timber land from a low of $100 an acre to a whopping $1000 an acre in a half decade.

So high has the price and taxation on mountain land become in the last few years, that the dream of a mountain farmer to have at least one son stay home to till the soil has changed to the nightmare that he may not even be able to maintain the farm for his own retirement.

Sons and daughters of small, subsistence farmers along the Blue Ridge Parkway in Carroll County, Virginia, have been returning home lately to learn that the Groundhog Mountain Development Corporation, a firm that sells lots to professional people from North Carolina cities, has used high-pressure tactics to force their parents to sell their land to them.

According to Larry Bowman, a law student at Wake Forest and a native of the area, "These old folks—many of whom can't read and write—believe that they are only leasing, not selling their land to these corporations.

"Others are so poor that the promise of a new roof or some worthless gratuity is traded for a small-print contract that in effect amounts to the theft of the land."

Only a few miles further down the Blue Ridge Parkway in Carroll County—the county that Mike Seeger says "has best preserved all those things that make up the Appalachian culture"—another firm is building, of all things, a ski resort.

The headline in the Carroll News on December 8, 1972, proclaimed, "Cascade Mountain—New Way of Life," and continued, "First there was Beech, then Sugar, and now Cascade. Yes Cascade Mountain Resort will have one of the finest ski slopes in southwestern Virginia."

As one of its "many features," the ski resort will have an "Olympic Village" with a lodge and motel named "Liebenschuer." And, of course, there will also be a county store. Carroll County needs a ski resort like San Francisco needs skyscrapers.

Thanks to these kinds of developments in this county, the price of farm land is far beyond the means of farmers to buy it.

An eighty acre farm in Carroll, for example, was recently offered for public auction—something that mountaineers have traditionally done when there are several heirs to a farm and the community is in need of a social event, something that auctions have always been. The hope has always been that one of the family or a close neighbor would "buy the old homeplace."

This farm was privately offered by the heirs to a local man for $7500, a figure that he considered excessive and rejected. At the public auction, flooded by land speculators and professionals from North Carolina in search of a "second home," the farm brought $20,000. A few weeks later one half of it was subdivided and sold for $40,000.

$40,000 for a hillside that once grossed only a crop of wheat sufficient for the family's bread, pasture for 4 cows for the family's milk, and a few cord of pulpwood to be sold to "put the kids in school" for the winter.

Carl Salmons, a small dairy farmer whose farm borders on the one mentioned above says, "These people from North Carolina now own land on all four sides of me. I guess I'm next."

The Salmons family is one of four families out of what was once thirty families in the same hollow who have not sold out. Land speculation, urban affluence and overcrowding, and the decline of small farmers, has led to a situation where the right to be a hollow dweller—as most mountaineers have been for centuries and want to be now—carries with it the attendant obligation to also be rich, an obligation that few mountaineers can meet.

The economic situation of small farmers in Appalachia is similar to that in the rest of the nation, though Appalachia has the greatest number of small family farms of any region in the nation.

Exact figures are not compiled by the U.S. Department of Agriculture for Appalachia but these statistics nationwide give an idea of how desperate the situation is:

—there were more than six million farms in 1940 but there are less than three million today, and the Department of Agriculture predicts that at least another million farms will shut down during the next eight years;

—in 1970, for the first time since the nation was settled coast to coast, our farm population fell below 10 million;

—during the past three decades, an average of almost 2000 farms a week have folded and there is no end in sight:

—by the year 2000, experts predict that little more than 500,000 farms will produce the nation's food and fiber;

—47.1 percent of the farm families in this country have annual incomes that fall below the minimum poverty level;

—1.5 million farm workers averaged an income of $1083 in 1970; another one million farm workers raised their average income to $2461 in 1970 by also doing some non-farm work. Less than 12 per cent of the farm workers were employed year-around. They were the highest paid, making a mere $3467 for 1970.

While this forced migration of the people from the land has been going on, the Federal Government and its agriculture extension stations at land-grant colleges throughout the nation have been spending the taxpayers' money to help annihilate the small farm and forever entrench the corporate farms as the source of the nation's food supply.

According to a report by Jim Hightower of the Agribusiness Accountability Project in Washington, here is how the agriculture extension services and the universities have been spending the public's money:

—1,129 scientific man-years (smy) on improving the biological efficiency of crops, and only 18 smy on improving rural income

—842 smy on control of insects, diseases and weeds in crops and 95 smy to insure food products free from toxic residues from agriculture resources.

—200 smy on ornamentals, turf and trees for natural beauty, and a sad seven smy on rural housing

—88 smy on improving management systems for livestock and poultry production, and 45 smy for improving rural institutions

—68 smy on marketing firm and system efficiency, and 17 smy on causes and remedies of poverty among rural people

Hundreds of proposals for rural development have been put forward in the past few years to revitalize the rural economy. Cooperatives, rural loan banks, and other kinds of palliatives have been advocated. All have failed to halt the stream of migration north. If the family farm is to survive in Appalachia, indeed, if Appalachia as a rural area is to survive, then more dramatic steps such as the following have to be taken:

(1) Corporate farming nationally must be stopped. It is a monopoly which allows high prices to be charged for inferior food.

(2) A regional producing and marketing system must be adopted which would forbid importing any food to Appalachia that could be grown locally by mountain farmers. This would entail the creation of a kind of Appalachian state, similar to a country of the European Common Market, which would protect mountain farmers at the expense of corporate farmers in Idaho and Colorado.

(3) Land reform must be instituted. The giant holdings of the corporations in Appalachia should be federalized and homesteaded just like the U.S. Government seized and homesteaded in the West. If we can do this to the poor Indians, there is no reason why we cannot do it to the rich corporations. This would simply be returning to the mountaineers the timber and land that they were swindled out of at the turn of the century. With this land, small family farms could again flourish in the mountains. Each homesteader would be required to sign a pledge that he would preserve his land for the next generation—not allowing it to be stripped or destroyed. The U.S. Government is presently forcing land reform on land barons in South Vietnam. It is also giving millions of acres of land back to the Indians. There is no reason it cannot give back the land of mountaineers, either.

(4) Resort complexes that serve only middle-class skiers and other kinds of intruders into the mountains should be prohibited. They bring only crime, high land prices, and disrespect for mountaineers with them to the mountains. Land is too precious to be used in the same way that we use our cities.

Homesteads are falling down all over the Appalachian area, priced beyond reach of the families that grew up in them.

Retaking the resources of the mountains by mountaineers is the only way to solve the problems of the mountains. Like the mountain Swiss who decided that they did not want to be Germans, British or French, mountaineers must decide that they want to remain mountaineers. Otherwise in a few short years we shall be like the Cherokee chief standing on the roadside, trying to get someone to take our picture for a quarter to make a living. We are fast becoming, as Harry Caudill has suggested, a paleface reservation, except that we will not even own our own reservation. We might take this warning of Hawk Littlejohn, a young Cherokee fighting to keep TVA from flooding the Cherokee graveyards: "The government and the corporations are not going to be happy until they have driven all the people out of the mountains. Mountain people are going to experience the Trail of Tears, too."

CANYON de CHELLY

Must have been early 1970 when I told Clyde Childress I thought we should do a photographic project together. He thought I was crazy. Also, he wanted to know where? I said give me six months and I would come up with something. Eventually I suggested Canyon de Chelly and Clyde wanted to know how many times I had been over there. I had never been there and I knew he hadn't either. All I had ever seen of de Chelly were a couple of T.H. O'Sullivan's and the great Edward Curtis photograph of the line of Navajo horsemen and a dog against a mammoth cliff. That one had been hanging on my wall for years.

So we rounded up Steve Jett, who had long wanted to pull together all the literature that ever existed on Canyon de Chelly, and in June, 1971, the three of us drove to Chinle on a political trip, to meet the National Park Service and ask their help in locating a guide for us and our proposed long-term project.

It was at Antelope House ruin in Canyon del Muerto that we met Chauncey Neboyia. Chauncey was foreman of the dig crew and he knew we were coming. He rose up out of those ancient walls with his hard hat on his head, walked on over and we shook hands. I don't think we said much, any of us, but it was agreed we would return in the fall and start work. And that's how it began. We're still working on it and we keep going back over there. We love the land and the great walls and the cornfields and the Rio de Chelly and the cottonwoods. But the other part of it is that we miss seeing Chauncey and Dorothy and the rest of the extended family. So as I said, we keep going back.

Berkeley, California
8 May 1973

The photographs:

Chauncey and Dorothy at home, mesa top
In Canyon de Chelly at high noon
The Rock-That-Lightning-Struck in Canyon de Chelly
The lower Canyon in winter, from Tsegi
White House ruin
Canyon de Chelly
Petroglyph B.P. 700 (?)

Dave Bohn

POETRY

OTHER MAN

Tli dogpaddles the October morning
ice in the pasture. As she breaks through
spreading in the sun
sparkling water, she drinks

the mowed field ringed by birch and fir like a lake.
Mountains of fading snow
the sky, over
the hogback rise behind my Maine house ships
slip up in the green swells, the six Holstein heifers.
They browse in the green apples.
Oaks frostbit gold and dark brown as sweet cider.
When I come up to them, skittish,
I realize how it is I never learned how to behave in hotels.
Larches and wrens I misunderstood deliberately.
Ice
I do not know how to break.
They lower their heads, weaving
rolling the round brown eyes up.
The black and white bellcow nips at my kneecap like an apple.
I stand still as a fir as she rubs her neck against my side,

light like piles of snow drifting under the scotch pine.
As if I am opening,
a crazily wrapped package,
throwing off my sheepskin coat in April,
taking the shirt off that you recognize me in,
and the pants only I would be caught dead in,
a sandpapery tongue laces into my Levis
as if I were a lump of sugar.

I stand up in my skin with delight.

As we head back through the early dark
I am beside myself.
The first stars are frost on a window.
Day cools like a small home.

by Robert Gillespie

KALAMAZOO (for Ben Tibbs)

> *"Life is good in Kalamazoo"—*
> *(the Kalamazoo Chamber of Commerce)*

I hear the razorblades breeding
in the November mist off Lake Michigan
while heaters seep their lie
across the chiseled fields.
Already the windbreaks are brittle with husk.
In town I sleep in knots,
shuddering dreams of legs
that taper miles beyond morning and snow.
I wake to a knee in the groin
and feel no better for owning it.

Born and bored in Indiana,
I used to ask what there was to do.
My mother would tell me,
"Spit in your shoe
and send it to Kalamazoo."

I thought it was in Africa
and now I have only boots
up to my knees
but life is good. life is good . . .

I remember women
who kept their shoes on
when every third day they rolled
the stone away and scattered
to the high tension wires of the spine
to caw the good life seeping from the tomb.

Below, the old man with one leg
is pounding the walls again,
dying by degrees
into the Masons and Miller High Life,
turning in his bed
to the beating of a purple heart—
the khaki ghost that haunts the mannequin.

The trees are growing older
than their rings tonight.
The bark splits like a dark wound.
Birds unfist themselves
and leave for better housing.
Soon they are only a code

among the stars. Clouds shatter
on the moon's talon.
God is having coffee at the Charsteak,
drinking from a used cup.
The old man is almost through the wall.
Where else can you go in this weather?

You can leave the good life—
travel to some hot land
with exotic birds
and women with deep eyes,
not know what to do
send back your shoes, get cold feet
and hobble back to Michigan.

DEER KILLING

California

Highway's an exercise run,
oiled growls through chrome fangs.
Yet somehow they find the break
in the fence and wander in
for the well kept grass,
then suddenly freeze on the yellow eyes
bearing down, guessing their moves
to a smear of blood and bone,
hardly a dark stain by morning.

Indiana

These small towns are vague
in their beginning—frozen shuck
strangles in the grass. Somewhere
the first fence remembers what was meant.
So they blunder in every Fall
panic down Lincoln Way East
jump at their reflection
in the bookstore window,
bleed to death in the outdoor section.

California

Midnight on a winding road,
tired and almost home
it was as if the full moon
pulled my foot up
as I rounded the last curve
and saw him delicately
stepping back into the shadows.

114

GERARD

for Nicole Pinsky

The easels went to the swift, namely
Irving Berman and me back
when I was in kindergarten, Nicole.
Two easels, so we raced, come arts
& crafts: I usually won, am strange
about winning yet, sometimes even
hang back a bit who early shoved
my way, intense to make it, first
to get there first, and only then
to love the giant bottles of yellow
and blue and schloshing around on the paper
various genius items, and all
this while Gerard would sit in his corner:
he always accepted the banging-sticks
in the orchestra, the rest of us calling
"Me! Me!" for the glockenspiel:
Gerard the heavily-mothered, lost
the first day, tearful, beating the door,
his mother gone and couldn't hear him
no matter how hard he cried, as teacher
explained, and next day the same, what luscious
sport: Gerard with his oval head
and museum guard demeanor, convenient
Gerard to take our jibes (to take our
shit)—he had to wear rubbers, galoshes,
black floppers every day, and every
day a man's black umbrella, imagine,
even in breathless June, grim
Mr. Junior Death Gerard with shame
on his feet, above his head, we almost
died, Lenny and Irving and Wilma
and Neil and Shirley and Marvin and me:
wizened Gerard, decked out with care
"just in case it should prove to rain"—Gerard,
Gerard, Gerard, we called your name
till you wept: that hushed us a bit, and then:

Gerard, Gerard,
Momma's pet!
Gerard, Gerard,
Don't get wet!

(am I telling you this for forgiveness, Nicole?
I hear at your kindergarten you flinch
at the sudden shrill of the schoolyard bell,
can't bear the noise and confusion: I'm glad
your teacher lets you in before
the rest, but please, if they start to shout

Nicole, Nicole,
Jump in a hole!

or other stuff like that, will you kindly
let us know, and we'll fix it up
somehow, we lords of creation?)—meanwhile
Gerard's a judge by now I'd guess,
or a millionaire, or both, with regular
habits—or what if he turned out folksy,
Just Plain Bill, why not? or a hairy
prophet, a poet, a singing waiter,
anything, engineer or enter-
tainer, amazement to wife and kids
and friends, no permanent damage—but oh
come back Gerard, and we'll take off your rubbers,
we'll fracture that damned umbrella in 12000
pieces, we'll lock your mother in
the room with the little chairs, we'll lift you
shoulder high, home to our ethnic
slovenly moms and pops who'll feed you
on kasha with bowties, flanken and gravy,
and let you stay up on a school night for Mr.
Keen, Gang Busters, Norman Corwin
Presents, and pack you off next day
happy, straight through the pouring rain!

by LOUIS PHILLIPS

BIRD-WATCHING
    (for Jack Violi)

Black-feathered
With a voice
For an eye,
Its round eye opens.
Flared
At the neck & high
Among branches, its choice
Is to widen

Our forest. It
Frets with color
As a mad painter,
Jet-blue, then brown,
& never sits
Still. It grows fainter
Then sails or
Soars, flits down

Into a fool's spectrum.
What fastens
Onto branches
The way blackbirds do?
Theirs is the dumb
Motion of panic, is
The beak that glistens
With food. Blue-

Black, the jackdaw thinks
Only of hunger,
Whistles its fast
Among high branches,
Its grackle head shrinks
To a thimble fist
In fear without anger,
Bobbing as

A wooden duck does
On the edge
Of a pan. Hops,
Flaps, in a climate
Of nerves, air flows
& twigs, it stops
Only to feed, to hedge
The lake, to mate.

Black birds are
Anything but black,
Are blue wiggles
& wags, purple tails
Jutting in the air,
Slightly invisible
Weather vanes, then back
To the isles

Of branches. Their
Universe
Is worm-centered,
An eye among storms.
Flattened in air,
They head
North, then reverse
To roost in swarms.

Boat-tailed,
The grackle chucks,
Chucks, keels
To the wind, lights,
Treads stately, then head
Up, wheels
To a ribbon of black
& sets its sight

For water. No
Tears for him,
He merely adjusts
To no avail.
The blackbird knows
Nothing as he thrusts
His feathers into a whim
& sail.

His head nods.
The wind is going some-
Where, but what
Flutters through branches
Is not wind,
But a polished flit
Of blackbirds handsome
As boots. The wind is

Going somewhere,
But what flutters
Through the branches
Is not wind, but grackles.

J.D.

Post your men along the bridge
in the darkness of the street lamps,
and instruct them carefully to whistle
the song of the pine grosbeake at
the approach of anyone suspicious.

Better still, they should whistle at
the approach of anyone as all are suspicious.
And I will place myself at the far end
of the bridge in a patch of skunk cabbage
and await the whistle.

Wait, there is a problem here.
Who are your men?
They are not trustworthy!
You must fire them all!

I will take their places, moving from lamp
to lamp every ten seconds, thus
covering the whole job myself.

Trust is not something I take lightly.
It comes only after extreme tests.
So far, no one has met these tests,
save for you, of course, my friend.
Should I meet you on the bridge
I can hold my pucker.
No need to whistle at your approach.

Ah, another problem has arisen!
To whom am I to whistle the warning?
For I am on the bridge and no one
waits in the skunk cabbage.
Why is life such a trouble?
And how does a pine grosbeake sound anyway?

SERMON ON MOUNT EVERETT

            Making
a sauna of old doors
and a tubful of rocks
            Showing
visitors the lookout on a branch,
the gallery on the ground,
and the lovenest slung in trees
with twine and twigs and eyes of god,
            Sleeping
on colored parachutes stuffed
with pine needles
            Growing
grass in thin mountain soil
            Letting
music out of bamboo flutes
and drums decked with flower tokens
and copper instruments Ron Boise strung
and voices from their strange throats,

            This band
of Wanted and unwanted live up
too high to be threatened by
the scattershot below.
They are attending to
the opposite direction.

When sparks fly from our cave,
does the squeal of primates bring us down
though some have been our brothers?

CHARLEY NOTHING

Charley signs his paintings
            Nothing.
He has given up a studio.
An artist makes it where he's at,
with what he finds,
            woodbark,
            crayons,
            old tin cans.
Let go of oils and canvas,
throw and throw away.
Use less, need less.
Charley wants the ultimate—
creation and enlightenment—
            Nothing
less will do, and so
he'll throw away the last material
to get it. His gesture
the work of art, the work of art,
his gesture.
            Nothing
there but God.

STUDIO UP OVER IN YOUR EAR
(12/26/72, Palo Alto)

The radiator's hissing hot
My Smith Corona's cleaned & oiled
with a fresh nylon ribbon
for the hard miles ahead

Gurney Norman's notes for his book
scribbled into this flaking wall
painted landlord green grow more
cryptic as the nights wear on
This used to be his workingplace

The sky over University Avenue
from my 2nd floor window is clean
clam & black again in this
sudden warm night in December

Sleepily my inner voice thins
as entering the world of my characters
I see all of life as unedited film
with no title, no lion, no paramount
spangle of stars to soften what's ended
tho everybody gets in on the credits

Downstairs a country/western band
calling itself Asleep at the Wheel
breaks em up as their lead singer
a little brunette with Woolworth's
in her voice belts out, "You wanna
        take me for a ride in the
            backseat of your car!"

Down on the sidewalk just below my
half-opened window 3 young men split
a 5th of Bali Hai & shoot the shit
& some craps 1940s-style to the music

Up here in freelance heaven
I got my own floating game going on

The ante's tremendous & side bets
are OK but youre lucky if you walk out
with the clothes on your back

CALIFORNIA PENINSULA: EL CAMINO REAL

In 15 minutes
the whole scene'll change
as bloated housewives
hems of their skirts greased
with love mouths wide open
come running out of shops
dragging their young
moon in their eyes
the fear upon them

Any minute now
the gas blue sky over El Camino Real's
gonna droop for good
shut with a squish &
close them all in like
a giant irritated eye

Theyll scramble for cars
the nearest road out
clutching their steering wheels
like stalwart monkeys

It couldve happened yesterday
It couldve happened while they
were sighing in Macys Walgreens 31 Flavors
Copenhagen Movies or visiting the Colonel
like that earthquake night
that shattered L.A.

Whatll they will their children then?
Whatll they leave for them to detest?
What tree, what lip print, what Jack in
what Box, what ugly hot order to go?

Already I can smell the darkness
creeping in like the familiar shadow
of some beloved fake monster
in a science fiction flick

In 15 minutes
48 hours days weeks months
years from now all of thisll be
a drowsy memory barely tellable
in a land whose novelty was speech

118

by WILLIAM PITT ROOT

SONG OF EMERGENCY

After dreaming the pure pleasure
of a being loose in clear water,
diving easily in and out
of the warm mud deep at the bottom,
I wake to the risks of light.

I kick free and I streak
joyous as a bird toward the sun
out of the earth, through water, into the air
where I hang for an instant
free of awareness of safety, free of danger
in the dominion of the heron.

From this height
I glimpse at a distance, tall and white,
the still gods where they bend
above the pond or hunch in trees
to dry those wings spread glowing in the sun.
They stare into the shallows.
They shine like clouds.

At night I have slept dreaming
    of those reed-legged gods whose eyes are small suns,
who are silent
    but whose rare calls pierce my world like claws,
who fly as we dream of flying
    and burn against the sun in a great tumult of wings,
whose slow grace threatens us
    and wooes us with its beauty,
who consume us to survive,
whose lives we dread and envy.

Now I wait the moment when,
suspended above the midworld of water,
I will know the presence of the white cloud loweing,
the explosive sun quick
above the pierce of the beak,
the shrieking wings.

SONG OF SHAKING

        —Today out in the woods
an old tree found me.
It said I am you

and a chorus of whispers
blew by where I shook.

I am you *it said*
with no words, no words.

Big tree, dead, huge memory
of itself collapsing
to feed the green shoots
ringing its base,

and the babble of whispers
blew by where I listened,

their small voices hard
to hear:

        we *they seemed to say*
        we
        are becoming you.

And the shaking stopped.—

SONG OF BENEDICTION

May light sweeten in your lungs
may your tongue shine

May you be grateful to your body
    for the offenses it forgives you
may your body please you
may your mind accept its form
    and guide you among dangers and pleasures

May you love yourself as you are loved

from *Striking the Dark Air for Music*, Atheneum Press, 1973.

THE DREAMBOOK

DREAMS AND DRAWINGS BY JON DA POET AND DREAMS AND PHOTOS BY JANE WATTENBERG

BOOK OF DREAMS

—jon da poet

im inspecting th cells in a bathroom jail cell
there ar 3 cells two big ones an one lil skinny one
in th lil skinny cell a huge creature is imprisoned
hes abt 7 feet tall w/ brite red skin
th skin is speckeled w/ brite wite spots like th skin
of an aminita mushroom
hes got 4 hands at th end of long floppy pupet
    rag doll arms
an 2 huge feet at th end of long wiggly legs
his eyebrows nose an lips all stick out frm his skull
his body is hairless an emooth
his skin looks dull evn tho th colors of it ar brite
a western sheriff w/ a long shotgun is cleanin
    out th cage
he notices me an begins to speek—sumthin aint he?
    its onea JKFs
illigetimate kids. had bad cromosones frm takin all
    that speed. this
thing is really a freak aint he? he starts to hit an
    push th creeture
an laff at him
th beast seems very docile almost drugged an pulls
    away like a
child or scared dog wod do
it dont defend itself an looks rather harmless
it sulks ovr to a corner of th cell an tries to push
    away th blos w/ week arms
th deputy laffs an kicks at him on th way outta
    th cell
i feel vry sad cause th creeture is sumhow familiar
                jan 26 73 oinkland

i am watching a figure emerg frm a dense wood
i realize its me
th branches ar thick an snap in my face
my face is scratched an bleeding
i hav antlers groin outta my head
bloody bandages ar hung on th sharp tips of antler
a crown of laurel leaves is on my head
i hav a slite headache were th antlers
    cum outta my skull
i feel very strong
                berkeley winter 70

i am sitting in a cold grey room at a large long stone
    table
my head starts to turn black
then it melts onto th table
th black spot begins to pulsate
a large golden worm undulates frm out of th hole
that usta b my head
it dances in th air
attached by one end to my head (or th spot or
    hole in th table
that usta b my head)
th other people at th table start to laff an carry
    on in a
roudy fashon th woman seated at my left laffs
till tears roll down her cheeks
                mar 12 70 berkeley

Dreambook, c/o Antelope All-Colors, Walnut Grove, Cal. 95690

TH VISION OF TH WHITE LADY

th white lady
she comes
th woman in white pants
th girl in pants of white
th naked female
she disturbs th grass
th white lady
she comes

i sit on a wall of stone
i sit alone
my poetry is th moss groin on th wrong side of a dead tree
th people pass by carrying dead animals
i do not see them
i talk to th wind
i dream of an unknown face
i see her dressed in white

th white lady
she moves silently
she is dressed in snow
she is dressed in th foam that rides on th lips of waves
she is dressed in th walls of white marble that line
    th shore of an undiscovered island
her face is framed by wings of soft angel hair
she stops
she returns
she goes back to th same place that she came from

i fly
i soar
i move silently
i pursue th white lady
th lady in white
th eyes that shine in caves of ice and fire
th white shirt th white pants th white hair
i lay my poetry in her hands
i give her a block of polished wood
i give her a brown pebble
i give her th song of an insect
i give her th life of a child
i lay myself at her feet

she smiles
she touches me w/her breath
she bows she bends she turns to liquid

a paperboat drifts under a bridge
a yello kite is lost against th sky
a cloud remains dark an motionless overhead

i turn
i walk away
i am wounded
i hear her ask my name i begin to limp
i stagger back into th green heart of th forest
i lie benieth th shelter of a pine tree
i weep
i will wait fr th moon to rise
th white lady th face of th white lady
i will hurl my tears into th sky

—jon da poet

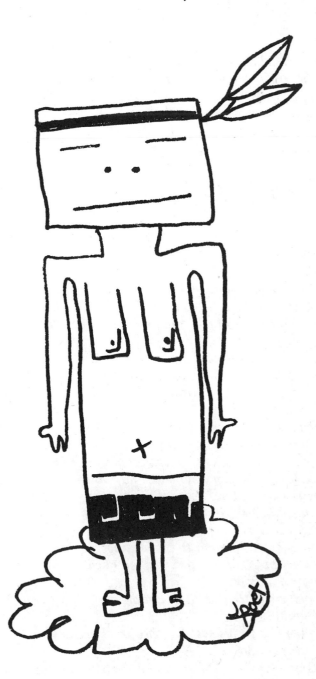

winter sky dull grey silent cold
there is th sound of a soft dead wind
i am standin in front of a huge gold bildin
    that shines w/ its own lite
there are baby gargoil faces carved into th thick
    oak doors
there is a large empty courtyard on th left handside
grey an empty dead vines crumble on th broken bricks
i go into th gold bildin
its warm inside
my hair is short an a golden lite radiates frm my body
i am in a large chamber like th eves of a church
as i walk into th bildin th walls close in an th roof
    lowers till
im walkin down an office building corridor
a commotion starts behind me a shot cums—
    theyre gonna try an stop me
a nam in a yello uniform suddenly blocks my way
he has an X on his chest were 2 blac leather straps
    cross
he looks unsure of himself so i decide to bluff him
—get outta my way motherfucker or ill tear u apart
    i growl
he panics an runs down th hall
i turn left an go down th hall
4 men in yello block my way
i run towords them an they vanish
i turn left again an cum to a ded end
in front of me is a windo that looks out on
    gradcenteral station
to my rite an open office where 2 men wait for me
X is due to arrive at any time now they say
an he will thro us out
i say—well see abt that
i turn around an 3 men stand there
a large goon w/ huge muscles a gangster strong arm
    stereo tipe
an two smaller mean pimp lookin tipes
all three grin as my two frends vanish
i run up an give th gorilla a kick in th belly w/ my
    left foot
he doubles ovr
i make a magic sine w/ my arms an th pimps vanish
i grab th man by his x strap an push my face into his
—talk i say in jon wayne tuff guy voice
he remains silent
i drag him ovr to th windo an dangle him out by
    his boots.
i admire th shine on th blac leather
we ar abt 20 or 30 stories up an i hear traffic noise
    pigeon coo
smell smog thousands of people go in an outa th
    station
th medals on his cest fall thru th air as does his
    spare change
its hard to hold him up an he starts to scream an cry

my two frends cum bac an grin at me as i let go of
    his foot
he remains dangling there in mid air as we all look
    on amazed
                    nov 29 71

i meet my brother marc in a huge waiting room were
    comuters sit zombie like
watchin a giant t.v. screen he sez—lets go take a
    shower
we go into another waitin room that has big open
    showers in th back
th shower is a lil rectangular cloud that pour water
    down onto a spot abt
1/2 an inch frm th floor where th water vanishes
each cloud has th name of a state on a funky wooden
    plaque
my clothin vanishes an i get in a shower
th water wont wet my body
in th shower next to me (mississippi) is a black man
he is very thin an lite brn in color an is singing a
    wild scat jazz song
that he makes up as he goes along—do bop de bop
    bop re bop do bop is so
much fun in th mississippi shower etc etc
th song is very lite an lilting an id expect his body to
    swing an sway
in time to th rythum but he stands there ridgid w/
    his eyes fixed on th giant
t.v. screen
only his lips move as he smiles to th music he makes
                27 dec 72 oinkland

MY GURU CAN LICK YR GURU
CAUSE HES GOT 3 EYES & A
LONG TONGUE TOO!
                fr guru maharaj gee

they got no stewardesses
on th astral plane
& long hed trips
gimme a
pane
so ill just stay here
an wallo
in th maya
an stick another log
into th
carnal fire
abusein drugs an kissin
women on th lips ·
& makin sexy undulations
w/ my buttocks an my hips

all dreambook photos by jane wattenberg

i get a job as a gardener in a subway station
th trains dont run any more an lawns ar planted on
   th platforms
i am waterin the lawn w/a long green hose
scrooge McDuck is walkin w/ me an takin to me in
   human talk

im tryin to get him to loan me sum money
he squaks an jumps up an down in a frenzy
a copy who is trimmin th lawn accidently cuts my
   hose in half
th water continues to cum out of th end
                 jan 1, 72

WHILE THE SUN WAS OUT MOONLIGHTING
—Jane Wattenberg

There I was making portraits of me and George. Three types I made. My favorite was the landscape with three tiers. A different type of fertile land on each tier. That was us alright, ho ho. A regular agricultural patchwork quilt of corn, peanuts and plenty. The one of us as cornerstones of a rocketship just didn't seem to fit our image too well. And the other, under the deep blue sea with the octopus bodies and urchin eyes was beautiful I'll admit but a bit too weakling like watercolor. No, we weren't weaklings. We spat at each other twice a day. If not spitting, howling curses. We just didn't make sense and that's why I was making these portraits. Drawing is telling I hear and I'll just show George, see what he thinks. But most probably he'll just spit on them and then the color will run and then it won't do any good anymore anyway.

Like the colors of that swimming pool so fashionable last week. We were swimming together in a pool indoors. I remember stopping swimming every so often while they sanitized the pool sides and water. There was a pool floor and a balcony above that pool floor. All spotless and white enameled it was.

Then a couple came right in the midst of our swimming, came to the pool to get married. All dressed up they stood on the duo-diving boards. I now pronounce you, spoke the lifeguard, husband and wife and with that they dove simultaneously into the water of chlorine and sanity, holy waters for the brow. O yes, George and myself were in the water below at the time and when the newlyweds rose to the surface the bride lady cried out; My brooch! My brooch! it's fallen off, o help me look for it anyone. The groom husky said; you weren't wearing any brooch dearie. But yes, I was. I wore one special for this day, said she. So naturally I dove to the bottom of this and naturally found the wife's brooch near the pool drain. Then we all dried up and went away.

It was the end of summer anyway and I was trying to find a ride to St. Louis but the ride always went to Ann Arbor.

* * *

Jonathan brought Grandma's ivy plants to me. Grandma . . . I loved her. She grew ivy and kept buttons and jars and hung out the clothes from her royal pantry tower with a button size window just big enough for clothes to be pushed out and travel down the rope line.

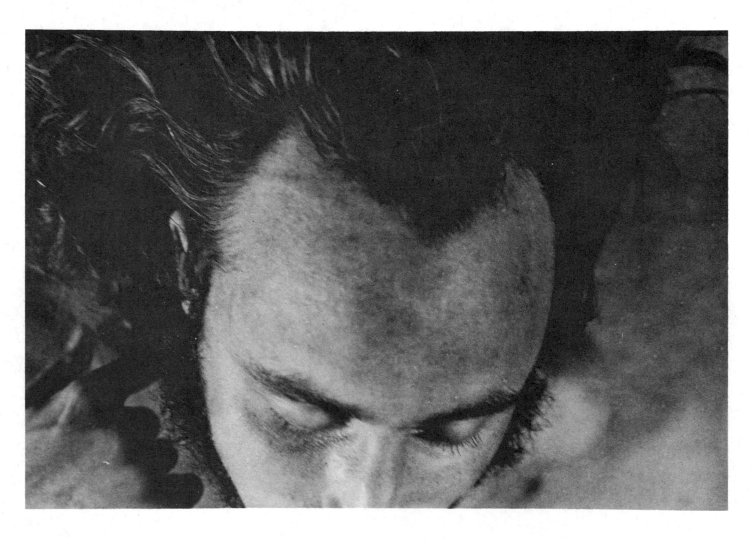

Jonathan brought me her ivy, a tiny pot, green plastic with a long wood stick supporting the slender spiral of that crawling. Now with Grandma gone and Grandpa not watching, the ivy was dulling and pale.

So Jonathan brought me the ivy. But I told him I was going to leave him now. Not to see him. No. No more. He stared into the spiral gently expecting these words as he held the ivy. Looking wistful, a crawling ivy.

But then Jonathan was no longer there. Now it was Owen's transparent figure before me, laughing and sneering. Running an arrow finger into my shoulder, a rough hand over my breast. Cruel Owen, no, standing there saying Rachel, then who will I have tonight, who will rip you this night? Owen, I cried, leave me.

But Jonathan had returned, sweet Jonathan. We lay under the ivy and talked in jars. Grandma made baked potatoes that I could smell all the days they weren't baking and she'd say Sam, Rachel's helped me clean all day, can't you give her a dollar?

* * *

Heard a scream. Got out of my car to find the danger. Climbed many stairs to find the sound. An apartment. I entered. It was nothing. A woman and her pet tiger. He bit her and the scream. I stayed and visited a bit. Ann was the scream and John, the tiger. I am Sandra Jean and how do you do? And why do your children sleep on a lazy susan? Does it rock them to sleep?

Well goodbye John, another time maybe. I gave Ann a ride to where she was going. Funny, she wouldn't leave my car at the end of the line. Please dear Ann, I must hurry off to where I am going. I'll see you and John and lazy susan and the children again, I promise you soon it shall be. Now leave. No? Leave me! and I pushed her from my car and sped away.

But she chased the car. She really chased me. And she was a fine runner. I had almost no margin and she was about to overcome my velocity when a hill came forth. A very steep hill it was and in low gear I sped to its top. Ann, go away I hissed stop it stop it. And I gained on her. The top was a cliff. I hadn't known. Then a rushing leap over it's top.

Then no car. It was I, flying freefall down onto the smoothest of sand dunes. And lo! this dune was an outdoor movie theatre. I feel deep and comfortable into the sand and settled in it's wave. Ah, I've hidden from that crazy lady. What does she want? I'll settle in more, hide in the dune, enjoy the movie. Later I'll slip away.

A hand on my shoulder, my scream, excuse me lady, no upset, it was the usher. No shoes on the dunes, please. I unzipped my shoes. Ann slipped into the seat next to mine.

* * *

FEAR

But What Was the Moral?

by Robert Stone

"Fear" is excerpted from
a forthcoming novel.
Robert Stone is also the
author of the novel, *Hall of Mirrors.*

arly in the spring, Converse had been away in the Mekong Delta and Madame had rented room Number Sixteen in his absence. The man who had taken it apparently had a thing about squashing lizards; Converse returned to find nearly a dozen of them mashed into the walls and the tiles of the floor. He had found it disturbing. Like most people he was rather fond of house lizards. They ate insects and were fun to watch when one was high.

The management had made a few gestures toward effacing the traces of carnage but there were still stains and remnants of tiny dinosaur skeletons. Murder haunted the room.

ILLUSTRATIONS BY PAUL PRATCHENKO

Whoever he was, he had spent hours stomping around his soiled grey hotel room wasting lizards with the framed tintype of Our Lady of Lourdes that stood on the night table.

Converse sat at his writing desk, drinking Sprite, looking at the lizard smears. It was just as well not to wonder why. There was never any satisfaction in that. Maybe the man had thought they would bite him. Maybe they kept him awake nights, whispering together. Probably, he just didn't like their looks. The man had also diligently crushed all his used batteries so that the hotel flunkies couldn't recycle them through Thieves Market.

An extrovert, Converse thought.

On the desk beside him was a thermos bottle filled with cold water. It was supposed to be bottled water, but Converse knew for a fact that the porter filled it from the tap. Every day he poured it into the shower drain. Every day the porter refilled it. From the tap. Every day Converse felt guiltier about not drinking it.

That was the liberal sensibility for you, he thought. It began to give in the face of such persistence. One day, perhaps, he would feel thoroughly obliged to drink it.

The thermos was somewhat original, an actual Vietnamese artifact—and Converse planned to take it with him when he left. Printed across it in bright colors was the picture of a wide winged bat; on the bat's breast was the brand name—"Lucky."

He stood up and went across the cement air shaft to the bathroom, carrying the thermos with him. When he had locked the door, he turned on the cold shower and poured the contents of the thermos into the drain.

Fuck it, he thought, why me? Let somebody else drink it.

There were plenty of other Americans around.

Converse was, by profession, an author. Ten years before he had written a play about the Yokasuka Naval Prison in Japan which had been performed and admired. But since the production of his play, the only professional good fortune which attended Converse had been the result of his marriage to the daughter of an editor and publisher.

His father-in-law, Elmer Bender, published imitations of other magazines. The name of each Bender publication was designed to give its preoccupied and overstimulated purchasers the impression that they were purchasing the more popular magazine which it imitated. If there were, for example, a magazine called *Collier's*, Elmer Bender would edit and publish a magazine called *Shmollier's*.

"Mine are better," Elmer Bender would say. He was a veteran of the New Masses and the Abraham Lincoln Brigade.

In addition to imitation magazines, Bender published several soft core tit books and *Nightbeat*—which was described by his attorneys as "A Weekly Tabloid With a Heavy Emphasis on Sex." For seven years, Converse had been *Nightbeat*'s editor. He supervised a staff of two—Mr. Douglas Cockburn who was a newspaper alcoholic with beautiful manners, and a Chinese Communist named Mike Woo who had once attempted an explication of the theory of surplus value in the weekly horoscope. (Don't be afraid to ask for a raise this week, Sagittarius. Your boss always withholds part of what your work is worth.)

He had been married to Margaret Bender for seven years.

On the morning of his daughter Janey's second birthday, Converse had awakened after two hours of wracked siniter sleep and gone to the living room window to watch the sun come up over the Bay. An enchantment of unremembered dreams clung to him; the floor was littered with colored balloons he had inflated for the birthday morning. As day broke, he had found himself engaged in an old childish exercise—he stared at the back of his hand and softly repeated his own name. The purpose of the exercise was to convince himself of his own reality.

Staring at his hand, he had become alarmed at its extraordinary whiteness. It was as though there were some unwholesome light burning under the skin. With every breath he drew, the light grew brighter until he felt as though his flesh had become phosphorescent. It was not to be borne.

But Converse was clever and resourceful and he had not died of the white light. He had persuaded Elmer to write a letter to the press authorities in Saigon requesting that he be accredited as a staff writer for Pacific Publications. Elmer had agreed to maintain Margaret and Janey and to forward Converse a portion of his former salary.

Elmer was sympathetic. He had been an author himself in the thirties and one of his stories had earned him a passionate letter of appreciation from Whittaker Chambers. Moreover, Bender cherished his daughter's marriage and it seemed to everyone that a period of constructive separation might restore its edge. Margaret's mother had been a left-wing Irish vegetarian who had committed suicide with her lover during the McCarthy times. It was often remarked that Margaret was very like her.

As for the girl herself—she had been resisting and sullen at first. When in the end she agreed—and even became an enthusiast—it was not the logic of the enterprise which carried her but its fatefulness.

In Vietnam, Converse had been able to extend his employment by taking over the positions of departing stringers and hustling a few of his own. And surely enough, the difficulties he had been having with his own reality were in time obviated. One bright afternoon, near a place called Krek, Converse had watched with astonishment as the world of things transformed itself into a single overwhelming act of murder. In a manner of speaking, he discovered himself. Himself was a soft shellless quivering thing concealed in a hundred and sixty pounds of pink sweating meat. It was real enough. It tried to burrow into the earth. It wept.

Converse had not been seeking such an encounter. He was naturally timid; in general he avoided the line. But the South Vietnamese Air Force, in its enthusiasm, had carried out a strike against its own positions and Converse had experienced his place in the scheme of things.

His nature was not unfamiliar to him and he recognized it at once. The quivering, the twitch—were really all there was of him. All there was to work with. All there had ever been.

He fled to Bangkok for a while and there, in a Dairy Queen on Phya Thai Road he met his friend Jack Hicks. Hicks had been the basis for one of the characters in Converse's play. They had been in the Marine Corps together, both of them serving as guards in Yokasuka. From time to time they had been running into each other around San Francisco Bay and Converse had once driven to Hayward to visit Hicks and his Japanese wife.

In Bangkok, Hicks and Converse went out to dinner and to a massage parlor to get laid. Hicks was divorced now, working as a merchant seaman for Sealift Command out of Oakland. Several times a year, aboard different ships, Hicks shipped from the west coast for the Saigon river—Camranh Bay run. He had taken to running dope—usually a few kilos of grass, sometimes blocks of hashish—between Nam and the Army Terminal.

During their time at Yokasuka, Converse and Hicks had passed many watches reading Playboy and evolving schemes which would leave them the tenants of terraced apartments opening on city nocturnes. It was the way people of that age were at that time and it gave them something to think about while they bullied the cringing court martial prisoners across the yard to breakfast. In Bangkok, they found themselves talking about dope smuggling. Hicks had become an adept in the moving of contraband. Entire ships' bakeries were at his disposal and he had come to know every lumber pile, deadhead and Dempsey dumpster on both sides of the Army Terminal's gate. It would be a shame, Hicks suggested, if they failed to run a little dope. He was thinking of hash.

Converse had a bank account in Berkeley with twenty-one thousand dollars in it. Most of it was the remains of his fee for a film version of the play which had never been completed. He had further the acquaintence of many like minded colleagues in Saigon, where

dope in all its variations was as common as rice. But the large score, as everyone was forever reminding everyone else, was not in blocks of hash. It was in heroin.

Charmian had been for it. She had contributed a matching twenty thousand and access to her friend Captain Tho. The heroin refinery of which Captain Tho was an executive was the fourth largest building in greater Saigon.

He had exchanged a lingering correspondence with Margaret about the moral objections and, with her taste for the fateful, she had gone along. It was exciting and she was bored.

His own reasons changed by the hour. He had been in the country for eighteen months and for all the discoveries it was by now apparent that there would be no book, no play. It seemed necessary that there be something.

Showered, he sat drying under the ceiling fan. It was difficult for him not to think of Charmian although to do so was painful to him. She had figured so largely in his finally deciding to do it that he sometimes became alarmed. He wondered suddenly if Captain Tho might perhaps hate her as much as he did.

t seven thirty, Jill Percy telephoned from the offices of the World Bank. The Percys would meet him in the Crazy Horse, which was a girly bar on Tu Do Street. Jill Percy was becoming an international social worker and she had conceived a professional interest in girly bars. She was always trying to get people to take her to them.

Converse dressed, pulled on his plastic anorak and went down to the street. It had started to rain again. As he walked toward Tu Do, he sifted through his pockets to find twenty piastres.

Half way up the street, midway between the market and Tu Do, there was always a legless man squatting in a doorway. Each time Converse passed, he would drop twenty piastres in the man's upturned pith helmet. He had been doing so for more than a year, so that whenever the man saw Converse approach he would smile. It was as though they were friends. Often, Converse was tormented by an impulse to withhold the twenty piastres to see what sort of a reaction there would be but he had never had the courage.

Having dropped the twenty P and exchanged smiles with his friend, Converse sauntered down Tu Do to the Crazy Horse. The Crazy Horse was one of the Tu Do bars in which, according to rumor, the knowledgeable patron might be served a bracing measure of heroin with—some even said in—his beer. As a result it was usually off limits, and on this evening Converse was the only customer. Facing him across the bar were fifteen uniformly beautiful Vietnamese girls in heavy make-up. It was as though he were the bartender and they had put the bottles on the wrong side. He took a stool, smiled pleasantly and ordered a Schlitz. The girl opposite him began to deal out a hand of cards.

Beer in the Crazy Horse cost two hundred and fifty piastres without heroin and Converse was not in the mood for cards. He glanced down at the poker hand on the chrome before him as though it was a small conventionally amusing animal and affected to look over the girls with a worldly expression. In spite of the glacial air-conditioning and his recent bath, his face was covered with sweat. The fifteen girls across the bar turned their eyes on him with identical expressions of bland, fathomless contempt.

Converse drank his beer, his sinuses aching. He felt no resentment; he was a humanist and it was their country. They were war widows or refugee country girls or serving officers of the Viet Cong. And there he was, an American with a stupid expression and pockets stuffed with green money and there was no way they could get it off him short of turning him upside down and shaking him. It must make them want to cry, he thought. He was sympathetic.

He was searching his Vietnamese repertory for an expression of sympathy when Jill and Ian Percy arrived. Jill looked at the girls behind the bar with a wide white smile and sat down beside Converse. Ian came behind her, stooped and weary.

"Well," Jill Percy said. "This looks like fun."

A girl down the bar blew her nose and looked into her handkerchief.

"That's what we're here for," Converse said.

The Percys ordered bottles of "33" beer; it was pronounced "bami-bam" and supposedly made with formaldehyde. Ian went over to the juke box and played "Let It Be."

"Staying through the summer?" Jill asked Converse.

"I guess so. 'Til the elections. Maybe longer. You?"

"We'll be around forever. Right Ian?"

"We'll be around all right," Ian said. Some '33' beer trickled from his mouth and into his sparse sandy beard. He wiped his chin with the back of his hand. "We're waiting around until we get an explanation."

Ian Percy was an Australian agronomist. He was also an engage', one of the few one saw around. He had been in the country for fifteen years—with UNRAA, with WHO, with everyone who would hire him, ending with the Vietnamese government which had him on loan from the Australian Ministry of Agriculture. A province chief up north had gotten him fired and he had taken accreditation with an Australian daily which was actually more of a racing form than a newspaper. As an engage' he hated the Vietcong. He also hated the South Vietnamese government and its armed forces, Americans and particularly the civilians, Buddhist monks, Catholics, the Cao Dai, the French and particularly Corsicans, the foreign press corps, the Australian government and his employers, past—and most especially—present. He was said to be fond of children but the Percys had none of their own. They had met in Vietnam and it was not a place in which people felt encouraged to bear children.

"Bloody lot of people leaving," Jill said. "We're getting possessive about our friends."

"Nobody wants to be the last rat," Converse said.

Ian ordered another "33" beer. He drank "33" unceasingly from about four in the afternoon until after midnight.

"Poor old last rat," Ian said. "God help him."

Jill took her beer along the bar and started a conversation in Vietnamese with a bar girl opposite her. The other girls, softened by curiosity, leaned together to listen.

"What's she saying?" Converse asked.

"She's telling them her troubles." The girls across from Jill had turned toward Ian and Converse and were nodding sympathetically. "Later she'll come back and want them to tell her their troubles. She's writing a report on Saigon bar girls."

"What for?"

"Oh for the information of the civilized world," Ian said. "Not that the civilized world gives fuck at all."

They drank in silence for a while as Jill told her troubles to the bar girls.

"One thing," Converse said, "this war is going to be well documented. There's more information available than there is shit loose to know about."

An image came to Converse's mind of the sheets of paper onto which the computers clacked out useful information for the conduct of the war. The prettiest were the ones that analyzed the loyalties and affiliation of country villages —these were known, known, with curious Shake-spearean under-tones as Hamlet Evaluation Reports. The thought of Hamlet Evaluation Reports made Converse hungry. Each Friday the Viet-namese used them to wrap food in.

"Let's eat," he said. "Before it rains again."

They went outside and walked down Tu Do toward the river. On the first corner they came to, the MP's had a soldier in fatigues up against the wall and were searching his many khaki pockets while a crowd of silent Saigonaise looked on. Converse bought Jill a marigold necklace from a sleepy child flower seller at the edge of the crowd. The marigolds when they were still fresh smelled wonder-fully on hot nights; they reminded Converse of Charmian.

"OK," Jill said. "The Guillaume Tell, the Tempura House, or the Floating Restaurant?"

The floating restaurant would be too crowded and Ian said that the chef at the Guillaume Tell had run away because someone had threatened to chop his hands off. They took the long way to the Tempura House, walking beside the lantern lit barges on the river front. Mosquitos hurried them on and reminded Converse of his fever. As they walked, they smoked Park Lane cigarettes, factory packaged joints with glossy filters. "33" beer was supposed to be made with formaldehyde, Park Lane cigarettes were sup-posed to be rolled by lepers. The grass in them was not very good by Vietnamese standards but if you smoked a whole one you got high. Little riverfront children ran up to them, fumbling at their arms to see their watches, calling after them—Bao chi, bao chi.

At the Tempura house they entered merrily, wafted on fumes of Park Lane, removed their shoes and set-tled down among the dapper Honda salesmen. Ian ordered more "33."

"Ever see Charmian," he asked Converse.

"I just left her. She's the same."

"Somebody told me," Jill Percy said, "that Charmian had a habit."

Converse essayed a smile.

"Bullshit," he said.

"Or else that she was dealing. I can't remember which."

"You never know what Charmian's into. But if she had a habit, I'd know about it."

"You don't see her so much now do you?" Jill asked.

Converse shook his head.

"Charmian," Ian said, "has a friend named Tho. He's an Air Force captain. In the cinnamon business."

"You ought to look into Tho," Jill told her hus-band. "He must be looming large around here if Charmian's found him."

"I don't think Tho is coup material," Converse said. "He has a very satisfied look."

The waitress, who was at least partly Japanese, brought them a plate of red peppers. They rinsed their flushed faces with cool towels.

"Ever hear Charmian's Washington stories," Jill Percy asked. "She tells super Washington stories."

"Charmian belongs to a vanished era in America history," Converse said. "Not many people can claim that condition at the age of twenty-five."

"Ghosts," Ian said. "The country's full of ghosts now."

Jill Percy whisked a pepper from the dish with her chopsticks and consumed it without flinching.

"You can hardly call Charmian a ghost. There are plenty of ghosts out here but they're real ones."

"Wherever you have a lot of unhappy people dying young," Converse said, wiping his hands on the cool towel, "you'll get a lot of ghosts."

"We had a right bastard of a ghost down in our village," Ian Percy said. "One of the sort they call *Ma*. He lived under a banyan tree and he came out during siesta to frighten the kiddies."

"After the war," Converse said, "they should fly over the Ia Drang valley dropping comic books and French dip sandwiches for all the G.I. *Ma*. It must really be a drag for them."

Ian started another beer, ignoring the food before him.

"I'm not sure you've been around here long enough," he told Converse, "to talk like that."

Converse rested his chopsticks on the side of his plate.

"The way I see it, I get to say any fucking thing I want. I had my ass on the line. I been to war." He turned to Jill, who was frowning at Ian. "Ain't I Jill? I appeared on the field of battle."

"I was there," she said. "I saw you, sport."

"We went to war, Jill and me," Converse announced to Ian. "And what did we do Jill?"

"We cried," Jill said.

"We cried," Converse said, "that's what we did. We wept tears of outraged human sensibility and we get to say any fucking thing we want."

Both Jill and Converse had gone to see the invasion of Cambodia and both had had experiences which made them cry. But Converse had not really wept tears of outraged human sensibility. He had cried with fear.

"You're an entertaining fella," Ian said. "But in general I object to your being around."

Secure behind her porcelain smile, the waitress placed bowls of fish and rice before them. A party of American reporters came in, followed by four Felipino rock musicians. The Honda salesmen and their Japanese girlfriends grew merrier as the saki flowed.

"I mean," Ian said. "I love this country. It's not the asshole of the world to me. I grew old here, man. Now when I leave all I'll be able to think back on is bastards like you in places like this."

"Sometimes," Jill said, "you act like you invented the country."

"They're a pack of perves," Ian said. "You're a pack of perves. Why don't you go watch some other place die. They've got corpses by the river-full in Bangla Desh. Why not go there?"

"It's dry," Converse said.

A Vietnamese soldier with dark glasses and a white cane had been led in from the street by a little boy of about eight. They moved from table to table selling copies of the Saigon Herald. The American reporters reclining at the table behind Converse were watching them.

"Listen," one of the reporters was saying, "he can see as well as you can. The guy uses about six different kids. He rents them in the market."

"Yeah?" another reporter said. "I think he's blind."

"You know why he's got fresh ARVN fatigues? 'Cause he's in the ARVN. And even the ARVN don't take blind people."

When the ARVN and his boy came round, Converse and Ian bought Saigon Heralds and set them aside without looking at them.

"I met a lady," Converse said, "who told me that Satan was very powerful here."

"Check it out," Ian said. "Don't dismiss anything you hear out of hand."

Jill was trying to watch the American reporters unobserved.

"They'd know," she said, nodding toward their table. "We could ask them."

Converse turned to look at the reporters; they were sunburned, they had impressive Mexican mustaches, they used their chopsticks well.

"They wouldn't go for it," he said. "Satan might be hot stuff to the montagnards but he's just another coconut monk to those guys."

They finished off the beef and rice and called for more "33." The waitress brought them some peanuts which were inhabited by tiny spider-like insects.

"Satan?" Jill said. "What do you think she meant?"

"She was a missionary," Converse said.

The Percys ate their peanuts one by one, patiently dislodging the insects. Converse did without.

"I wonder who Tho is," Jill said after a while. "I wonder what's in it for Charmian."

"Fancy fucking," Ian said.

Converse said nothing.

"An ARVN captain."

Jill thoughtfully sucked on a peanut. "What can that be like I wonder?"

"Exsquisite," Ian said.

"Do you really think so?"

"Best fucking east of Suez," Ian assured her. "I have it on good authority."

"I have it on good authority," Jill said, that Kuwait has the best fucking east of Suez."

"If you like Arabs. Some do some don't."

"There's an Arab blessing," Converse informed them, "May the poetry of your love never turn to prose."

"There you are," Jill said, "Kuwait for me."

"I know a parsee in Karachi," Converse said, "who knows the Sultan of Kuwait very well. He's a caterer. When the Sultan goes falconing my friend the parsee supplies his every need. He could fix you up."

"Crikey," Jill said. "We'd falcon under the merciless sky. And at night while I'm asleep—into my tent he'll creep."

"Exactly," Converse said, "and you'll tickle his prostate with an ostrich feather."

Jill affected to sign. "With a peacock's wing."

Ian had turned to watch the waitress bend over her hibachi stove.

"This is sheer racism," he said. "It's shocking."

"Well," Converse said, "that's fucking. East of Suez."

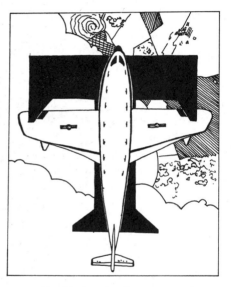

he shock came up at them from under the floor; Converse experienced a moment of dreadful recognition. When the noise ended, they looked, not at each other, but toward the street and saw that the glass window was gone and that they were looking directly on the metal grill that had stood in front of it. There was food in everyone's lap.

"Incoming," Jill Percy said. Someone in the kitchen cursed shrilly, scalded.

They kneeled on the tea stained mat, trying to find their shoes. The proprieter, who was a man of mild and scholarly appearance, was forcing his way toward the door in grim fury; people had begun to leave without paying. Through the space where the window had been Converse could see a fine layer of white dust settling on the wet pavement.

The street outside was strangely quiet, as though the explosion had blown a pocket of silence in the din of the city.

Converse and the Percys walked toward the river; they could see the four American reporters at the corner ahead of them. Every one seemed to know better than to run. Half way to the corner they passed the ARVN newspaper seller and his rented little boy; the pair of them stood motionless on the sidewalk facing the street. The ARVN still had his glasses on; the boy watched them pass without expression, still holding the ARVN's hand. On the corner

itself was an old woman who held her hands pressed to her ears in the position of hearing no evil.

"The Tax office," Ian said. And when they turned the next corner they saw that it had indeed been the tax office. The street before it was in ruins; a whole section of the concrete pavement was blown away to show the black earth on which the city was built. Nightlights in the nearby buildings had been blown so it was a while before they could see anything clearly. By now there were plenty of sirens.

The Tax Office had been a Third Republic Drollery, Babar the Elephant Colonial, and the bomb had made toothpicks of its wrought iron fence.

One of the balconies was lying smashed in the forecourt, surrounded by shredded personifications of Rectitude and Civic Virtue and the Mission Civilatrice. As they stood watching, a jeep with four ARVN MP's shot passed them and pulled up on the sidewalk.

In the light of the MP's torches, they could see that there were people sitting down in the street, trying to pick the concrete chips out of their flesh. It had been very crowded in the street because of the stalls. Families of refugees sold morsels of fish and noodles to the petitioners who stood all day outside the building and at night they settled down to sleep among their wares. Since the building had been empty when the charge went, the street people had taken the casualties.

Converse and the Percys moved back against the metal shutters of a building across the way, as ARVN Marines arrived in canvass covered trucks to seal off the street to traffic. The ARVN's came picking their way through rubble, nervous as rats, poking people aside with the barrells of their M-16's.

After a few minutes, the barbed wire arrived. The emergency services in Vietnam always carried immense quantities of barbed wire for use in every conceivable situation. There was still no sign of an ambulance but the National Police had arrived and were unloading their coils of wire. Some of them rolled the coils along the street to spread at each end of the block. Others were poking among the ruins by the fence, shining hurricane lamps. Now and then Converse could see marvelously bright gouts of blood.

When the ambulances came, fastidious men in white smocks got out and walked carefully toward the pile; when the wire caught their clothing they swatted at it with quick delicate gestures. Jill Percy followed them across the street and peered over their shoulders and over the shoulders of the National Policemen making a short patrol the length of their line. Converse tried to see her face in their lights.

From the way she re-crossed the street Converse and Ian could tell what she had seen. Her steps were slow and deliberate and she appeared confused. If one stayed in the country long enough one saw a great many people moving about in that manner.

"Crikey," she said. She made a small fluttering gesture with her hands. "Kids and . . . all."

Ian Percy had brought his beer bottle from the Tempura House; he let it fall from his hand to shatter on the street. The Vietnamese nearby turned quickly at the sound and stared at him without expression.

"Somebody ought to set a plastique at the London School of Economics," he said. "Or in Greenwich Village. All those bastards who think the Front are such sweet thunder—let them have their kids guts blown out."

"It could have been anybody," Converse said. "It could be an irate taxpayer. Anybody can make a plastique."

"Are you going to say it's the Front," Jill asked her husband. "It probably wasn't you know."

"No," Ian said. "I'll say it probably wasn't. It could have been anybody."

He began to curse in Vietnamese. People moved away from him.

Converse went across the street and watched the ambulance people lug body bags over the rubble. Dead people and people who appeared to be dead had been laid out on the exposed earth where the cement had been blown away and the blood and tissue were draining into the black soil. There were chop sticks, shards of pottery and ladles lying about and on close inspection Converse saw that at least some of what had appeared to be human fragments might be chicken or fish. Some of the bodies had boiled noodles all over them.

As he went back to where the Percys were, four men wearing rubber gauntlets came carrying large aluminum cans. When they reached the wreckage, they upturned the cans and scattered white powder over it.

"What it is?" Converse asked Ian.

"Chloride of lime."

Jill Percy stood with her shoulders hunched, arms folded.

"If you get run over in the street," she said, "they'll come and string barbed wire around you. If you don't get up fast enough they'll sprinkle you with chloride of lime."

They walked down the street a few yards until they stood before the glassless windows of a Buick agency. In the glare of the lights, they could see the office inside with its charts and wall calenders and tiny electric fans on each desk. Reams of paper were scattered over the floor. Because of the angle of the windows the office had absorbed a great deal of the concussion. One of the interior walls was dappled with blood that looked as though it had been flung from a brush. Converse stopped for a moment to look at it.

"What?" Jill Percy asked.

"Nothing. I was trying to think of a moral."

He could not think of a moral. It reminded him of the lizards smashed on his hotel wall.

n his office just off the tiny lobby of the Hotel Coligny, Monsiuer Colletti was watching Bonanza on the Armed Forces Television Network. Monsieur Colletti had taken eight pipes of opium during the afternoon; he had taken eight pipes of opium every afternoon for forty years. When Converse entered, he turned from the set with a welcoming smile. He was the most courteous of men. Converse and Monsieur Colletti watched Bonanza for a while.

On the screen, two cowboys were exchanging rifle fire at a distance of thirty meters or so. They were fighting among enormous rounded boulders and as far as one could tell each was trying to move as close to the other as possible. One cowboy was handsome, the other ugly. There was music. At length, the handsome cowboy surprised the ugly one loading his weapon. The ugly cowboy threw his rifle down and a attempted to draw a sidearm. The handsome one blew him away.

Monsieur Colletti, who spoke no English, brought his palms together silently.

"Hoopla," he said.

"It's the same in Saigon," Converse ventured. Monsieur Colletti always seemed to understand his French.

Monsieur Colletti shrugged.

"Here, sure. Everywhere it's the same now." Monsieur Colletti had been everywhere. "Everywhere it's Chicago."

He said it Sheeka-go.

"There was a bombing tonight," Converse said. "At the office of taxes. It's all ruined there."

Monsieur Colletti made his eyes grow larger in an expression of surprise that was purely formal. It was not easy to bring him news of Saigon.

"But no," he protested mildly. "Any dead?"

"Some certainly. Outside."

"Ah," the patron said, "it's cruel. They're bastards."

"You think it was the Front."

"These days," Colletti said, "it could be anybody."

When Bonanza was over, they shook hands and

Converse went upstairs. Back inside his room, he turned on the overhead fan and the air conditioner. The air conditioner did not work very well but it provided a busy, and to the American ear, vaguely reassuring noise which drowned out the sounds from the street. The sounds from the street were not reassuring to anyone's ear.

He switched on the lamp on his writing desk to provide his room with the most agreeable cast of light. Small tricks, picked up all over. He took a bottle of PX Johnnie Walker Black Label from a locked suitcase and drank two large swallows.

There it is, he said to himself. That was what everyone said; G.I.'s, reporters, even Arvins and bar girls. There it is. It would have been good not to have had a bomb that night. To get stoned with the Percys and then sleep. Because of the bomb he felt numb and stupid and although there were situations in which stupidity would do almost as well as anything else he was not in one of them.

And getting drunk wouldn't do. Nor would smoking more grass. Better to have stayed downstairs and watched more westerns with Monsieur Colletti.

In his own despite, he took another swallow of whiskey, lit a Park Lane, and began to walk up and down the length of the room. In the next room, the Dutch flower-lover was playing Highway 61 on his tape recorder. After a few tokes, he decided that he was experiencing no more than a vague dissatisfaction.

Nothing serious. See them all the time. Side effect of low grade fever.

After a while, he stopped pacing and went across the airshaft to the bathroom to squat over the hole. The hole had treaded foot grips beside it to put your feet on; it was a vestige of the Mission Civilatrice. Unlike some American guests, Converse did not object to using the hole.

Often, especially if he was high, using it made him feel as though he were entering into communion with the tight lipped *durs* of vanished France Ultra-Mer— the pilots of St. Exupery, General Salan, Malreaux. Sometimes he whistled *non, j'ne regret rien* as he left the toilet.

Straining, trembling with the fever that stirred in his intestines, Converse took his wife's letter from his trouser pocket and began to re-read it.

"Re Cosa Nostra—why the hell not? I'm prepared to take chances at this point and I don't respond to the moral objections. The way things are set up the people concerned have nothing good coming to them and we'll just be occupying a place that someone else will fill fast enough if they get the chance. I can't think of a way of us getting money where the money would be harder earned and I think that makes us entitled."

Perhaps, Converse thought, as he managed the business of the banknote sized tissue paper and wash-ed his hands, perhaps the vague dissatisfaction was a moral objection. Back across the airshaft, he secured the rusty double locks and took another swallow of Scotch. He stood facing the wall where the lizard stains were, rubbing the back of his neck, and thought of Charmian. Her body under the white linen, her Chinese soap, the garden, the smack chilling his eyes.

She had one of those faces, he thought—for all her rounded sensuality, extend the soft Carolina smile and you saw the skull beneath the skin. If smack had a body it would be like hers. Cool-out, languor, unmaking.

When Converse wrote thoughtful pieces for the small European publications which employed him he was always careful to assume a standpoint from which moral objections could be inferred. He knew the sort of people he was addressing and he knew the sort of moral objections they found most satisfying. Since his journey to Cambodia, he had experienced a certain difficulty in responding to moral objections but it seemed to him that he knew a good deal about them.

There were moral objections to children being blown out of sleep to death on a filthy street. And to their being burned to death by jellied petroleum. There were moral objections to house lizards being senselessly butchered by madmen. And moral objections to people spending their lives shooting scag.

Everyone felt these things. Everyone must or the value of human life would decline. It was important that the value of human life not decline.

Converse had once accompanied Ian Percy to a color film made by the U.N. soil conservation people about the eradication of termites. In a country that looked something like Nam, where there was elephant grass and red earth and palm trees, the local soldiery drove over the grasslands with bulldozers destroying immense conical termite colonies. There was a reason, as he remembered; the mounds caused erosion or the termites ate crops or people's houses. The termites were doing something bad. When the conical mounds were overturned termites came burrowing up from the ruins in frantic tens of thousands, flourishing their pincers in futile motions of defense. Soldiers with flame throwers came behind the bulldozers scorching the earth and burning the termites and their eggs to black cinders. Watching the film one felt something very like a moral objection. But the moral objection was overridden. People were more important than termites.

So moral objections were sometimes overridden by larger and more profound concerns. One had to take the long view. It was also true that at a certain point the view might become too long and moral objections appear irrelevant. To view things at such length was an error. The human reference point must be maintained.

Really, Converse thought, I know all about this. He pressed his thumb against the wall and removed a

dry particle of reptile spine from its cool surface. It was an error to take the long view in the face of moral objections. And it was an error to insist on moral objections when they were overridden.

In the red field when the fragmentation bombs were falling out of what appeared to be a perfectly empty blue sky he had experienced no moral objections at all. He had cried as they fell but his tears had not been those of a philosopher.

The last moral objection that Converse experienced in the traditional manner had been his reaction to the Great Elephant Zap of the previous year. That winter, Mac V—Military Advisory Command, Vietnam—, had decided that elephants were enemy agents because the NVA used them to carry things, and there had ensued a scene worthy of the Ramayana. Many-armed, hundred-headed Mac V had sent forth steel-bodied flying insects to destroy his enemies, the elephants. All over the country, whooping sweating gunners descended from the cloud cover to stampede the herds and mow them down with twenty caliber machine guns.

The Great Elephant Zap had been too much and had disgusted everyone.

Even the chopper crews who remembered the day as one of insane exhilaration had been somewhat appalled. There was a feeling that there were limits.

And as for dope, Converse thought, and addicts—if the world is going to contain elephants pursued by flying men, people are just naturally going to want to get high.

So there, Converse thought, that's the way its done. He had confronted a moral objection and overridden it. He could deal with these matters as well as anyone.

But the vague disatisfaction remained and it was not loneliness or a moral objection; it was of course fear. Fear was extremely important to Converse; morally speaking it was the basis of his life. It was the medium through which he perceived his own soul, the formula through which he could confirm his own existence. I am afraid, Converse reasoned, therefore I am.

Fear redeemed. It purified motives. Applied to a suitable object it was, as the bible plainly stated, the beginning of wisdom—not merely an excuse but a virtue.

the coming of the fairies
sir arthur conan doyle

Stranger than fiction? Open your mind and suspend your disbelief for a while. There follows a real-life detective story, featuring Sir Arthur himself and a whole passel of Theosophists. They have a particularly English approach to the matter of fairies which is a far cry from either Walt Disney or folk tradition. Here are the five photos taken by Elsie and Frances Wright (referred to in the first section by the pseudonyms of Iris and Alice Carpenter.) Whether or not you are convinced, the notion of proving the existence of fairies has its charm.

THE FIRST PUBLISHED ACCOUNT—"STRAND" CHRISTMAS NUMBER, 1920

Should the incidents here narrated, and the photographs attached, hold their own against the criticism which they will excite, it is no exaggeration to say that they will mark an epoch in human thought. I put them and all the evidence before the public for examination and judgment. If I am myself asked whether I consider the case to be absolutely and finally proved, I should answer that in order to remove the last faint shadow of doubt I should wish to see the result repeated before a disinterested witness. At the same time, I recognize the difficulty of such a request, since rare results must be obtained when and how they can. But short of final and absolute proof, I consider, after carefully going into every possible source of error, that a strong *prima facie* case has been built up. The cry of "fake" is sure to be raised, and will make some impression upon those who have not had the opportunity of knowing the people concerned, or the place. On the photographic side every objection has been considered and adequately met. The pictures stand or fall together. Both are false, or both are true. All the circumstances point to the latter alternative, and yet in a matter involving so tremendous a new departure one needs overpowering evidence before one can say that there is no conceivable loophole for error.

It was about the month of May in this year that I received the information from Miss Felicia Scatcherd, to the effect that two photographs of fairies had been taken in the North of England under circumstances which seemed to put fraud out of the question. The statement would have appealed to me at any time, but I happened at the moment to be collecting material for an article on fairies, and I had accumulated a surprising number of people who claimed to be able to see these little creatures. The evidence was so complete and detailed, with such good names attached to it, that it was difficult to believe that it was false; but, being by nature of a somewhat sceptical turn, I felt that something closer was needed before

Excerpts from The Coming of the Fairies *by A. Conan Doyle ($2.95) available from Samuel Weiser, Inc. New York, NY 10003.*

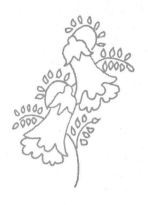

I could feel personal conviction and assure myself that these were not thoughtforms conjured up by the imagination or expectation of the seers. The rumour of the photographs interested me deeply, therefore, and following the matter up from one lady informant to another, I came at last upon Mr. Edward L. Gardner, who has been ever since my most efficient collaborator, to whom all credit is due. Mr. Gardner, it may be remarked, is a member of the Executive Committee of the Theosophical Society, and a well-known lecturer upon occult subjects.

He had not himself at that time mastered the whole case, but all he had he placed freely at my disposal. I had already seen prints of the photographs, but I was relieved to find that he had the actual negatives, and that it was from them, and not from the prints that two expert photographers, especially Mr. Snelling, had already formed their conclusions in favour of the genuineness of the pictures. Mr. Gardner tells his own story presently, so I will simply say that at that period he had got into direct and friendly touch with the Carpenter family. We are compelled to use a pseudonym and to withhold the exact address, for it is clear that their lives would be much interrupted by correspondence and callers if their identity were too clearly indicated. At the same time there would be, no doubt, no objection to any small committee of inquiry verifying the facts for themselves if this anonymity were respected. For the present, however, we shall simply call them the Carpenter family in the village of Dalesby, West Riding.

Some three years before, according to our information, the daughter and the niece of Mr. Carpenter, the former being sixteen and the other ten years of age, had taken the two photographs—the one in summer, the other in early autumn. The father was quite agnostic in the matter, but as his daughter claimed that she and her cousin when they were together continually saw fairies in the wood and had come to be on familiar and friendly terms with them, he entrusted her with one plate in his camera. The result was the picture of the dancing elves, which considerably amazed the father when he developed the film that evening. The little girl looking across at her playmate, to intimate that the time had come to press the button, is Alice, the niece, while the older girl, who was taken some months later with the quaint gnome, is Iris, the daughter. The story ran that the girls were so excited in the evening that one pressed her way into the small dark-room in which the father was about to develop, and that as she saw the forms of the fairies showing through the solution she cried out to the other girl, who was palpitating outside the door: "Oh, Alice, Alice, the fairies are on the plate—they are on the plate!" It was indeed a triumph for the children, who had been smiled at, as so many children are smiled at by an incredulous world for stating what their own senses have actually recorded.

OBSERVATIONS OF A CLAIRVOYANT IN THE COTTINGLEY GLEN, AUGUST 1921

Wood Elves. (Under the old beeches in the wood, Cottingley, August 12, 1921.) Two tiny wood elves came racing over the ground past us as we sat on a fallen tree trunk. Seeing us, they pulled up short about five feet away, and stood regarding us with considerable amusement but no fear. They appeared as if completely covered in a tight-fitting one-piece skin, which shone slightly as if wet. They had hands and feet large and out of proportion to their bodies. Their legs were somewhat thin, ears large and pointed upwards, being almost pear-shaped. There were a large number of these figures racing about the ground. Their noses appeared almost pointed and their mouths wide. No teeth and no structure inside the mouth, not even a tongue, so far as I could see. It was as if the whole were made up of a piece of jelly. Surrounding them, as an etheric double surrounds a physical form, is a greenish light, something like chemical vapour. As Frances came up and sat within a foot of them they withdrew, as if in alarm, a distance of eight feet or so, where they remained apparently regarding us and comparing notes of their impressions. These two live in the roots of a huge beech tree—they disappeared through a crevice into which they walked (as one might walk into a cave) and sank below the ground.

Fairies. Frances sees tiny fairies dancing in a circle, the figures gradually expanding in size till they reached eighteen inches, the ring widening in proportion. Elsie sees a vertical circle of dancing fairies flying slowly round; as each one touched the grass he appeared to perform a few quick steps and then continued his slow motion round the circle. The fairies who are dancing have long skirts, through which their limbs can be seen; viewed astrally the circle is bathed in golden yellow light, with the outer edges of many hues, violet predominating. The movement of the fairies is reminiscent of that of the great wheel at Earl's Court. The fairies float very slowly, remaining motionless as far as bodies and limbs are concerned, until they come round to the ground again.

There is a tinkling music accompanying all this. It appears to have more of the aspect of a ceremony than a game. Frances sees two fairy figures performing as if on the stage, one with wings, one without. Their bodies shine with the effect of rippling water in the sun. The fairy without wings has bent over backwards like a contortionist till its head touches the ground, while the winged figure bends over it. Frances sees a small Punch-like figure, with a kind of Welsh hat, doing a kind of dancing by striking its heel on the ground and at the same time raising his hat and bowing. Elsie sees a flower fairy, like a carnation in shape, the head appearing where the stalk touches the flower and the green sepals forming a tunic from which the arms protrude, while the petals form a skirt, below which are rather thin legs. It is tripping across the grass. Its colouring is pink like a carnation in a pale, suffused sort of way. (Written by the light of the moon.) I see couples a foot high, female and male, dancing in a slow waltz-like motion in the middle of the field. They appear even to reverse. They are clothed in etheric matter and rather ghost-like in appearance. Their bodies are outlined with grey light and show little detail.

Elsie sees a small imp reminiscent of a monkey, revolving slowly round a stalk to the top of which he was clinging. He has an impish face and is looking our way as if performing for our benefit.

The brownie appears during all this to have taken upon himself the duties of showman. I see what may be described as a fairy fountain about twenty feet ahead. It is caused by an uprush of fairy force from the ground—and spreading fish-tail fashion higher into the air—it is many-hued. This was also seen by Frances.

Elf. Elsie sees a kind of elf who seems to be going so fast that it blows his hair back; one can sense the wind round him, yet he is stationary, though he looks to be busily hurrying along.

Goblins. Elsie sees a flight of little mannikins, imp-like in appearance, descending slantwise on to the grass. They form into two lines which cross each other as they come down. One line is coming vertically down, feet touching head, the other comes across them shoulder to shoulder. On reaching the ground they all run off in different directions, all serious, as if intent upon some business. The elves from the wood appear to be chiefly engaged in racing across the field, though no other purpose appears to be served by their speed or presence. Few of them pass near us without pulling up to stare. The elves seem to be the most curious of all the fairy creatures. Frances sees three and calls them goblins.

Fairy Band. There has suddenly arrived in the field a fairy director with a band of fairy people. Their arrival causes a bright radiance to shine in the field, visible to us sixty yards away. She is very autocratic and definite in her orders, holding unquestioned command. They spread themselves out into a gradually widening circle around her, and as they do so, a soft glow spreads out over the grass. They are actually vivifying and stimulating the growth in the field. This is a moving band which arrives in this field swinging high over the tree tops as if from a considerable distance. Inside a space of two minutes the circle has spread to approximately twelve feet wide and is wonderfully radiant with light. Each member of the band is connected to the leader by a thin stream of light. These streams are of different colour, though chiefly yellow, deepening to orange. They meet in the centre,

ELSIE AND THE GNOME

Elsie was playing with the gnome and beckoning it to come on to her knee. The gnome leapt up just as Frances, who had the camera, snapped the shutter. He is described as wearing black tights, a reddish jersey and a pointed bright red cap. Elsie said there was no perceptible weight, though when on the bare hand the feeling is like a 'little breath.' The wings were more moth-like than the fairies and of a soft neutral tint. Elsie explained that what seem to be markings on his wings are simply his pipes which he was swinging in his grotesque little left hand. The music of the pipes can only just be heard as a tiny little tinkle if everything is quite still. Neither of the children could distinguish any tune.

merging in her aura, and there is a constant flow backwards and forwards among them. The form produced by this is something like an inverted fruit dish, with the central fairy as the stem, and the lines of light which flow in a graceful even curve forming the sides of the bowl. This party is in intense activity, as if it had much to do and little time in which to do it. The director is vivified and instructed from within herself, and appears to have her consciousness seated upon a more subtle plane than that upon which she is working.

Fairy. Elsie sees a tall and stately fairy come across the field to a clump of harebells. It is carrying in its arms something which may be a baby fairy, wrapped in gauzy substance. It lays this in the clump of harebells and kneels down as though stroking something, and after a time fades away. We catch impressions of four-footed creatures being ridden by winged figures who are thin and bend over their mounts like jockeys. It is no known animal which they bestride, having a face something like that of a caterpillar.

Elsie sees about a dozen fairies moving towards us in a crescent-shaped flight. As they drew near she remarked with ecstasy upon their perfect beauty of form—even while she did so they became as ugly as sin, as if to give the lie to her words. They all leered at her and disappeared. In this episode it may be that one contacts a phase of the antagonism and dislike which so many of the fairy creatures feel for humans at this stage of evolution.

Golden Fairy. One specially beautiful one has a body clothed in iridescent shimmering golden light. She has tall wings, each of which is almost divided into upper and lower portions. The lower portion, which is smaller than the upper, appears to be elongated to a point like the wings of certain butterflies. She, too, is moving her arms and fluttering her wings. I can only describe her as a golden wonder. She smiles and clearly sees us. She places her finger on her lips. She remains watching us with smiling countenance in amongst the leaves and branches of the willow. She is not objectively visible on the physical plane. She points with her right hand, moving it in a circle round her feet, and I see a number, perhaps six or seven, cherubs (winged faces); these appear to be held in shape by some invisible will. She has cast a fairy spell over me completely subjugating the mental principle—leaves me staring wild-eyed in amongst the leaves and flowers.

An elf-like creature runs up the slanting branch of the willow from the ground where the fairy stands. He is not a very pleasant visitor—I should describe him as distinctly low class.

* * *

In the literature of Theosophy, I know no one who treats the elemental forces of nature more fully than Bishop Leadbeater, whom I met in my Australian travels, and who impressed me by his venerable appearance, his ascetic habits, and his claims to be remarkable clairvoyancy which has, as he alleges, opened up many of the Arcana. In his book *The Hidden Side of Things* he talks very fully of the fairies of many lands.

"No contrast could well be more marked than that between the vivacious, rollicking, orange-and-purple or scarlet-and-gold mannikins who dance among the vineyards of Sicily and the almost wistful grey-and-green creatures who move so much more sedately amidst the oaks and furze-covered heaths in Brittany, or the golden-brown 'good people' who haunt the hillsides of Scotland.

"In England the emerald-green kind is probably the commonest, and I have seen it also in the woods in France and Belgium, in far-away Massachusetts, and on the banks of the Niagara River. The vast plains of the Dakotas are inhabited by a black-and-white kind which I have not seen elsewhere, and California rejoices in a lovely white-and-gold species which also appears to be unique.

"In Australia the most frequent type is a very distinctive creature of a wonderful luminous sky-blue colour; but there is a wide diversity between the etheric inhabitants of New South Wales or Victoria and those of tropical Northern Queensland. These latter approximate closely to those of the Dutch Indies. Java seems specially prolific in these graceful creatures, and the kinds most common there are two distinct types, both monochromatic—one indigo blue with faint metallic gleamings, and the other a study in all known shades of yellow—quaint, but wonderfully effective and attractive.

"A striking local variety is gaudily ringed with alternate bars of green and yellow, like a football jersey. This ringed type is possibly a race peculiar to that part of the world, for I saw red and yellow similarly arranged in the Malay Peninsula, and green and white on the other side of the Straits in Sumatra. That huge island also rejoices in the possession of a lovely pale heliotrope tribe which I have seen before only in the hills of Ceylon. Down in New Zealand their speciality is a deep blue shot with silver, while in the South Sea Islands one meets with a silvery-white variety, which coruscates with all the colours of the rainbow, like a figure of mother-of-pearl.

"In India we find all sorts, from the delicate rose-and-pale-green, or pale-blue-and-primrose of the hill-country to the rich medley of gorgeously gleaming colours, almost barbaric in their intensity and profusion, which is characteristic of the plains. In some

FRANCES AND THE LEAPING FAIRY

The fairy is leaping up from the leaves below and hovering for a moment—it had done so three or four times. Rising a little higher than before. Frances thought it would touch her face, and involuntarily tossed her head back. The fairy's light covering appears to be close fitting: the wings were lavender in colour.

FAIRY OFFERING A POSY TO ELSIE

The fairy is standing almost still, poised on the bush leaves. The wings were shot with yellow. An interesting point is shown in this photograph: Elsie is not looking directly at the sprite. The reason seems to be that the human eye is disconcerting. If the fairy be actively moving it does not matter much, but if motionless and aware of being gazed at then the nature spirit will usually withdraw and apparently vanish. With fairy lovers the habit of looking at first a little sideways is common.

parts of that marvelous country I have seen the black-and-gold type which is more usually associated with the African desert, and also a species which resembles a statuette made out of a gleaming crimson metal, such as was the orichalcum of the Atlanteans.

"Somewhat akin to this last is a curious variety which looks as though cast out of bronze and burnished; it appears to make its home in the immediate neighbourhood of volcanic disturbances, since the only places in which it has been seen so far are the slopes of Vesuvius and Etna, the interior of Java, the Sandwich Islands, the Yellowstone Park in North America, and a certain part of the North Island of New Zealand. Several indications seem to point to the conclusion that this is a survival of a primitive type, and represents a sort of intermediate stage between the gnome and the fairy.

"In some cases, districts close together are found to be inhabited by quite different classes of nature spirits; for example, as has already been mentioned, the emerald-green elves are common in Belgium, yet a hundred miles away in Holland hardly one of them is to be seen, and their place is taken by a sober-looking dark-purple species."

Very interesting indeed is his account of the Irish fairies. Speaking of a sacred mountain in Ireland, he says:

"A curious fact is that altitude above the sea-level seems to affect their distribution, those who belong to the mountains scarcely ever intermingling with those of the plains. I well remember, when climbing Slieve-na-mon, one of the traditionally sacred hills of Ireland, noticing the very definite lines of demarcation between the different types. The lower slopes, like the surrounding plains, were alive with the intensely active and mischievous little red-and-black race which swarms all over the south and west of Ireland, being especially attracted to the magnetic centres established nearly two thousand years ago by the magic-working priests of the old Milesian race to ensure and perpetuate their domination over the people by keeping them under the influence of the great illusion. After half an hour's climbing, however, not one of these red-and-black gentry was to be seen, but instead the hill-side was populous with the gentler blue-and-brown type which long ago owed special allegiance to the Tuatha-de-Danaan.

"These also had their zone and their well-defined limits, and no nature spirit of either type ever ventured to tresspass upon the space round the summit, sacred to the great green angels who have watched there for more than two thousand years, guarding one of the centres of living force that link the past to the future of that mystic land of Erin. Taller far than the height of man, these giant forms, in colour like the first new leaves of spring, soft, luminous, shimmering, indescribable, look forth over the world with wondrous eyes that shine like stars, full of the peace of those who live in the eternal, waiting with the calm certainty of knowledge until the appointed time shall come. One realizes very fully the power and importance of the hidden side of things when one beholds such a spectacle as that."

FAIRIES AND THEIR SUN-BATH

The central ethereal cocoon shape, something between a cocoon and an open chrysalis in appearance, lightly suspended amid the grasses, is the bower or cradle. Seated on the upper left-hand edge with wing well displayed is an undraped fairy apparently considering whether it is time to get up. An earlier riser of more mature age is seen on the right possessing abundant hair and wonderful wings. Her slightly denser body can be glimpsed within her fairy dress. Just beyond, still on the right, is the clear-cut head of a mischievous but smiling elf wearing a close-fitting cap. On the extreme left is a demure-looking sprite, with a pair of very diaphanous wings, while just above, rather badly out of focus, however, is another with wings still widely extended, and with outspread arms, apparently just alighting on the grass tops.

143

Judy Dater

Things unsaid and unsayable.

A poem in gray.

Souls captured in a bell jar,

Waiting for examination.

The mind contracts

as the light penetrates its blackest corners.

Don't try to talk!

Always making yourself more vulnerable.

But keep your mouth shut,

This is just a comedy.

San Anselmo, Ca.

Valerie Vancleeve   1972

Daydreams 1973

Maureen   1972

Laura Mae   1973

Aarmour Starr   1972

Libby   1971

Danville   1972

Gwen   1972

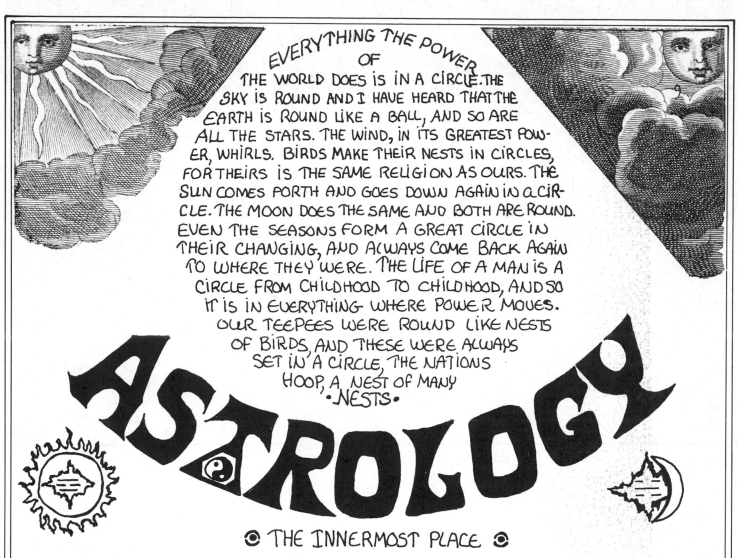

EVERYTHING THE POWER OF THE WORLD DOES IS IN A CIRCLE. THE SKY IS ROUND AND I HAVE HEARD THAT THE EARTH IS ROUND LIKE A BALL, AND SO ARE ALL THE STARS. THE WIND, IN ITS GREATEST POWER, WHIRLS. BIRDS MAKE THEIR NESTS IN CIRCLES, FOR THEIRS IS THE SAME RELIGION AS OURS. THE SUN COMES FORTH AND GOES DOWN AGAIN IN A CIRCLE. THE MOON DOES THE SAME AND BOTH ARE ROUND. EVEN THE SEASONS FORM A GREAT CIRCLE IN THEIR CHANGING, AND ALWAYS COME BACK AGAIN TO WHERE THEY WERE. THE LIFE OF A MAN IS A CIRCLE FROM CHILDHOOD TO CHILDHOOD, AND SO IT IS IN EVERYTHING WHERE POWER MOVES. OUR TEEPEES WERE ROUND LIKE NESTS OF BIRDS, AND THESE WERE ALWAYS SET IN A CIRCLE, THE NATIONS HOOP, A NEST OF MANY •NESTS•

ASTROLOGY

⊙ THE INNERMOST PLACE ⊙

These twelve pages constitute a
    Whole
A Whole Idea a Whole System a Whole
    Feeling
Cycles and Circles and Seasons and Centers
    The Beginning
      The End
A Mandala of Life with Spirit the
    Center
The life force of all Creation in the Center
    You in the Center
      Me in the Center
And from within the Seed Center
All Cyclic Motion of the Universe Revolves.
    Continual Movement
    Change
Change is the Support of Stability
    True Stability is Movement
    Stability in Movement
    is called Duration in
    the Book of Changes
There is the fullness and emptyness of the entire
Rhythmic cycle of life, known as Tao,
the interplay of Yin and Yang in the Book of Changes,
the movement of the moon around the earth,

the earth and the planets around the sun.
The sun as the Center, and that centered
system as a small part of a greater whole.
There is also the harmonious interweaving of the
elements of fire, earth, air, and water in constant movement in the greater constant motion of the whole.

There is the relationship between the Microcosm
and the Macrocosm, the Rhythm of the Universe,
the Study of Cycles as the basis of *all* Knowledge.
    The Circle is the Symbol of the Cycle.
The Circle is Complete—Whole—Total
    Cycles & Circles
    The Circle has a Center
    The Law of the Center is the Basic
    Principle of Nature
The Center is the Source of Power Wisdom and Life
    The Center is the Innermost Place

The Structure of the Cycle of Changes is apparent
    through understanding the process
    of Seeds
    Birth and Death
Spring Summer Winter Fall

Edited by Ann Marie Gretsch

dane rudhyar
on
cycles and person-centered, holistic astrology

Astrology, a Technique
For the Study of Life-Cycles

Astrology can be defined as a technique for the study of life-cycles. Its main purpose is to establish the existence of regular patterns in the sequence of events constituting man's inner and outer experience; then, to use the knowledge of these patterns in order to control or give meaning to these experiences. As a man learns to control the genesis, development and recurrence of his experiences, he achieves mastery. This is the goal of the "adept" or the scientist—a goal which deals with the accurate timing of actions and the adjustment to expected reactions. On the other hand, as man gives meaning to his experiences by referring them to the cycles of his individual being or of humanity at large, he develops a conscious and inclusive attitude to life. He gains understanding and wisdom, which is the goal of the philosopher. Indeed, the study of cycles—that is, of periodical activities in nature, human and otherwise—is the root of all significant knowledge, be it scientific or philosophical. And the study of cycles is a study of time.

There has been much unnecessary confusion as to the nature of time. And the confusion originates mainly in the failure to differentiate between "generic" time and "individual" time. Generic time—*objective* time—is the time measured by the calendar and by clocks; the time which makes the peasant plough the field and reap the harvest, which establishes the normal, natural rhythm of biological functions in human bodies. It is the very matrix into which the common activities of human beings flow. Just as the social activities and common reactions to life of the average person are structured by the cultural-religious traditions and the laws of his country, likewise, at a still more basic level, man's generic activities and his objective sense of time are structured by celestial cycles. The latter not only serve to "measure" time; they are the very substance of generic time. And the fundamental characteristic of this time, of which all men are compelled to be aware, is that

it is cyclic. It is cyclic because it is established by periodical changes in the cosmic environment of mankind—that is, by the ordered activities of cosmic wholes, of which our globe is only a very small part.

Beside this objective time, valid for all human beings, there is an individual time, which is experienced by individual entities as *subjective duration.* It is experienced as a normally unconscious, organic psychic feeling; and this feeling eludes standardization, depending as it does upon the more or less individualized rhythm of the experiencer and upon particular, unduplicatable conditions. Subjective duration is a resultant of the state of organic wholeness. It is an expression of the particular rhythm of a particular organic whole functioning truly as a whole and not merely as part of a larger whole.

At the level of strictly animal life, duration is an expression of the rhythm of the entire species rather than of the rhythm of a particular specimen thereof; this, because individual characteristics reside in the species and not in the individual organisms manifesting the species' biological characteristics. With human beings, however, as the process of individualization begins to operate and a particular man or woman develops increasingly individual (thus, relatively unique) characteristics—biological and, above all, psychological—"individual time" begins to be felt. Felt at first in the dim, almost poignant way in which the first longings of adolescence reach the consciousness, this sense of subjective duration becomes sharper, the more the human person functions as an individual. Moments of great emotional stress—of intense living or "dying"—arouse this latent realization; but techniques have also been devised deliberately to induce and accelerate such an inner development. Hindu yoga is a typical example of such a conscious effort to individualize time—a result obtained by the control of organic energies and by a refocusing of the ego.

RUDHYAR

The co-existence of objective time and subjective duration in the consciousness of the individualized human person produces at a certain stage of evolution a deep-seated inner conflict. This conflict is parallel to, and a function of the struggle between the collective and the individual factors of the personality; between the desire to participate in, or be subservient to, collective and social patterns, and the will to express one's unique identity; between the inbred realization that one is a part of a large whole (society or mankind) and the innermost feeling that one is a whole, unique and self-sufficient.

Astronomy and all precise sciences deal solely with objective time—clock time—regulated by a universally accepted standard. This standard is fundamentally the sidereal day, the period between two successive returns of a star to the meridian—the time needed for a complete daily rotation of the earth around its axis.

Astrology, in so far as it is based on astronomical data, deals with objective time and its cycles. But astrology is not merely a study of celestial cycles in themselves; it is *a technique of interpretation of the meaning of these cycles with reference to the possibilities for growth in individuals.* It does not aim merely at telling what will happen at a definite moment of objective time. Its essential purpose—when true to its highest and truest function in human affairs—is to indicate the possibilities for individual development inherent in the significant turning points in the cycle of a human life. It does not—or should not—deal with the compulsions of generic, cosmic fate; but, instead, with the opportunities which the individual has to emerge from the compelling, structuring matrix of objective time into the creative freedom of subjective duration.

Astrology can be understood as a technique for the discovery of one's own individual structure of being. And this structure is the foundation of individual immortality; for immortality is the power to dwell in a world of one's individual making, and to hold the structure of that world intact (and one's creative thought-powers firmly established within it), even against the shock of the disintegration of the biological organism, which we call death. Immortality is the victory of subjective duration over objective time. It is the triumph of the consciousness of being a whole with a unique identity over the consciousness of being merely a part of the human species subject to generic and social patterns of living and behavior.

The individual birth-chart, erected for the exact first moment of independent existence as a living organism (the first breath), is a cosmic symbol of the individual structure of being. But the astrologer must be able to see it as such! If he thinks of the birth-chart as a mere reading of the clock of objective time for a particular moment; if he adds up the positions of the sun, the moon and the planets as a man looking at a clock adds up the indications given by the hour, the minute and the second hands; then, what the astrologer discovers is only the sum-total of compulsions which the newborn must meet according to the laws of action and reaction of his genetic human nature. Indeed the newborn is seen, then, as merely a combination of natural drives, ancestral tendencies and unavoidable allegiances to environmental patterns.

If, on the other hand, the astrologer is able to visualize the entire birth-chart as an *individual and indivisible structure* revealing the potentiality of manifestation of a unique and original identy, creative of its own subjective duration and establishing the beginning of its own era—dawning point of its immortality—then, the astrologer can perform a spiritual function. He evokes and summons forth the image of the wholeness of the person whose birth-chart he studies. This is a spiritual act, because spirit deals only with wholes. Spirit is the wholeness of every living whole; and it is, in its operations, that which ever tends to re-establish wholeness, balance, harmony, integration, health, plenitude of being—wherever there is the consciousness of lack, of need, of greatness yet unrealized, of fullness yet unattained . . . and, at the same time, the faith which alone can open the gates of the empty structure to the inrushing tide of spiritual abundance.

Objective time establishes limitations and boundaries for human beings because it is the product of the activities of vast celestial cosmic bodies within the electro-magnetic fields of which a man appears as a most unimportant part. The position of the sun, or the moon, or any one planet or star in a birth-chart represents, therefore, the particular kind of subservience the person experiences in relation to the natural energies symbolized by the cyclic motion of this one celestial body productive of objective time. Likewise as a child is born into a certain family belonging to a certain social class, this fact indicates his subservience to the particular kind of social prejudice or preferment which is associated with that class. It is a limiting fact. To be born on July 30th of any year is a limiting fact. It establishes one's particular mode of subservience to the factor of solar vitality—the Leo kind of response to this solar vitality.

If, however, the birth-chart is seen as a whole—as the "Name" of the individual-in-the-making—the wholeness of it represents the particular potentiality of freedom of the person from this, that or the other natural energy and from this, that or the other natural energy and social prejudice which tend to clock his reactions to life. To see the birth-chart as a whole means seeing it as a complex relationship between the many factors it contains: planets, cusps, nodes, parts, etc. A sum-total is not a relationship. To add up the indications given by separate factors has statistical value; it has no spiritual meaning. Spiritual meaning is an expression of relatedness. Likewise, a tone produced by a great musician on a violin is a complex entity, composed of many overtones, each of which has a particular frequency, dynamic intensity, phase, etc. When we hear the tone, we hear an organic synthesis of all these component sound-vibrations, and what we call the "timbre," the moving quality, the emotional power of the tone are the results of the relatedness of all these sound-vibrations. This is the "character" of the tone; just as the character of an individual is an expression of the relatedness of all the constituent parts of his total being. And character is creative freedom.

from *The Lunation Cycle*
by Dane Rudhyar

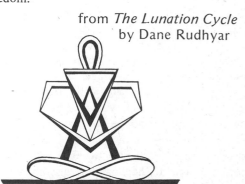

Astrology is a Symbolic language. It is a language attempting to formulate, by means of symbols based on the common experiences of men facing the all-surrounding sky, an immensely complex structure of relationships between the universe and man, relationships we cannot explain in other ways. The form that stands at the center of this chart is symbolical rather than a reference to astronomical facts. It suggests that the person whose birth chart it is, lives on the surface of the globe—

yet in some manner has his roots at the very core of the earth where, symbolically, all men commune. The standing figure is the Eyptian ansated Cross, symbol of Man. The center of the mandala is in the region of man's heart. It is for every person the center of his or her universe. The mandala has twelve petals, recalling the ancient symbolism of the Lotus. The planets are marked inside of the petals, the zodiacal degree at the cusps of the Houses.

MANDALA BIRTH CHART

A CHART MANDALA for a Person-Centered Astrology

INDIVIDUAL, COLLECTIVE, CREATIVE and CYCLIC PROCESS

. . . Astrology is philosophically meaningless unless it rests on a thorough understanding of cycles and of the creative potency of every moment—especially those "seed-moments" which become such by reason of their being the points of departure of cycles. The "Formula of Change" of the *Yi King* is a cyclic formula, which purports to determine symbolically the universal and essential structure of all cycles; better still, of *the* Cycle or of *cyclicity*. As all life-processes are cyclic—in essence, if not in outer appearance—such a formula becomes the basic law of all life-processes. Thus a truly universal synthesis of being and becoming is reached—a synthesis probably grander and more absolute, in its symbolical applicability, than that contemplated by Einstein through his "unified field theory" reducing all natural phenomena to a simple law.

Individual and Collective

All manifestations of life can be seen to involve a dualism of elements or tendencies. Where the Chinese spoke of *Yang* and *Yin* we shall use the terms: "individual" and "collective"; and we shall presently see that this dualism is resolved through the operation of a third principle: the "creative." The words themselves, of course, are not new. They have been used especially in psychology and in relation to social organization, politics—and even, of late, have been implied in the recent theories of modern physics (especially in the dualism of "particle" and "wave"). What, however, has not yet been done—as far as we know—is to use these basic concepts in an attempt at integrating the whole of human knowledge and at offering a consistent interpretation of being and becoming. Again, we must repeat that we are here barely suggesting how such an attempt could be made, and this in order to establish our re-

interpretation of astrological symbols on a foundation truly all-inclusive in its scope.

The philosophy of Holism, to which General Smuts gave a most interesting though not by any means complete formulation, will help us greatly in showing how the evolutionary life-process and its contributive factors can be re-interpreted in a way that is true to the spirit of the future civilization. Whole and parts are presented as the two terms of the life-process. And the introduction of these two terms as cosmic ultimates is a tremendous step—even though General Smuts appears somewhat shy of truly metaphysical and cosmic generalizations. However, he characterizes the nature of the World-process thus:

> This is a universe of whole-making . . . The ultimate reality of the universe is neither matter nor spirit but wholes. . . . Holism as an active creative process means the movement of the universe towards ever more and deeper wholeness. This is the essential process, and all organic and psychic activities and relations have to be understood as elements and forms of this process . . . The rise and self-protection of wholes in the Whole is the slow but unerring process and goal of this Holistic universe.
>
> *(Holism and Evolution, 1926)*

Such a picture, when completed by the idea that soul or self must be understood as the wholeness of the wholes, constitutes a revolutionary revaluation of man's attitude to life. The dualism of spirit and matter, which was another form of physiological dualism, as it meant originally that of motion and inertia, is replaced by that of wholeness and parts. And the unity of the process is stressed in that "Holism is a process of creative synthesis . . . the movement of the universe towards ever more and deeper wholeness.

from *The Astrology of Personality*
by Dane Rudhyar

from *My Stand on Astrology*

It was the realization that what was happening in astrology parallels or reflects in many ways what I saw occurring in our society which led me in February-March 1969 to initiate the International Committee for Humanistic Astrology. In the series of six booklets which followed—now available in one volume entitled *Person-Centered Astrology**—I tried to formulate clearly the distinction between an "event-oriented" and a person-centered astrology. I extended and reformulated the concept of "aspect" and planetary *gestalt,* the meaning of astrological nodes, and I presented basic ideas applicable to the holistic interpretation of a birth-chart.

What I probably did not emphasize enough in my presentation is what could be called "the *mandala* approach" to astrological charts. Such an approach was mentioned already in my 1963 book *The Astrology of Personality.* The present popularization of the mandala concept (especially through the beautiful book by Jose and Miriam Arguelles, entitled *Mandala**) makes the use of the phrase "the mandala approach to astrology" particularly significant at this time. It also should bring more clearly than ever the meaning of the difference between *person-centered* and *zodiacally circumscribed* astrological charts—between the continental European, and the traditional English-American chart-forms.

In *The Astrology of Personality* I defined a mandala as "a magic circle containing a cross or some other basically fourfold formulation," adding that "every birth-chart is the mandala of an individual life. It is the blue-print of the process of individuation for this particular individual. To follow it understandingly is to follow the 'conscious way,' the way of operative wholeness, that is, the way of the active fulfillment of the wholeness of being that is Self" (as Jung understands this term).**

As the Arguelles' book *Mandala* clearly states: The universality of the mandala is in its one constant, the principle of center. The center is the beginning of the mandala as it is the beginning of all forms and of all processes, including the extensions of form into time...The center is symbolic of the external potential. From the same inexhaustible source all seeds grow and develop, all cells realize their function— There is a structural law, a cosmic principle by which perceptible forms are sustained and which governs the processes of transformation in all things. This can be realized only because the center principle manifests itself through man in the same ways as it does through a flower or a star; in it we may discover our cosmic commonality- our cosmic community....At the core each man is the center of his own compass and experiences, his own cardinal points. CARDINAL POINTS; north, south, east, west.

We are defined not only by our place on the physical level, but by our position in consciousness, and these are an interdependent whole . . . universally inherent in man's consciousciousness, the mandala has continually appeared in his construction, rituals, and art forms. From its various manifestations we can derive three basic properties: A center—symmetry—cardinal points.

(Mandala, p. 12-13)

* * *

When people seem to complain that they have to read twice my books in order to really understand what I wrote, I always feel like asking if they would expect to be a concert pianist by at most playing twice a passage, or to solve problems of calculus after reading once a textbook on mathematics. Living a life of self-actualization and transcendent development is the most arduous process there is in our materialistic and competitive society dominated by profit values and ideals of personal self-aggrandizement at others' expense.

* * * * * * *

The worst enemy of the individual attempting to emerge from the mass-vibration of his culture and of his more or less unconscious urges and ego-patterns is confusion. Alas, today, an extraordinary amount of confusion prevails not only in astrology, but in psychology, medicine and nearly all intellectual pursuits , the arts included. This is so because we are living through a transitional period. We still cling emotionally and fearfully to the past and to ego- saving devices, while our creative mind and more individualized and idealistic aspirations are " reaching to the stars ". But in order to reach to the stars as an individual, free from the collective past of the human race, one must first of all be centered. The individualized consciousness of a man has to be established and steady at the center of a vast Mandala, his universe. It is truly " his " Universe, his individual universe. It is a universe with which he can directly communicate and of which he can learn to decipher the great message of his birth; birth at a particular time, at a definite point on the earth—surface—his center. He should be able , sooner or later, to communicate without intermediaries, from his center to the cosmic center that most people call " God "

* * * * *

Soul Form and Ego— Rudhyar '53

How can astrology help a person while in the process of integration and self-liberation, and in fulfilling his or her destiny? Not by the negative device of telling what is wrong with the human nature of this person, or by foretelling future events. Help here means guidance along the lines marked by the essential structure of the birth-chart and the whole solar system at the time of birth, and also as the process of individuation and destiny-fulfillment unfolds year by year. The guidance must be based on a holistic perception of the chart or charts being considered. It must be an attempt to make as clear as is possible, at the time and under the circumstances of the contact with the individual, what the chart indicates to be *the best possibilities of action or reflexion and meditation.*

This can be done only if the astrologer has come to understand that the astrological mandala outlined by the sky at the place and time of birth reveals *not what necessarily is, but rather what should be.* It does not tell how the basic drives in the human nature of the individual inevitably *will* operate, but instead *how they should operate,* if the individual destiny is to be fulfilled, whatever be the external means for this fulfillment.

The means may be pleasant or unpleasant, easy or difficult, inducing happiness and well being or causes of pain, sorrow, and repeated crises. This is of no importance. No one will ever profit from knowing which of these alternatives is "most likely" to unfold. The person who deliberately seeks to actualize as completely as possible his birth-potential as a would-be individual should not dwell in his brain-consciousness upon the nature and results to himself of the means, but only on whether he can marshal the strength, courage, wisdom or equianimity to make a meaningful and eventually constructive use of them. The "means" I am speaking of here are simply the things which every day will confront him; but *at the time* they confront him, and not before. Nothing is more futile, and often more dangerous, than predictions of external events or inner changes whose modes of operation can never be definitely ascertained on a strictly astrological basis. Most predictions can be to some extent self-fulfilling—either directly or indirectly. The fear of a predicted crisis, subconscious as it may be, is a negative kind of self-fulfilling.

What, then, is the function of the astrologer, if it is not to indicate what his client is to face, and not even to analyze his character with the use of statistical techniques based on collective values and mass-averages?

The astrologer's function is very similar to that of a spiritual guide. He may not have the ability to see clairvoyantly where the client stands in his development, and what are his weaknesses and strengths at the personal and superpersonal levels; but he has in front of him a "celestial message" or "revelation," the client's birth-chart—and also his own birthchart considered in relation to that of the client. What he theoretically should be able to see in this client's birth-chart is *what the universe (or God) sought to achieve by the birth of a human being at that particular time and place.* Essentially nothing else; but this alone should be the astrologer's and the client's concern—indeed the concern of any individual throughout his life.

What we call "events" are—generally speaking—means to produce, in the best possible conditions what the birth of a person was meant to achieve. The only modification one should make to such a statement results from the evident fact that, as any

man is born in a family, community and nation and within the earth's biosphere, he is unavoidably subjected to a multiplicity of pressures which tend to distort, sometimes tragically, the rhythm of destiny inherent in his birth situation. He may be caught in maelstroms of war, revolution or epidemics; or, put in more occult terms, his individual *dharma* may be swept away by and become meaningless in a destructive precipitation of collective *karma* upon his racial group or his nation. He may survive the crisis, but it may have permanently distorted the pattern of his individual destiny, because too much power was released for him to withstand *as an individual.*

One can say, of course, that it was part of the person's karma to be placed in such devastating life-situations; but, as I see it, the birth-chart should not be interpreted in terms of "karmic retribution." The past is past; what the birth-sky reveals is how to build the future—that is, how to actualize what is only potential at birth. The birth-chart is a *set of instructions.* I repeat that its essential meaning lies NOT in giving you an analytical diagram of what your character and organic bodystructure are, but in showing you *how in your particular case, the ten basic energies of human nature should be used to the best advantage;* that is, in order to enable you to consciously work with all of them at all times. In modern astrology, these basic energies are represented by the ten planets (Sun and Moon included). Where these planets are located indicates where (by zodiacal signs, and especially by Houses) they can be used by you to produce the most valuable results—not necessarily valuable in terms of social success, health or money, but in terms of the only thing that should concern you, that is, the actualization of your birth-potential.

I have ceaselessly repeated during the last 40 years that there are no "bad" planets, signs, Houses or aspects. Everything in the birth-chart is as it should be. But *it is there to be used consciously and effectively.* It is to be used so that it may serve the purpose of self-actualization and of liberation from the compulsions of human nature and collective patterns of society and culture. I have repeated that astrology has value only in so far as it helps man to *tread "the conscious Way."* It can help not only to expand but to objectivize the consciousness of an individual and in a larger sense, when vast planetary cycles are considered, the consciousness of mankind in its dealings with the biosphere, the whole planet and eventually the solar system (what I call the "heliocosm").

Events come into a man's life in order to make him conscious of what his life is about. As we are still so involved in collective patterns of value and meaning, the events have very often indeed to hammer at the shell of our unconsciousness, or at the fortress of our ego. The study of our birth-chart, and of progressions and transits, should help us to realize *the meaning* of what happens *as it happens*—and more often than not *after* it has happened, because our mind then is probably clearer, more objective. This is what humanely and spiritually matters. We can change the past by giving it the meaning of a prelude to our fulfillment instead of a heavy weight of frustration or guilt.

* * *

A person-centered astrology, not only founded upon a humanistic approach—in the basic, non-dogmatic and not antireligious sense of the term, humanistic—but also challenging the validity of popular beliefs and expectations, has evidently not a "mass appeal." This does not mean that it can appeal only or mostly to our present intellectual elite, because the collective mentality of such an elite is still permeated with materialistic, quantitative and analytical concepts, and with what I consider a false ideal of individualism, of progress and of personal success. Since I began to speak of "humanistic astrology" the many hundred unsolicited letters which I received asking to join the movement have come mainly from young people, the great majority of whom are struggling to overcome the official college-mentality of our culture. The problem these young people are facing is how to define convincingly, even to *themselves,* what they are searching for. Yet they are today our only hope for a "humanistic" future and a social order founded upon qualitative values and upon that freedom which actually means allegiance and commitment to spiritual principles.

The first principle is that the individual person should be able to stand, erect and open, at the center of the universe around him. Erect in the "tallness" of his or her own truth of being; open to the downflow of the "star" at the precise zenith of his own individual destiny—what he was born on this earth-surface to perform for the sake of mankind and the whole earth.

When I speak of a person-centered astrology I refer to a kind of astrology, and to the type of astrological tools, which can be used to assist the individual to stand, consciously and deliberately, at the center of a great mandala: *his own particular universe.* Ideally he should be able to stand without crutches and to read by himself the message of the sky—his birth-sky and the yearly evolving sky overhead. Yet, sometimes, an intermediary may be needed, so as *to clarify* issues and individual problems. A person-centered astrology has only this one essential purpose: to clarify the meaning and purpose of what daily existence and daily relationships bring to the individual who is committed to significant and purposeful living. Such a commitment implies a "structured" living.

As I speak here of "structured living" I do not have in mind the type of structuring imposed from the outside by collective socio-cultural patterns—though these of course can be accepted as directives, *provided* they have been objectively studied, understood and consciously assimilated. I mean a kind of structuring which is the concrete manifestation of an individual's essential relationship to *his* universe. To work out this relationship consciously and in utter intellectual and emotional honesty—beyond all the tricks of the ego—this is what fulfilling one's destiny actually means.

* * *

During the 40 years or so that I have been definitely and intently working with astrology I have stated as clearly as I could where I stood. During that period, I have altered somewhat my approach to the formulation of my ideas; but I believe that my basic stand has been consistent. Where the emphasis has changed this was due to an increased ability to see through a number of rather deceptive claims, and to define more sharply what I felt I could best offer to the new generations. The terms I am using are not ideal. Both "humanistic" and "person-

cnetered" fail in many ways to convey all that I wish to state. The humanistic label can cover a broad spectrum of activities and beliefs; and, as I have explained in many places, it was selected in 1969 to indicate a stand which somewhat paralleled that of the humanistic psychologist. It essentially indicates an alternative to the superficial game of fortune-telling, and to the serious business of statistical research and quantitative devices for chart-interpretation.

The term "person-centered" is used to show the basic difference between my approach and the collectivistic geocentrism of a zodiac-based astrology. My approach is oriented to the possibility of developing in every person a steady eagerness for self-transformation and independence from the sociocultural patterns of the past. On the belief that there is latent in every man and woman the power to be greater than they are, more creative, freer, yet more deeply committed to a process of world-transformation, I stand. I hope to awaken the sleeping god in every person. By sounding the true "name" of an individual one may arouse to life the divine in him. Every person is a "celestial," if only he gains the strength and has the courage to stand by the truth of his being and to fulfill his place and function on this earth by following the celestial "set of instructions" revealed by the sky.

A PARTIAL LIST OF BOOKS BY DANE RUDHYAR

THE ASTROLOGY OF PERSONALITY
THE PULSE OF LIFE
THE LUNATION CYCLE
THE PRACTICE OF ASTROLOGY
PERSON—CENTERED ASTROLOGY
MY STAND ON ASTROLOGY
AN ASTROLOGICAL MANDALA

A complete booklist (with publishers and prices) may be obtained by writing to:
Tana Rudhyar..p.o. box 636..san jacinto..california..92383
or when in palo alto, california visit The Seed Center on university avenue, where some of Rudhyar's paintings are on display and all of his books are available.

TWO HEXAGRAMS from THE I CHING or THE BOOK OF CHANGES

The Richard Wilhelm Translation

T'AI / PEACE

The Receptive, which moves downward, stands above; the Creative, which moves upward, is below. Hence their influences meet and are in harmony, so that all living things bloom and prosper. This hexagram belongs to the first month (February-March), at which time the forces of nature prepare the new Spring. *THE JUDGMENT: PEACE. The small departs, The great approaches. Good fortune. Success.* This hexagram denotes a time in nature when heaven seems to be on earth. Heaven has placed itself beneath the earth, and so their powers unite in deep harmony. Then peace and blessing descend upon all living things. In the world of man it is a time of social harmony; those in high places show favor to the lowly, and the lowly and inferior in their turn are well disposed toward the highly placed. There is an end to all feuds. Inside, at the center, in the key position, is the light principle; the dark principle is outside. Thus the light has a powerful influence, while the dark is submissive. In this way each receives its due. When the good elements of society occupy a central position and are in control, the evil elements come under their influence and change for the better. When the spirit of heaven rules in man, his animal nature also comes under its influence and takes its appropriate place. The individual lines enter the hexagram from below and leave it again at the top. Here the small, weak, and evil elements are about to take their departure, while the great, strong, and good elements are moving up. This brings good fortune and success. *THE IMAGE: Heaven and earth unite: the image of PEACE. Thus the ruler Divides and completes the course of heaven and earth; He furthers and regulates the gifts of heaven and earth, And so aids the people.* Heaven and earth are in contact and combine their influences, producing a time of universal flowering and prosperity. This stream of energy must be regulated by the ruler of men. It is done by a process of division. Thus men divide the uniform flow of time into the seasons, according to the succession of natural phenomena, and mark off infinite space by the points of the compass. In this way nature in its overwhelming profusion of phenomena is bounded and controlled. On the other hand, nature must be furthered in her productiveness. This is done by adjusting the products of the right time and the right place, which increases the natural yield. This controlling and furthering activity of man in his relation to nature is the work on nature that rewards him.

HENG / DURATION

The strong trigram Chen is above, the weak trigram Sun below. This hexagram is the inverse of the preceeding one. In the latter we have influence, here we have union as an enduring condition. The two images are thunder and wind, which are likewise constantly paired phenomena. The lower trigram indicates gentleness within; the upper, movement without. In the sphere of social relationships, the hexagram represents the institution of marriage as the enduring union of the sexes. During courtship the young man subordinates himself to the girl, but in the marriage, which is represented by the coming together of the eldest son and the eldest daughter, the husband is the directing and moving force outside, while the wife, inside, is gentle and submissive. *THE JUDGMENT: DURATION. Success. No blame. Perseverance furthers. It furthers one to have somewhere to go.* Duration is a state whose movement is not worn down by hindrances. It is not a state of rest, for mere standstill is regression. Duration is rather the self-contained and therefore self-renewing movement of an organized, firmly integrated whole, taking place in accordance with immutable laws and beginning anew at every ending. The end is reached by an inward movement, by inhalation, systole, contraction, and this movement turns into a new beginning, in which the movement is directed outward, in exhalation, diastole, expansion. Heavenly bodies exemplify duration. They move in their fixed orbits, and because of this their light-giving power endures. The seasons of the year follow a fixed law of change and transformation, hence can produce effects that endure. So likewise the dedicated man embodies an enduring meaning which gives things their duration, we can come to understand the nature of all beings in heaven and on earth. *THE IMAGE: Thunder and wind: the image of DURATION. Thus the superior man stands firm And does not change his direction.* Thunder rolls, and the wind blows; both are examples of extreme mobility and so are seemingly the very opposite of duration, but the laws governing their appearance and subsidence, their coming and going, endure. In the same way the independence of the superior man is not based on rigidity and immobility of character. He always keeps abreast of the time and changes with it. What endures is the unswerving directive, the inner law of his being, which determines all his actions.

NOTES TOWARD AN INTEGRATIVE PSYCHOLOGY

by C. Singh Wallia, Ph.D.

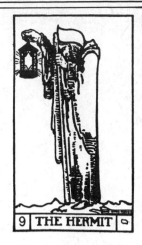

Human-Potential psychology today stands in sharp contrast to Behavior psychology and to Freudian psychology, both of which are rooted in a mechanistic-deterministic model of science. Human-Potential psychology asserts that this mechanomorphic model, though useful in the physical sciences, is not applicable to human beings. Guided by this model, Behavior psychology holds the image of man as a stimulus-response mechanism, while Freudian psychology regards man as driven by his instincts. But between these external pulls and internal pushes, what becomes of the person? He is diminished to a nihil. Human-Potential psychology opposes these mechanomorphic views of man's Being.

Human-Potential psychology views man as phylogenetically unique for he has the unique capacity to become aware of his self-awareness; this capacity enables him to transcend the determinate situation of his spatio-temporal specificity. Because of man's unique self-awareness the experimental results and observations of mechanomorphic psychology which generalize from animals to man can be held valid only on the physiological—not psychological—level. Further, Human-Potential psychology suggests that a person can be understood only as a unique whole. Fragmentary explanations in terms of stimulus-response schema alone, or with Freudian abstractions such as instinctual drives and unconscious needs, give a truncated, distorted image of man. Human-Potential psychology attempts to understand man's experience and to make salient the potentialities in his choices of experience; mechanomorphic psychology attempts to explain man's behavior and to make salient the possibilities of predicting and controlling his behavior.

Human-Potential psychology views man as directing his actions toward goals he selects to actualize his potentialities, as seeking to find meaning in his existence by relating affectively with others, by creating symbols of art, and by opening himself to transhuman, cosmic experiences. Its image of man is derived from existential philosophy in Western thought and from Upanishadic philosophy in Eastern thought.

On the existential-phenomenological view, the Cartesian dichotomy of subject (mind, consciousness) and object (body, environment) is false. Consciousness is never separate from its object; it is always a "consciousness-of." Man, too, is never separate from others; he is always a "Being-in-the-World." Man is the Being-in-the-World who separates and at the same time unites subject and object. His essence is becoming, or actualizing his potentialities in the world. He is always oriented toward the future; the particular orientation he chooses determines how he will structure his present and will reconstruct even his past. The emphasis, here, is on the self-aware person making choices, in contrast to the mechanomorphic view that the past determines the future—for example, in the alibi, "Not I but my unconscious did it." Authentic choices attempt to resolve the dialectic polarity between the limitations imposed by the finite, concrete situation (facticity) and the fulfillment of potentialities (transcendence).

On the Upanishadic view, the fourth state of consciousness, the *Turiya,* is pure consciousness where knowledge is intuitive.

The *Turiya*—which includes the other three states of consciousness of waking, dreaming, and dreamless sleep—is eternal and beyond dualities. Unlike perceptual and inferential knowledge, it is not as directly communicable to others. The *Turiya* reveals that the Self of man, the *Atman,* is identical with the universal Self, the *Brahman*—"this Self of man is Brahman" *(Ayam Atman Brahman).* The *Turiya* can be attained through choosing to practice disciplined meditation *(Sadhana).* The emphasis in the Upanishads, as in later Hindu thought, is on the individual person choosing to develop his Self-Realization; the doctrine of Karma emphasizes individual responsibility.

The act of choosing between authentic existence *(Vidya)* and inauthentic existence *(Avidya)* is emphasized in both existential and Upanishadic philosophies. Their image of man gives him the freedom to choose authenticity and concomitantly imposes the responsibility to actualize his potentialities.

This vision of man has been embodied in many works of creative literature at least as forcefully as in more abstract philosophical works. The precursors of contemporary existential philosophy and psychology such as Kierkegaard, Dostoyevsky and Nietzche, whose work was done against the background of a world increasingly dominated by mechanomorphic concepts, were as much creative artists as they were moral philosophers and social psychologists. An integrative approach to the study of Human-Potential psychology should stress the works of these writers and others such as: Kafka, for whom literature was "like an ice-ax to break the sea frozen within us;" Rilke, who perceived art "as a penetration into the confidence of things;" Wallace Stevens, who saw in poetry the "unofficial view of being." (The official view of being, assigned by Stevens to philosophy, would, at least in America, be that of logical positivism and linguistic analysis, which consider questions about view of being to be simply meaningless and unsuitable for philosophical investigations.)

In conclusion, it is proposed that an integrative approach to Human-Potential psychology studies should stress existential philosophy, Eastern philosophy, modern literature, creative arts, humanistic psychology and experiential workshops.

Psychology at the hands of the mechanomorphs sequentially lost its soul, its will, its mind, its consciousness. It is time now to recover those losses and to reaffirm psychology as the science of the soul.

Dr. Wallia is the founder and director of The Institute of Human-Potential Psychology in Palo Alto, California.

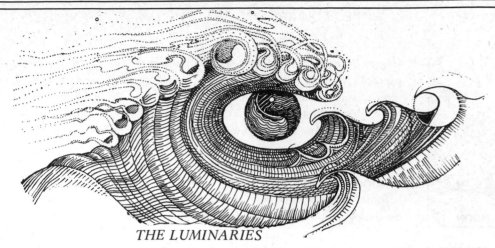

THE LUMINARIES

☉ SUN: The Source of Life: spirit, the conscious state or ego-center; source of power of the individual itself; individuality.

☾ MOON: The Mechanism of Response: the maternal intercession that recycles and interprets the solar power, the subconscious state; the channel to the Collective Unconscious.

THE TRADITIONAL PLANETS

☿ MERCURY: The Messenger: the conscious mind, the horizontal mind; perception, thought, and expression; communication.

♀ VENUS: The Goddess of Love and Beauty: the feminine part of the psyche; esthetics and the value system, harmonization; sympathy and the higher forms of love; attraction.

♂ MARS: The Warrior: the masculine part of the psyche: forcefulness and energy, stamina and the desire for self-expression; projection.

♃ JUPITER: The Prophet: the vertical mind; aspiration for growth and the capacity to assimilate; foresight; expansion of the consciousness into society.

♄ SATURN: The Lawgiver: the limitations and disciplines of the ego-structure; focalization of consciousness; restraint.

THE OUTER PLANETS

♅ URANUS: The Awakener: originality; revolt against the dogmas of older forms, with new-found inner awareness of the non-egoic state; the projections from the Unconscious; transformation.

♆ *NEPTUNE:* The Lord of the Sea: the wisdom that cannot be learned, vision, the transverse mind; dissolution and repolarization toward the Collective; transcendence.

♇ PLUTO: The Lord of the Netherworld: determination; the regeneration that lies at the center of the Maelstrom of Chaos; birth=sex=death; resurrection.

The composition of the planetary glyphs:

○ The symbol of spirit; Will; the concept.

+ The symbol of soul; Wisdom; the method.

∪ The symbol of matter; Activity; the raw material.

FOR A CHILD IT'S ALL THE SAME

Sometimes we forget the holistic awareness we had as a child. Both the child psychologist Jean Piaget and the philosopher Dane Rudhyar say that holistic thought and cyclic awareness are an important part of a child's world. We think that the tendency to look empirically at the parts of existence is natural. We "adults" feel that relationships must be "cause and effect," that a linear view is more natural than a cyclic view. We should realize that it is not as much a matter of learning to look at wholes in time (cycles) and wholes in space as it is a matter of remembering our world as a child.

Rudhyar describes the infant's primary experience of consciousness coming from an awareness of two basic factors: "On the one hand he experiences the continuous flow of existential activity as if it were a tumultuous and haphazard sequence of unrelated events . . . On the other hand man becomes aware either *through or beyond* the existential tumult, of patterns of order and periodicity, of rhythmic processes and cyclic recurrences, thus of essential *order.*" (Rudhyar, *Planetarization of Consciousness,* p. 221). Not only is the young child aware of order and cycles, but he uses this awareness to learn.

The child has an ego-centric view of existence—that is he feels one with the "external world." His early imitation experiences can be thought of as an effort by the child to sustain an experience as a whole or to maintain a cycle. Piaget uses the term "circular reaction" to describe the early learning experiences where a child's random response is imitated by the parent in order to get the child to repeat the response. Since the child is not yet aware of himself as an individual, he is not learning by a process of copying an external model, but by participating in a larger whole, by reinforcing order. Piaget describes the child's reaction to the movement of a hand in front of his face. The child begins moving his head, when the hand stops moving the child continues to move his head as if to keep the movement going. (Piaget, *Play Dreams and Imitation in Childhood,* p. 21). For the child both the hand moving in front of the child and the appearance of the hand moving caused by the child moving his head are the same. The child does not identify one action as his own and the other action and being caused by an external force. Both actions have the same result; they are part of a larger whole.

Both the awareness of wholes and order and the awareness of parts and chaos are a part of man's experience. Both intuitive and empirical knowledge are valid and important to use. But our Western culture supported by its educational system emphasizes empirical knowledge and the logical function of language. The child is taught to respond to the chaos, but not to the order. He is taught that language is for communication: to demonstrate facts. But Piaget points out that young children do not use language that way. The questions that the typical six year old asks do not involve causality; children's explanations are not causal. When thought is intuitive there is no need for proving a proposition. (Piaget, *The Language and Thought of the Child*).

The child knows through experiences of wholes. He has an intuitive understanding of the cycles of existence. For us to learn to respond to the cycles of life we must become as little children.

Joan Lewis

Astrology, psychology, Eastern Thought, Mandala-symbolism, and Cyclic Awareness are all manifestations of a Single Source of Energy. To understand any one symbol system, thoroughly, is to be in communication with the Spirit of all Cosmic Truth. To be One with the Spirit is to live. *"I believe a leaf of grass to be no less than the journey-work of the stars."*—Walt Whitman.

While reading these interpretations of the twelve Signs of the Zodiac, the Luminaries, and the Planets it is good to be reminded of the greater WHOLE, as expressed by the great Paracelsus: *Constellations are subordinate to the wise man; they have to follow him, not vice versa. Only a man still on the animalistic level is ruled by the planets, just as a thief cannot escape the gallows, a murderer cannot escape hanging, a fisher cannot escape the fishes, a hunter cannot escape the animals. But this stems from the fact that such a man does not know himself, and does not know how to use the forces that lie within him. Justly he must be regarded as unwise and be in bondage to all earthly mortal factors. The key, as always, lies within.*

THE ZODIAC

	Sign	Element	Mode	Principle	Quality	Keyword
♈	ARIES	Fire	Cardinal	Action	Initiative	I am
♉	TAURUS	Earth	Fixed	Reaction	Appreciation	I have
♊	GEMINI	Air	Mutable	Interaction	Awareness	I think
♋	CANCER	Water	Cardinal	Containment	Reserve	I feel
♌	LEO	Fire	Fixed	Individuation	Centeredness	I will
♍	VIRGO	Earth	Mutable	Differentiation	Analysis	I analyze
♎	LIBRA	Air	Cardinal	Equilibrium	Harmony	I balance
♏	SCORPIO	Water	Fixed	Regeneration	Penetration	I desire
♐	SAGITTARIUS	Fire	Mutable	Direction	Planning	I see
♑	CAPRICORN	Earth	Cardinal	Crystallization	Responsibility	I use
♒	AQUARIUS	Air	Fixed	Distribution	Universality	I know
♓	PISCES	Water	Mutable	Redemption	Synthesis	I believe

Descriptions of the signs based on the element and mode followed by the seasonal cycle related to the signs:

♈ The spark, acting as electrical catalyst, creating life. The spring equinox, the day-force overcomes the night-force, emergence.

♉ The fertile soil, nourishing the seed of life within. The day-force becomes steadier and more persistent, stability.

♊ Exhalation, the moving winds of intelligence. The day-force is at its strongest, with its ever-shifting eagerness for new things.

♋ The fountainhead, the source. The summer solstice, the ingathering night-force increases in strength; focusing and responsibility.

♌ The glowing coal from which spirit emerged. The personal day-force still rules, but there is a desire for social recognition.

♍ The sands of eternity that lie at the edge of the primordial sea. Through technique and repolarization social responsibility is realized.

♎ Inhalation; objectification of experience, the breath itself. Fall equinox, the triumph of social co-operation over individual self-expression.

♏ The glacial ice that grinds matter down; the cycle itself. The night-force grows as the individual merges in absolute union with others.

♐ The leaping flame that aspires; inspiration and search. Collectivism overpowers individualism; new abstract, metaphysical mental horizons.

♑ The high granite peaks of the mountains. The winter solstice, the individual yields to completely organized social living.

♒ The held breath, space and spacial thought. Social man overcomes bondage to the conservative state, humanitarian reform.

♓ The mists of residue that lift from the primordial sea. The night-force breaks down under the weight of social crystallization.

DONUT
HOLES

JAMES
MOTLOW

Truckstop   1972

S & G Donut Hole   June, 1972

February 1973

Truckstop   December 1972

Coney Island Cafe   1972

December   1972

May 1972

July 1972

S & G Donut Hole   July 1972

Cornucopia

Laura Alpert

3. And when I awoke I lay in a soft quilted bed.
A pitcher of water and towels were placed by my head.
From somewhere soft music came gaily in thru the night.
By the window I gazed, and felt the soft breeze,
And watched Cornucopia's lights.

4. Across the hallway my partner was still sleepin' sound.
He too had been cared for, all of his wounds had been bound.
He opened his eyes and spoke of the quiet he knew;
Then we slept thru the night, and at morning's light,
Stepped in Cornucopia's dew. (Chorus)

5. As we walked through the streets we saw not man, not a horse.
The houses were empty though sometimes we did hear a voice.
Then just about noontime a rider came into the place;
We told how we strayed, and how we were saved,
Then we saw fear in his face.

6. The rider stepped down and he told us of prosperous days:
"Cornucopia's mines were the richest of all some folks say.
But with greed came disaster and the miners were buried
    in the sand.
And since those days, no one has stayed,
No one's lived in this part of the land." (Chorus)

Columbia

flowing

Laura Alpert

With plumes on the peaks Canadian Rockies stand bleak, vast
(Now a) man wrote a song a-bout the Grand Coulee Dam, and the
(From the) green forest shores thru the dry—barren hills, Co—

glaciers crack cold in the day. Then the summer winds come and the
power it gives to our land. But Co-lum-bi-a's roll gives a
lum-bia—roll by my home. From the tower-ing falls to lake

wild waters run to the o-cean, a life-time a-way.
power to—soul much greater than trapped by our hands.
Roose-velts shore, Co—lum-bi-a—roll where I roam.

Refrain

From the bright city lights to the cool des-ert nights— Co-

lum-bi-a flows— where I roam.— And no mat-ter how

far I may fol-low this star,— Co-lum-bi-a's land is my

home.— Now a / From the

star, Co—lum-bi-a's land is my home—

173

Mother of Trees

lively   john green

1. Well she's my — on·ly dia·mond sparkling in the light, she'll
2. (Well she) teases my head with a stream of tales, she'll

calm me down or work me up to — fight. I see her in the forest at the
Tell me who's hap·py and who's in jail. She'll grow her — plants — and

fall of — day — standing in the river read·y to play. She's the
keep them green. Read — in the paper where she's just been seen. She's the

1.3.
Mother of Trees — Sis·ter to the Breeze. Well she
Mother of Trees — Sister to the Breeze. Men are

2.4.
breeze — Well I — feel her a·round me now, working out the knots. I feel

bet·ter now than I — have in months. Good sister — good

mother — good daughter — good lover. — Good sister — good

mother — good daughter — good lover. — 3. Well, I

3. Well, I see her in the garden
With a fistful of weeds.
Walking on the hillside
With an apron full of seeds.
You won't catch her in town
On a warm spring day,
By the time you're out of work
She'll be miles away.
She's the mother of trees
Sister to the breeze.

4. Men are wild without her
They don't know what to do.
They raise up armies
And they wear out shoes.
But once they've seen her
They'll throw down their guns.
She'll watch the change
And she'll show them the sun.
She's the mother of trees
Sister to the breeze.   (chorus)

174

3. Well the turkey got up off the platter
   And he trotted out the door.
   He gobbled back over his shoulder
   He said,' I've been through this movie before.
   You eat like a machine....'

4. So I chased down the turkey
   As he got into his cadillac.
   I said, 'We've been waiting for this meal a long time
   I'm goin' to have to bring you back.
   I'm so hungry I could die....'

5. Well the turkey rolled down the window
   As he put on his hat.
   He said,' Buddy try me next year
   When I've gained back all my fat.
   You eat like a machine....'

6. So I trudged back in the kitchen
   And Mabel pulled out her stash.
   We smoked some Gunga Din
   And we ate some corn beef hash.
   I'm so hungry I could die....

Frog Song

Peter Music

1. Frog woke up and he called his friends: "you're all missin' what the
2. Frog lay down and he closed his eyes, an'he filled his heart full of

mornin'— sends! The dawn is a-breakin' through the fat oak tree and— if
lonely— sighs; The wind started blowin' all his fears a-part —— The

you ain't a-look-in' you won't ev-er— see— so get out of bed and come an'
sun started shin-in' love in-side of his heart; an angel came and ordered him a

sit here with me — we'll laugh and talk and croak and hop 'till quarter to three."
dream a-la-carte — and all at once he woke up feeling clev-er and smart—(so)

Frog wondered what that he might think a-bout and Then he saw his friend, Mister
Frog hopped back to his grassy— home —— hap-py just to know he wasn't

Rain-bow Trout. "Well, how are you this mornin', it's a beauti-ful day— my whole
so a-lone. A cricket laughed and turning to the for-est said, ——"Trees, i'm

family's still a-sleep and i sure hope you can stay; would you like to play some chess or maybe
Tel-ling you I think that frog is out-of-his-head!"— His family missed it all 'cuz they were

Turtle croquet—?" "Sorry no, i've got to go, i've no time to play——!"
still— in bed-and poor old frog, he wondered if they might not be dead——!

why do all pass by me? Is my skin too slim-y?

well,

176

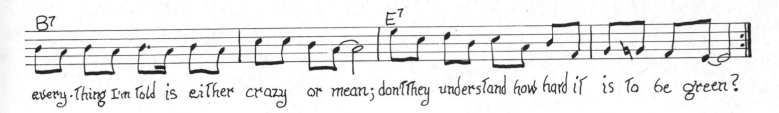

every-thing I'm told is either crazy or mean; don't They understand how hard it is to be green?

Down in the swamp next to New Orleans
There's a frog who's wonderin' what reality means;
Anyone who thinks that he might understand,
The questions that a frog might ask or even a man,
Just introduce yourself to anyone in the band,
We'd all like to tell that frog so he'll understand.

Why do all pass me by?
Is my skin too slimy?
Everything I'm told is either crazy or cruel,
Don't they understand I'm nowhere near such a fool.

Don't You Know That Jesus Loves You

Jacques Derge

Folky not polky

Don't you know That Jes-us loves you more Than — The Grateful Dead do

and They said it Them-selves it's True. Fill your soul with The

love of Jes-us, let your music sing his praises ———

and The glory of God will be with you. you can be

dead in Christ grateful-ly ——— 'cuz he gives you back your life for

all e-Ter-ni-Ty ——— Don't you Know That Jes-us loves you more Than The

Grateful Dead do ———

1. My love's a-cross yonder mountain range, I grow to miss him more every day. I have tried and I've tried to send him word, he just lives too far a-way. — I've got a bird that whistles, a-nother little bird that sings, but I ain't got a bird can cross those mountains on a pair— of i-ron wings.

2. Ain't no phones across yonder mountain range, so I can't make a long dis-tance
3. The sea breaks out-side ———— his kitchen door where his sup-per's a-cook by an
4. If you see my family and they ask after me ———— Tell 'em I'm runnin' with my

call. And they don't know a stamp from a pocket bible- be-yond that piney wall. I've got a

eff; and the sea quail totter and the sea biscuit sing, tho I swear I've never seen it my-self. I've got a

love; I can't go on like this, it's too gooda thing to miss, I have found me the wings of a dove. I've got a

Handsome

down-home lonesome

Lia Holdorf

1. (I) Hand-some you're a lot of fun you make my nights so gay. But
2. got this way by thinkin'— that I was much too good to

handsome I don't think you're the one 'cause you're al-ways goin' a—way.
set-tle down and have-a home in a qui-et neigh-bor—hood, and from

1. It ain't very sensi-ble to live the way I do,
2. thinkin' I's too smart to be a wife. Now

1. half the time I'm jumpin' for joy and half I'm craz-y blue.
2. every bit of peace I get, I steal from a-nother gal's life.

The life of a honky tonk girl should never be ad-mired; Saturday night you're sweet sixteen but
So handsome put your clothes back on and get out of my sight. I don't think I care to hear a-

Sun-day mornin' you're much too tired to go to church the way you ought to do, when you
nother dirt-y joke to-night, and when you tell your children how to be, tell them

1. got a feel-in' it ain't no help for you. I
2. to for-get a-bout being free.

179

Northern Girls

3. Now I had no choice, to enjoy myself,
   But to guzzle down more blockade.
   And Jack he felt the very same way,
   But he was late comin' to my aid,
   Well, late comin' to my aid.

4. There's three sober ones, and then there's me.
   And I long to drive that Ford.
   But its hair-pin turns and boulders and mud
   And I drive down on the floorboards
   Yeah I drive that awful floorboard. (Chorus)

5. Pretty soon everybody's mad and scared
   Doing 95 on a flat tire.
   Those girls were black and blue from bangin'
   Their bodies against the doors
   Yeah, their bodies against the doors.

6. We're runnin' down chickens and dogs and geese
   And there's hub caps flyin' in the air.
   Jack he's shakin', the girls are cryin'
   But I have not a care
   No, I have not a care. (Chorus)

7. At last we piled into the dirt
   And I made a happy face,
   But Jack and the girls they hailed a car
   To take them to a safer place
   Yeah, to take them to a safer place.

8. When later I was questioned why
   I gave those girls such a shock,
   I said, "They just hawked hell outa me
   With their everlasting talk
   Yeah their everlasting talk." (Chorus)

Rut___love

emphatically

dave smith

Call on that man when you —— see him fall. Fall on that
Call on that hand when it's —— just a bluff. Say that the
Call on that man when he's —— in a rut. If he don't

man —— when he's down.
way —— home is rough.
Jump it he'll drag you in.

If he don't regret it don't let him for-
If he don't admit it you can't let him
You can't sac-ri-fice that so just put on your

get it. —— He's got a lot to do —— a —— lone.
Quit it. —— Hold him down un-til he —— gets back up.
high hat. —— Tell him if he loses —— he won't win.

refrain

'Cause he might go through the same old things a-gain—— and

That old ditch with-out an end, you know it ain't no place for woman or man a-

men

181

See America First

2. So Harry borrowed money to take his family;
He said he'd meet the payments every time.
He bought a motor-coach just jammed with luxuries,
And just a little trailer for behind.
Then he went to packin' with rover and the kids,
And there wasn't many things they didn't load.
They took a little beer like the folks on T.V. did,
Then Harry wife and family hit the road. (Chorus)

3. They had a little trouble, a little past Des Moines;
They paid the fella' twenty for the tow.
Oh breakfast, lunch, and supper they was eatin' up the coins
And Harry got to feelin' kinda low.
They hit a cow in Kansas, bumped a Chevy near Pikes Peak.
They blew an alternator in Salt Lake.
In Reno there was boozin' and a little losin' streak.
And San Francisco Bay looked like a lake. (Chorus)

4. *Oh then they headed northward along the ocean coast*
   And back across the mountains and the plains.
   They went down to see the geyers and a bear or two at most,
   And every other night it seemed to rain.
   Home was looking better than it ever had before,
   And even good old Rover missed the lawn.
   The kids were never quiet, spillin' milkshakes on the floor
   And Harry wished to christ he'd never gone.   (Chorus)

5. *They finally hit Chicago and began to feel at home,*
   The traffic on the freeways wasn't bad.
   They had a trailer full as proof that they had roamed
   Even though they owed on all they had.
   Then finally to the driveway of their little home they pulled
   And they told the neighborhood about their thrills.
   They all went back to work, their lives were once more filled
   Of nine to five and football games and bills. (Chorus)

MICHAEL S. MOORE: FIVE AUTO BIOGRAPHIES, 1968-1973

"GOOD HOUSEKEEPING IN AMERICA, THE SECOND WORLD WAR": SPRING 1968 - SUMMER 1971
1956 DODGE FORMER TELEPHONE TRUCK PURCHASED THROUGH WEIRD NEGOTIATIONS
WITH BREEZE IN SAN RAFAEL IN LATE SPRING 1968. NEEDED GAS TANK IMMEDIA-
TELY, ENGINE SOON AFTER AND MANY EXTRAS. STND TRANS (THREE ON
THE TREE) 15" WHEELS, CAMPER ON REDWOOD FLATBED OF TRANCAS WAS-
TEWOOD, FLATHEAD SIX LAMELY LABORED TO NEW HAVEN WHERE IT
DIED A MARTYR'S DEATH WHEN TOWED + STORED UNDERWATER, BRIEFLY
REVIVED BY VALVE JOB SPRING 1969 BUT SOON PERISHED FOR GOOD.

REINCARNATION WAS SWIFT IF
NOT SURE BUT TOOK MONTHS
OF CARELESS WORK TO
ACCOMPLISH: REBUILT 273
DODGE V-8, 4 (COMPOUND)
ON THE FLOOR, STRANGE
DE CUSTOM BODY WORK
WHICH LASTED CROSS
COUNTRY WITH THE AAA
AND MANY BREAKDOWNS)
UP TO SEATTLE AND THEN
FINALLY THREW A ROD
NEAR PESCADERO WITH
JEANNE AND THE KIDS ON
OUR WAY BACK FROM A
FIRST TRIP TO BIG SUR
(AUTUMN 1969) BUT MADE IT
BACK TO MILL VALLEY WHERE
IT REMAINED AS STORAGE
SPACE UNTIL FINALLY JUNKED
SUMMER 1971 AFTER MANY PLOTS FOR RERESTORATION WENT UN
IMPLEMENTED THOUGH THE WASTEWOOD OF THE CAMPER WENT
FOR OTHER PROJECTS AND THE GREASY REDWOOD BEDPLANKS
BECAME A SOLID KITCHEN TABLE, WHICH GREASILLY SURVIVES
TO THIS DAY, THOUGH ITS DAYS MAY NOW BE NUMBERED....

"OIL SALAD"; OCT 1969 - MAY 1971

1956 FORD V-8 4 DOOR WAGON FOUND SEMI ABANDONED AT BREEZE'S DUE TO COOLING PROBLEMS, TEST-DRIVEN TO LA AND BACK AND PURCHASED FALL 1969 // MANY TRANSMISSIONS LATER, THREE ON THE FLOOR ADAPTED; REAR RISERS A CHRISTMAS GIFT FROM BREEZE 1969. CAR WENT TO PYRAMID LAKE (SPRING 1970) ESSENTIALLY LIKE THIS, PERFORMED ADMIRABLY, AND WAS RECAMOUFLAGED DURING THE RETURN, THE FIRST OF MANY RECAMOUFLAGINGS, AND LATER ON IN THE SUMMER A NICE BIG HOLE WAS TORCHED (THEREAFTER NEVER ADEQUATELY CLOSED FROM THE WEATHER) IN THE ROOF. THE SEATS WENT QUITE EARLY FIRST REPLACED BY A PAIR OF ARMCHAIRS, THEN A BENCH TIED TO THE DOOR POSTS AND FINALLY A FREESTANDING BENCH TYPE CA. SPRING '70 (PERHAPS FOR THE P.L. TRIP)... LATER A PERMANENT RACK WENT AROUND THE HOLE WITH A BLUE PLEXI HATCH THAT GAVE NICE LIGHT BUT ALWAYS LEAKED. TOWARDS THE END THE STEERING BECAME QUITE BIZARRE AND THIS FACT WAS FINALLY APPREHENDED, NEAR MORRO BAY TRAVELLING SOUTH WITH PULSA TO LA IN MAY (OR MARCH) 1971 AFTER A SEAFOOD DINNER, AT A CHP

SAFETY CHECK. COST OF REPAIRS WAS PROHIBITIVE, SO A COMPROMISE SOLUTION WAS ARRIVED AT, INVOLVING, AT THE END OF ITS ROAD, JAKE TURRINI'S MASHER, RESULTS OF WHICH WERE FILMED, PHOTOGRAPHED, AND OTHERWISE ENGRAVED ON OUR BRAINS ONE SUNNY MARIN AFTERNOON WITH A PICNICLIKE ATMOS JUNK SPHERE.

OIL SALAD SQUISHED

THOUGH SQUISHED FLAT ON A WARM, MAY 'SATURDAY' AFTERNOON MAY SEEM AN IGNOMINIOUS FATE FOR THE FIRST CAR TO CROSS MENDOCINO PASS BARELY A YEAR BEFORE, WHICH IS ANOTHER WAY TO SAY 'SPRING 1970' ALL WAS NOT REALLY LOST NOR WAS IT SO IGNOMINIOUS AS IT MAY SEEM FOR PRECEDING JAKE TURRINI'S 'SATURDAY' SQUISH OF THE CAR WE ALL HAD COME TO KNOW SO WELL WERE SEVERAL GREASY WEEKS OF REINCARNATION WHEREIN THE INNARDS OF THE STATION WAGON (56 FORD V-8, 56 MERC TRANS, OVERLOAD SHOCKS, 12 VOLT ELECTRICALS, RADIO, TACHOMETER ETC.) WERE NOT ONLY DEPOSITED BUT INSTALLED IN A MORE OR LESS FUNCTIONAL CAPACITY AT APPALLING EXPENSE IN THE EMPTY SHELL OF A 1949 FORD PANEL TRUCK FROM ALBANY WHICH THEN WENT THROUGH A RAPID AND RADICAL SERIES OF PAINTED TRANSFORMATIONS BUT FEW ACTUAL MALFUNCTIONS (OTHER THAN VERY VERY LOW OIL PRESSURE) WHILE BREEZE'S CORVETTE POWERED 1949 STUDEBAKER PICKUP WAS ALSO READIED FOR THE ANNUAL PYRAMIDAL

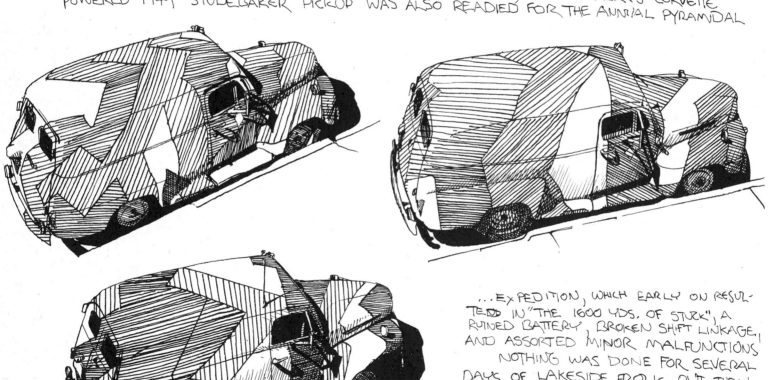

...EXPEDITION, WHICH EARLY ON RESUL-TED IN "THE 1600 YDS. OF STUCK", A RUINED BATTERY, BROKEN SHIFT LINKAGE, AND ASSORTED MINOR MALFUNCTIONS NOTHING WAS DONE FOR SEVERAL DAYS OF LAKESIDE FROLIC BUT THEN EVENTUALLY THEY ALL DID GET DONE (AND A REBUILD ON THE STARTER MOTOR IN - WHAT BETTER PLACE - SPARKS NEVADA AT - WHAT BETTER PLACE - ART'S "GARAGE".) AND BACK IN DOCT OR JOHN'S CAMOUFLAGED 1954 DESOTO (THE "DODO") WITH A CASE OF BEER AND ALL RAN WELL ALL THE WAY HOME (WITH OCCASSIONAL HESITATION SUBSEQUENTLY 'TEMPORARILY' TRACED TO A FOULED ROTOR) SAVE FOR A FLAT TIRE BETWEEN DAVIS AND VACAVILLE. BREEZE'S STUDEBAKER DIDN'T FARE QUITE SO WELL - BLEW THE REAR OIL SEAL IN RENO, FLOODING THE FLOOR OF THE CAB, BUT HE MADE IT HOME TO FINALLY LOSE THE REAR END IN HIS MILL VALLEY DRIVEWAY, WHERE THEN THE TRUCK REMAINED FOR ABOUT A YEAR. THIS ONE THOUGH KEPT RUNNIG, ER, RUNNING, AND ADVENTURES/DISASTERS WITH IT WERE FAR, FAR FROM OVER...EVEN WITHOUT MORE OF A NAME THAN "FROD" IN RAISED LETTERS UNDER LAYER OF PAINT

"FROD" (SPRING 1971 - JAN 1972) AND
"YOTA" AT PYRAMID LAKE, JUNE 71

THE 1971 PYRAMIDAL JAUNT, FOR ALL ITS MISHAPS, PROVED TO BE THE HIGH POINT IN THE TRUCK'S CAREER AS WELL AS A BENIGN INFLUENCE ON THE ART, SO AS THE ENGINE GREW PROGRESSIVELY LOUDER THOUGH LESS POWERFUL THE CHANGE WAS PERHAPS MORE EASILY IGNORED DUE TO THE RELATIVELY EXCITING INCEPTION OF THE PYRAMID LAKE DRAWINGS AND THEIR SUBSEQUENT REALISATION AS A SUITE OF SCREENPRINTS CALLED "PYRAMID LAKE 1971." WITH NEW IGNITION WIRING AND REBUILT DISTRIBUTOR THE TRUCK RAN ~~THREW~~ THROUGH THE SUMMER BUT WITH WORSEN ING CLUTCH. REPLACING THE CARBURETOR AND MUFFLER DIDN'T HELP THAT PROBLEM ~~~~ SO FINALLY IN JANUARY CLAIRE AND I SET OUT TO PULL A QUICK CLUTCH EXCHANGE, BUT ALONG THE WAY MY RADICAL TOOTH-KARMA GOT IN THE WAY OR RATHER MY TOOTH GOT IN THE WAY OF THE SPLINE ALIGN, THOUGH AFTER TIME OUT FOR AN EMERGENCY ROOT CANAL WE NONE THELESS GOT THE NEW CLUTCH & THROWOUT BEARING IN ONLY TO IN PRACTICE DISCOVER THAT THE HORRIBLE SHIMMY WAS STILL THERE: GLAZED FLYWHEEL; A BUMMER TO BE PUT OFF TILL A MORE LUCRATIVE LATER, LATER; RIDING EASY ON THE (NEW)

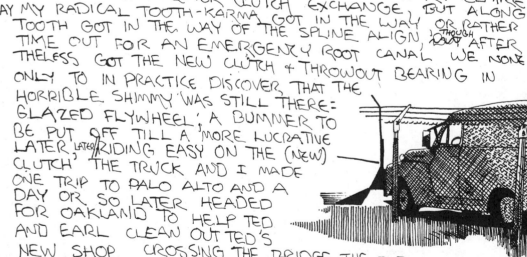

CLUTCH THE TRUCK AND I MADE ONE TRIP TO PALO ALTO AND A DAY OR SO LATER HEADED FOR OAKLAND TO HELP TED AND EARL CLEAN OUT TED'S NEW SHOP. CROSSING THE BRIDGE THE OLD ENGINE STARTED TO KNOCK **REAL** BAD; IT THREW THE ROD COMING OFF THE SECOND SPAN AND SEIZED UP JUST PAST THE TOLL BOOTHS, BUT WE COASTED INTO A CLUMP OF BUSHES AND TED CAME OUT WITH EARL AND TOWED ME TO THE SHOPYARD, WHERE WE LEFT THE TRUCK (NEVER EVEN BROKE DOWN THE ENGINE TO SEE WHAT HAD HAPPENED.) TILL SOMEONE I NEVER SAW BOUGHT IT AND TOWED IT OFF IN OCTOBER 1972. I GUESS ALL THOSE YEARS WITH ONLY FIVE POUNDS OF OIL PRESSURE FINALLY GOT TO THAT OLD V-8 FORD, BUT IT WAS A BAD ONE WHILE IT LASTED.

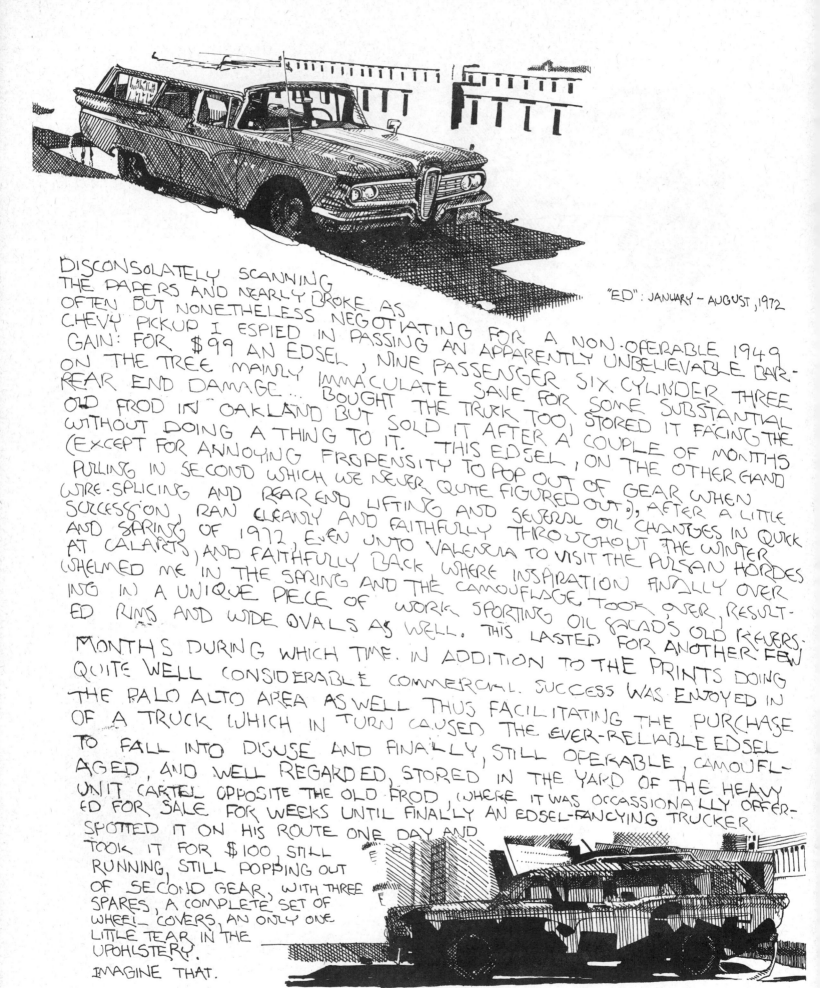

"ED": JANUARY - AUGUST, 1972

DISCONSOLATELY SCANNING THE PAPERS AND NEARLY BROKE AS OFTEN BUT NONETHELESS NEGOTIATING FOR A NON-OPERABLE 1949 CHEVY PICKUP I ESPIED IN PASSING AN APPARENTLY UNBELIEVABLE BAR- GAIN: FOR $99 AN EDSEL, NINE PASSENGER SIX CYLINDER THREE ON THE TREE, MAINLY IMMACULATE SAVE FOR SOME SUBSTANTIAL REAR END DAMAGE... BOUGHT THE TRUCK TOO, STORED IT FACING THE OLD FROD IN OAKLAND BUT SOLD IT AFTER A COUPLE OF MONTHS WITHOUT DOING A THING TO IT. THIS EDSEL, ON THE OTHER HAND (EXCEPT FOR ANNOYING PROPENSITY TO POP OUT OF GEAR WHEN PULLING IN SECOND WHICH WE NEVER QUITE FIGURED OUT), AFTER A LITTLE WIRE-SPLICING AND REAR END LIFTING AND SEVERAL OIL CHANGES IN QUICK SUCCESSION, RAN CLEANLY AND FAITHFULLY THROUGHOUT THE WINTER AND SPRING OF 1972, EVEN UNTO VALENCIA TO VISIT THE PULSAN HORDES AT CALARTS, AND FAITHFULLY BACK WHERE INSPIRATION FINALLY OVER- WHELMED ME IN THE SPRING AND THE CAMOUFLAGE TOOK OVER, RESULT- ING IN A UNIQUE PIECE OF WORK SPORTING OIL SALAD'S OLD REVERS- ED RIMS AND WIDE OVALS AS WELL. THIS LASTED FOR ANOTHER FEW MONTHS DURING WHICH TIME, IN ADDITION TO THE PRINTS DOING QUITE WELL CONSIDERABLE COMMERCIAL SUCCESS WAS ENJOYED IN THE PALO ALTO AREA AS WELL THUS FACILITATING THE PURCHASE OF A TRUCK WHICH IN TURN CAUSED THE EVER-RELIABLE EDSEL TO FALL INTO DISUSE AND FINALLY, STILL OPERABLE, CAMOUFL- AGED, AND WELL REGARDED, STORED IN THE YARD OF THE HEAVY UNIT CARTEL OPPOSITE THE OLD FROD (WHERE IT WAS OCCASSIONALLY OFFER- ED FOR SALE FOR WEEKS UNTIL FINALLY AN EDSEL-FANCYING TRUCKER SPOTTED IT ON HIS ROUTE ONE DAY AND TOOK IT FOR $100, STILL RUNNING, STILL POPPING OUT OF SECOND GEAR, WITH THREE SPARES, A COMPLETE SET OF WHEEL COVERS, AN ONLY ONE LITTLE TEAR IN THE UPOHLSTERY.

IMAGINE THAT.

ED CAMOUFLAGED ON CARL STREET, EARLY SUMMER.

1960 CHEVROLET ½ TON PICKUP 6 CYLINDERS, FOUR GEARS (COMPOUND LOW) PURCHASED FROM A CONFESSED BUT ALLEGEDLY REFORMED CAR THIEF LIVING IN A MISSION STREET HOTEL, JUST IN FROM ARIZONA. AND THE BRAKES WENT OUT. TRUCK HAD ARIZONA PLATES TOO AND I WORRIED ALL THE WAY TO DMV IN CORTE MADERA IN THE EDSEL, WAS FURIOUS ALL THE WAY BACK FOR HAVING FORGOTTEN THE REGISTRATION, ATE LUNCH, DROVE BACK (IN THE EDSEL) TO EXCHANGE THE PLATES AND GET THE PAPERWORK STARTED. MEANWHILE LENNY FIXED THE BRAKES AND THE FOLLOWING WEEK SAVED THE REAR END AS WELL IN THE COURSE OF A THOROUGH CHECK-OUT. TRUCK WEIGHED IN HEAVY FOR ITS SIZE (4080) SO MORE REG MONIES WERE REQUIRED. I REPLACED THE TWO WORST TIRES WITH 7:00-16 MUD AND SNOW TIRES, REPLACED THE ANTI-SWAY BAR, AND WITH TED'S HELP BUILT THE GREEN BOX, AND PAINTED IT GREEN. WITH BREEZE'S HELP MOUNTED AM-FM RADIO FROM HIS OLD STUDEBAKER, ANTENNA, AND REPAIRED EXISTING BUT PREVIOUSLY DISFUNCTIONAL SPOTLIGHT. MOUNTED GATES' 'COMMANDOS' ON 15" FRONT RIMS, REPLACED FRONT SHOCKS AND TOOK OFF FOR THE DESERT IN JUNE, 1972 WITH THE DOCTOR AND HIS LADY. A WEEK LATER, IN ALTURAS, I'D LEARNED MY LESSON ABOUT BOTH SIDEMOUNTED JERRY CANS (WHICH CAUGHT ON ROCKS IN THE CAÑONES, CAVING IN FENDERS AND EACH OTHER) AND THE SMALL FRONT WHEELS (WHICH CAUSED THE NOT NECESSARILY SOFT BUT NONETHELESS VULNERABLE UNDERBELLY A LOT OF UNNECESSARY CONTACT WITH BOTH GRANITIC AND BASALTIC OUTCROPS). SO THE LITTLE WHEELS AND TIRES WERE TRADED OFF FOR A PAIR OF 7:50×16 8 PLY MONSTER GROBBERS, CHIPPED AND BROKEN TORSION BAR ANCHORS WERE REPLACED, LOST HELPER SPRINGS WERE ALSO REPLACED, AND, THIS TIME WITH BROTHER BRYAN, I HEADED OUT AGAIN. BUT NOT FOR LONG: FIVE HOURS NE OF ALTURAS I STRIPPED THE REAR AXLE GEARS TRYING TO CLIMB HART MOUNTAIN IN THE TRUCK ON A ROAD NOT MEANT FOR IT. AFTER A LAST STOP IN ALTURAS, HOWEVER MANY RELATIVELY TROUBLE FREE MILES HAVE PASSED AS WELL AS AN APPALLING AMOUNT OF GAS. "AFLAME ON INTERSTE 80E" FOR INSTANCE, WAS AMUSING, BUT I STILL HAVE THE TRUCK, STILL RUNNING, SO

"CACTUS PATCH SOUP": MAY 1972 —

189

PARANOID BUT NOT NECESSARILY STONED BART ANDITZ AGAIN ELUDES THE DIVINE INERT
PART 3

Friday 19 Jan 1973
eat crap ex buy crack ers soup matches
centralize open plasticover downstairs herbroom
move fish up   open window
hangdoor
three packs truck   gas
leave

Pyramid Lake
Over Donner no chaining four hours
to Sparks and ice, the new paved
road beyond Sutcliffe to Warrior
Point a surprise an ecologic neces-
sity I guess and great comfort in my
rush for the phone but all that erosion at the beach since last summer
makes one wonder. Not much snow,
just patches stuck under the bushes
down here like little scraps of paper
by the ceaseless wind. In truck en-
camped and coldly at interims through
the night stoned out stone cold by
black on silver moon in water end-
lessing into mind-warping light-
globules gobble chromium rivers
swallowed as they are followed into
matte black watervoid. Woke late to
sun light light pristine clear soon to
disappear, coffee frozen and the sky
shutting down North and West like
hollowed lead heading north for
Sand Pass past a rusted burntout
fourdoor Ford alone at the end of a
big beige valley by the railroad. On
beyond and down then in the Smoke
Creek Desert raising dirt back behind
but not so much as summer. Wet
alkalai mirrors muddy scudding
clouds across the basin to the rail-
way causeway running bent around
the southern edge to eventually Gerlach as does this northern road on
the high ground.

We weren't going to Winnemucca anyway
The Gerlach-Sulphur-Winnemucca
road's ruined and all the more so
since last night when one of the
local maniacs swam his four-wheel
drive shortbed through in doordeep
mud with fifty gallons of fuel for
the plane up here acting as fortui-
tous ballast, tearing up anything
still passible and closing down the
entire dubious route (except when
frozen) until it dries out some, like
in about six months. All while I was
freezing my knees down at Pyramid
Lake.

That's How We Taught Leonard to Swim
January rarity: clouds breaking up
and no fog save the hot springs
steaming away in their own pecu-
liarly self-sufficient mists out on
the barrens back of town edging
the great winterwet expanse of the
Black Rock Desert Alkalai extending east past Sulphur past halfway
to Winnemucca, northeast bumping
Desert Valley and turning crossing
the Winnemucca-To-The-Sea Highway, follows it nearly to Denio on
the northern border, while just east
of here it juts its seasonally muddy
finger north up on an obsidian-
strewn alluvium ending abruptly at
Soldier Meadow amongst a rash of
springs and obscure historic sites.

Just the other side of the rise raised
by the Granite Range's southern
tooth the Smoke Creek lopes off
around Pah-Rum Peak west and
south to Sand Pass, while due south
lies the partially irrigated San Emido
Desert with its stash of abandoned
art works, maybe, left by the Art
Bandits in June, 1971. Gerlach has
the railroad, two gas stations, and a
bunch of bars. There's a pretty good
Mexican restaurant attached to the
last bar on the left on the way out
to the springs, or at least there was
when I ate there in 1968 and since
Gerlach hasn't changed much since
I wouldn't be surprised to find it
still is, though stumbling over a
vaguely mysterious beernursing
stairdweller in the springs' winter
fogs was something of a surprise
some four years three months later.
Also the winter's water's cooler,
but so's the air as illustrated when
the mist broke briefly revealing
bunches inches from my nose of
bunch grass, iced. Right about then
Aileen and Mrs. Smith drive up in a
'60 Chev coupe with a flag decal,
styrofoam dice from the mirror and
exclamations of "Yuk, who cut the
cheese?" as the load of kids, inner-
tubes and lively shrieks hit the cold
air and warm oozebottomed pool
in quick succession, disappearing
shouting, reappearing shouting, disappearing all most surreal. "That's
how we taught Leonard to swim,
just ignored him and swam all
around him," says Aileen, breast-
deep in the steaming outdoor pool
but still into her cigarette looks sort
of like the girl I had dinner here
with in 1968.

You Filthy Bastard

The dressing room walls at Gerlach Hot Springs are covered by an epic poem beginningly entitled "The Western Trail" which degenerates many words and several walls later to "The Hobo's Road." I had intended to copy it all down but the task seemed altogether too epic so I hacked my way partway into a badly frozen grapefruit instead, then headed up Highway 81 towards the snow and Saturday after noon, having determined the crapper's poetry to be somewhat more concrete: "DO NOT SPIT ON WALLS DO NOT SPIT ON FLOOR YOU FILTHY BASTARD."

Leonard's Hot Springs

Highway 81: not really plowed past Poodle Mountain nor even down in Surprise Valley past small snow-sprinkled spreads and frighteningly hoglike men in hunter's caps, late-model pickups and bulky plaid jackets with guns, so still slushing through near dead Eagleville and a somewhat livelier Saturday Cedarville to County Road 17 and east to a desperate steaming shit in the middle of the dining room floor at Leonard's Hot Springs through a hole a few miles northeast of Middle Alkalai Lake at three p.m. The big swimming pool, abandoned with the bathhouse and the rest, held old snow and black menacing chunks of wood, but steam above a nearby ditch in turn led to warm hillside springs presently rerouted for cattle, irrigation. East of CO15B about halfway between CO 17 and CO15, another spring, but brutalized by tire tracks cat tracks and garbage, real ugly. 4:00 P.M. advanced upon Fort Bidwell for a slightly paranoid reconnaissance and just north of town (California's most northeasternmost) found a truly remarkable art work atop a snowy knoll with a road leading right up one side and down the other, a pile of huge abandoned logs burning fiercely unattended.

Curious Visions

Camped in last light back against the hills in sight of Leonard's by the springs and felt the power there. The north and western skies closed in as in the a.m. but now it was night and I slept after curious winter visions dangled slightly madly among the wetly persistently falling snow muffling coyotes east and southeast and hiding completely the few lights across the valley.

Painfully Clear

Sunday dawned painfully clear witn fog thickly quickly spreading out of the valley as I did the morning things and tracked untracked snow down CO17B along the northeast end of Middle Alkalai Lake until just midway where the causeway dumps 299 just before it comes unpaved at the border on its way to Vya (was this the road on which we disappeared into the desert in a red Ford in 1967?) although with snow pavement's end made no matter, tracing the maintenance truck's morning tracks in sweeping uphill curves to the ridge and pause to scan the expanse beyond without a clue as to whether 34 south was weathered beyond all passability until the Sheriff came along on his Sunday day run out Long Valley to assure me that 34 was under water a lot and pass on such climatoillogical curiousities as two days -34o preceding snow preceding rain and its consequent backcountry all time nemesis, The Mud, as well as making it tactfully but painfully clear that my left side chains were on inside out.

After a Slight Collision

After a thrilling sequence of high velocity skids in the fresh powder recrossing Duck Flat and a slight end on collision on the Poodle Mountain upgrade, rechaining was easy remembering the Sheriff's advice, though I kept losing my hat and therefore disguise underneath the truck but soon was safe over and down the treaching frozen mud of the canyon to clear pavement and the Smoke Creek Desert fogged in right down to its fresh-snowed socks with only one set of tracks coming off the Sand Pass road and ominous as shit.

Back to the Confusion and the Outdoor Baths of Moscow

While replacing the headlight lost in the crash at Gerlach's lone Texaco, learned of last night's washout twenty-five miles out on the Smoke Creek and was glad not to be blindly roaring towards it in the fog, so roared blindly down the pavement instead, the fog clearing, to reveal the justly named Limbo Range, Winnemucca Lake and lurking near the Truckee Delta, Nixon. One last cold campnight at the usual Pyramid Lake campsite and one last primus morning unfreezing the coffee as dawn broke somewhere above behind low silvery overcast bringing with it great inverted pyramids of dimensional light in the snowy canyons across the water as well as a psychology student on the last leg of some insomniac journey with his dog whose ultimate purpose may have been to inform of the outdoor baths of Moscow, vast and steaming in a winter partway round the world, which he duly did before I drove back to, as was said in Gerlach only Sunday, "The Confusion," San Francisco, where Willie, two and a half years late from Aspen, had been waiting since about the time I got to Pyramid Lake, Friday 19 Jan 1973.

Natural Wonders Transportation Co. announces: THE BALLOONERY

Transportation of the near future will be different from today's. People are going to get choosier about how they and their goods get around. It just won't do any more to propel yourself around the earth wasting energy and scattering trash. And the skies will be a lot friendlier when our space buggies stop belching out all that sludge. Travel in general has gotten a bad name lately because people have no other way to get around but by exploding gasoline, fouling the air and stealing energy from the earth. Nowadays the only way to get from California to Chicago is to creep into the belly of a big dead bird, sit back and be jellified with air, moisture, food, liquor, and darkness, while leaving behind 2,000 miles of dirty air.

These drawings are sketches of the first WORKINGMAN balloon. It is a heart-shaped hydrogen balloon, with a varnished canvas bag 55ft tall, 50ft long, and 30 feet across. The overall height is 87 feet. Its 3055 cubic yards of hydrogen provide about 6100 pounds lift. Durable steel cables of various widths encircle the gas bag and cradle the cabin. The heart shape of the balloon and cabin will allow for the positioning of the balloon with respect to the wind - this being accomplished by the use of a wind turbine, rotating around a central

shaft between the cabin and the bottom balloon box, and a set of large wind vanes on the other end of the turbine's axle (this assembly not drawn on sketches). By rotating these vanes the balloon can be positioned flat against the wind, on edge with it, or somewhere in between. While these vanes will provide some lateral direction in respect to the wind, most of the direction of the balloon will come through seeking out favorable winds.

The cabin holds three people, hangs securely in a cable

cradle, is 12 feet from top to bottom and from end to end, and eight feet across at its widest. Cables are buried in the lightweight wooden beams of the cabin, binding it together in barrel fashion. Shatterproof glass covers the structure and inside, woven leather strapping is used extensively for floors, bunks, platforms, and seats. Being substantially transparent, the cabin is meant to support, not enclose the passengers. Designed with four living spaces, and with adequate heating, cooking, and sleeping facilities, and an on-board supplemental hydrogen production system, the balloon will be capable of floating for weeks at a time without taking on supplies.

This first WORKINGMAN craft will be in the air (hopefully) by Spring of 1974 and will take three regional tours during the summer of 1974. They are:

A. Down California's central valley, from Mt. Shasta to the Tehachapis (June)

B. from the black prairies of central Texas, northeast over the Missouri, Mississippi, and Ohio valleys (July, August)

C. the Shenandoah and Great valleys, from Southwest Virginia up into Pennsylvania and New York (September)

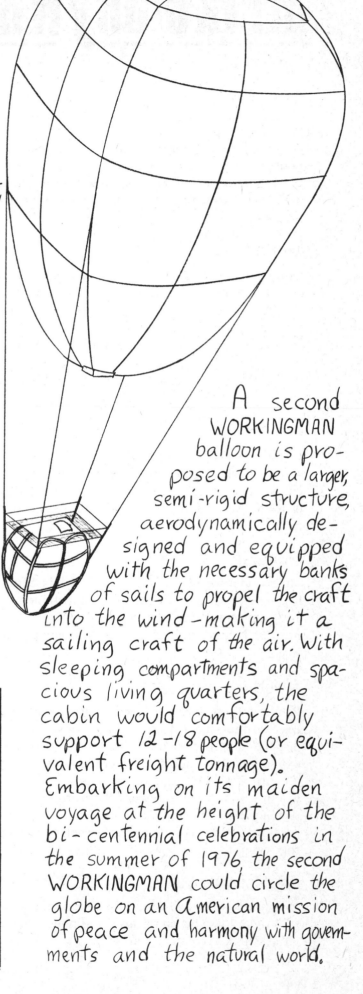

A second WORKINGMAN balloon is proposed to be a larger, semi-rigid structure, aerodynamically designed and equipped with the necessary banks of sails to propel the craft into the wind — making it a sailing craft of the air. With sleeping compartments and spacious living quarters, the cabin would comfortably support 12–18 people (or equivalent freight tonnage). Embarking on its maiden voyage at the height of the bi-centennial celebrations in the summer of 1976, the second WORKINGMAN could circle the globe on an American mission of peace and harmony with governments and the natural world.

If you're interested enough to want to support the operations of the Balloonery, and fool enough to want to spend 24 hours aboard the first WORKINGMAN, for five hundred dollars we'll send you a one day ticket on the regional tour of your choice. Send ride preference and vital statistics, and keep us informed of your whereabouts. Bill me reservations, when accompanied with 20% cash down, will be accepted. We'll gladly refund your money at any time (on 30 days notice), or if ride is not delivered before October 15th 1974. Address all correspondence to: BALLOONERY
Natural Wonders, Inc.
Walnut Grove, Cal. 95690

strike anywhere *

As a special bonus to our left-handed readers, all **Strike Anywhere** * articles begin on the inside column.

a few things about staples

j.d. smith

They are easy to dry. Just gather them as you will, cut out the bruises and the core, and slice them thin. (If the apple pieces were orange segments, you'd cut each one into four or five wedges.) Then take down your screen door and use it for a drying rack. Keep everything warm and dry for a few days, without the little pieces touching each other, then store them in a pillow case.

RICE, brown

Don't get into mystical numbers, just wash the rice as well as you would anything else you were going to eat. Then get a little salt, if you please, and two times as much water as rice, and boil all ingredients until the rice gets soft and the water gets gone. Pay some attention to it during the last fifteen minutes. If you think it takes too long that way, pour off a little of the water and eat harder rice.

CHEESE

Its melting properties are what you would expect, the softer the cheese, the faster the melt. Some processed cheeses chrystalize in the oven, and you end up with brittle flakes and macaroni. Like cheese? Learn to love mold.

CABBAGE?

The wonder vegetable. Kept cool it will last forever. It is mock lettuce until boiled, then its boiled cabbage until sour kraut. The Matanuska Moonlight cabbage gets much larger than the average refrigerator can handle.

POPCORN

Pam and I saw "Claire's Knee," during which Pam discovered that, like fingerprints and snowflakes, no two popped kernels were the same. Based on the idea that expanding water and steam were responsible for the blowup, I tried freezing raw popcorn to pre-partial pop it, but it didn't seem to work. Popcorn makes good packing material, and good fire starter, and a quick breakfast. Pop a couple of test kernels before you put the rest in the pan.

MISCELLANEOUS

Evaporated milk will whip up like cream, but it won't stay there long. Seven raisins per almond is a nice mouthful. Chocolate is a drug.

MEAT

You are what you imagine.
Imagine you and a cow are sharing a cheeseburger you bought.
Does she know your relatives as well as you know hers?
Does she care for the cheese?
Do you take care of your body?
Is she a sloppy eater too?
Was the lettuce crisp or flabby?
Is it gone?
Would you like another?

POTATOES

Boil them, bake them, whip them with a spoon,
Eat them if they're frozen or they're dried.
Ink them, drink them, grow them on the moon,
Solanum tuberosum glorified.

Homecut, Lincolnlog, greasy, Frenchy fries,
Salt them as you eat them if you please.
Old Gram Dolbin looked them in the eyes,
And wore them in her shoes to cure disease.

Alaskan Nuggets have a pretty skin.
Eat them till you see them in your dreams.
Feed them to the cattle, fry them up again,
And throw them like a baseball in between.

BEANS, dry

Beans cooked in the most delicate way still cause farts. The people concerned with the energy crisis should light a fart sometime, as a study in the power they flush down their toilets. Beware, baby limas can be vicious.

APPLES

A crisp semi-sour apple in bed in the morning makes it seem that going to the doctor would be a bummer.

THE LADY has just landed her catch and doesn't know what to do about it.

WATCH your nose, madam.

ANYTHING under control and a happy smile for the photographer.

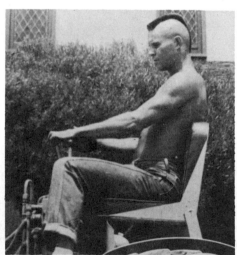

manhattan beach ★

by glen stillwell

GONE YESTERDAY BUT HAIR TODAY. The gent on the left, with the flowing locks, was photographed last summer (1972) near the Manhattan Beach pier. The construction worker, with the "Mohican" . . . remember that one? . . . was photographed in 1963 a few blocks up from the same pier. Those barbers still in business are probably wondering what next?

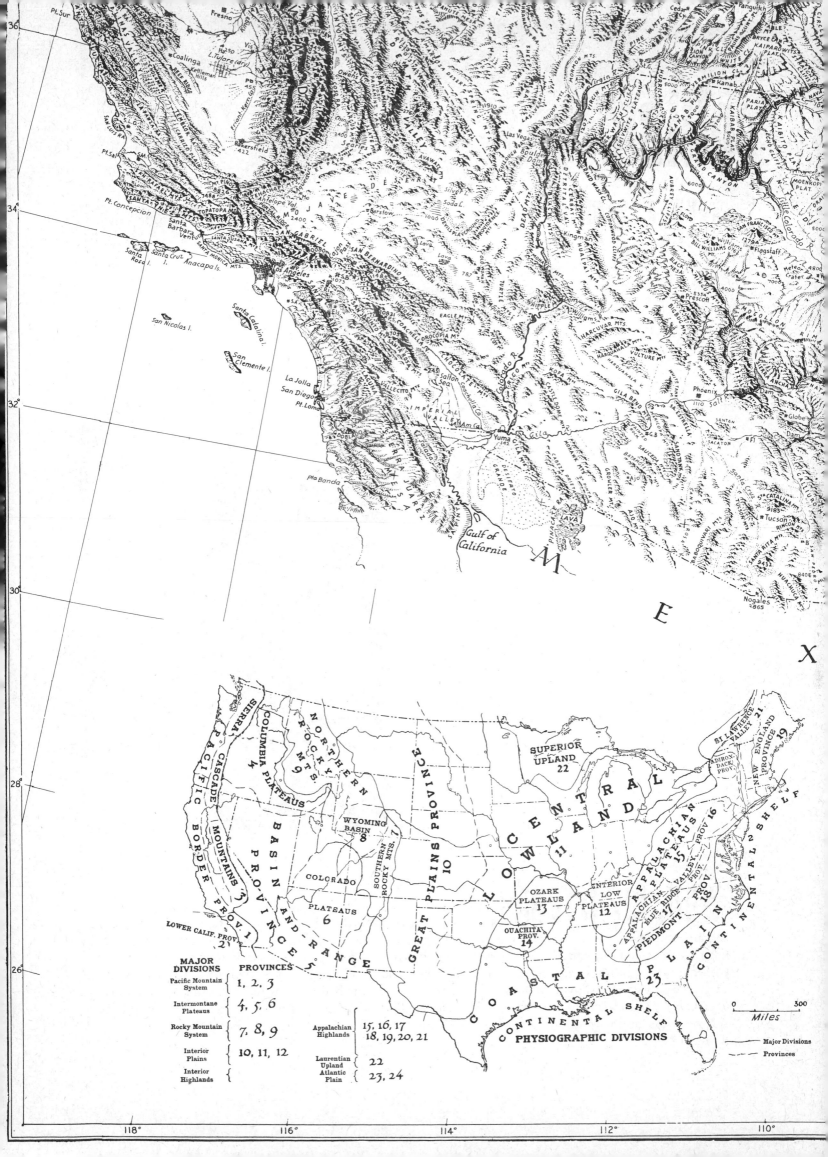

MAJOR
DIVISIONS | PROVINCES

Pacific Mountain
System | 1, 2, 3

Intermontane
Plateaus | 4, 5, 6

Rocky Mountain
System | 7, 8, 9

Interior
Plains | 10, 11, 12

Interior
Highlands | { Appalachian
Highlands | 15, 16, 17
18, 19, 20, 21

Laurentian
Upland | 22

Atlantic
Plain | 23, 24

PHYSIOGRAPHIC DIVISIONS

0 ———— 300
Miles

——— Major Divisions
– – – Provinces

rolling thunder

Gigi Carroll

well, my friends, began Rolling Thunder, "I'll speak to you as clearly as possible. This is my first association in spiritual matters with white people. Indians out where I live sit and talk all night long about spiritual things. As long as ten years ago I could not talk to you about spiritual things regarding the American Indians because after the conquest of this continent, those things were hidden. We go by signs and they change as we go along. The pattern of life changes and we were shown about six years ago that the time had come when we could communicate with people and travel and mix with people and would find people in different places with good hearts and we could talk with them." *April 15, 1971, Council Grove Meeting, Menninger Foundation, Topeka, Kansas.* ★

Free University, Berkeley (Fall '70 Cat.)

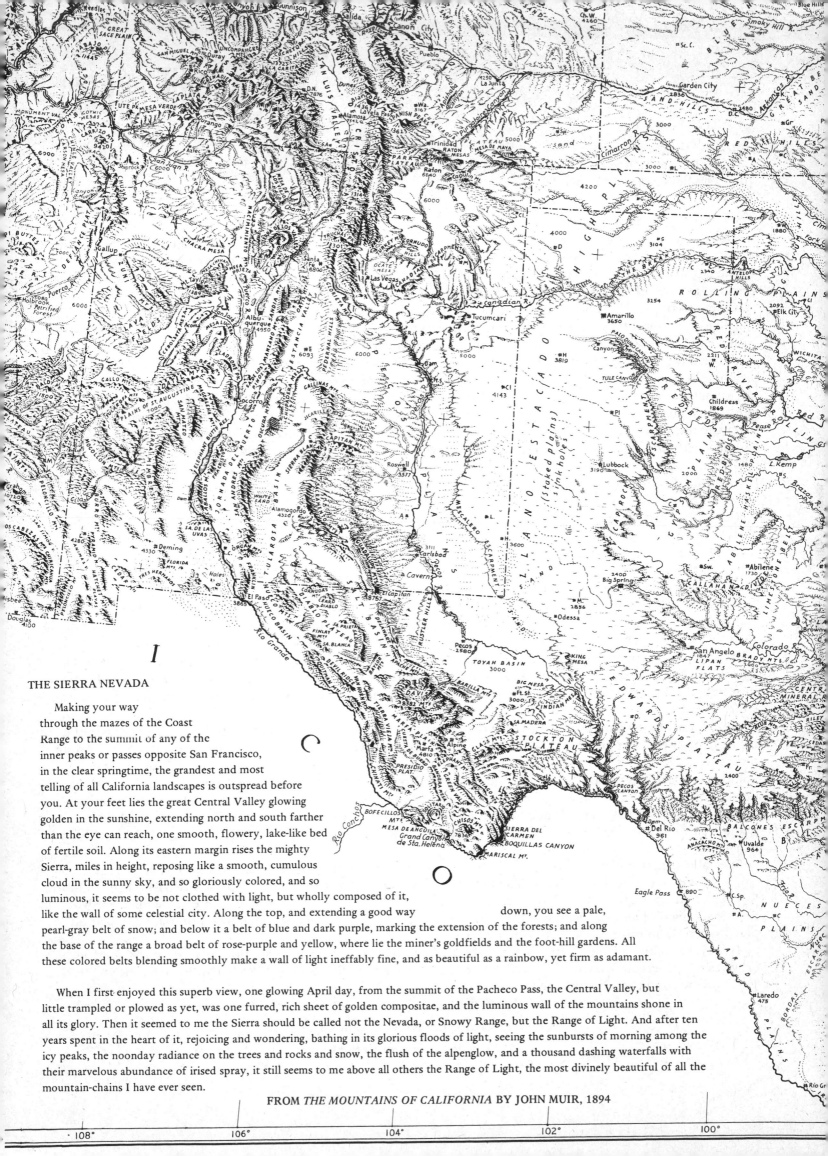

I

THE SIERRA NEVADA

Making your way through the mazes of the Coast Range to the summit of any of the inner peaks or passes opposite San Francisco, in the clear springtime, the grandest and most telling of all California landscapes is outspread before you. At your feet lies the great Central Valley glowing golden in the sunshine, extending north and south farther than the eye can reach, one smooth, flowery, lake-like bed of fertile soil. Along its eastern margin rises the mighty Sierra, miles in height, reposing like a smooth, cumulous cloud in the sunny sky, and so gloriously colored, and so luminous, it seems to be not clothed with light, but wholly composed of it, like the wall of some celestial city. Along the top, and extending a good way down, you see a pale, pearl-gray belt of snow; and below it a belt of blue and dark purple, marking the extension of the forests; and along the base of the range a broad belt of rose-purple and yellow, where lie the miner's goldfields and the foot-hill gardens. All these colored belts blending smoothly make a wall of light ineffably fine, and as beautiful as a rainbow, yet firm as adamant.

When I first enjoyed this superb view, one glowing April day, from the summit of the Pacheco Pass, the Central Valley, but little trampled or plowed as yet, was one furred, rich sheet of golden compositae, and the luminous wall of the mountains shone in all its glory. Then it seemed to me the Sierra should be called not the Nevada, or Snowy Range, but the Range of Light. And after ten years spent in the heart of it, rejoicing and wondering, bathing in its glorious floods of light, seeing the sunbursts of morning among the icy peaks, the noonday radiance on the trees and rocks and snow, the flush of the alpenglow, and a thousand dashing waterfalls with their marvelous abundance of irised spray, it still seems to me above all others the Range of Light, the most divinely beautiful of all the mountain-chains I have ever seen.

FROM *THE MOUNTAINS OF CALIFORNIA* BY JOHN MUIR, 1894

the BunaB report ★

QUARTERLY (Halfterly) REPORT TO KEY PERSONNEL IN THE FIELD
from Orville K. Snav & Associates

Dear Sirs & Brothers:

Our President, Mr. Orville K. Snav, regrets that circumstances, namely the protracted and uninhibited high glee of our current gala Annual New Year's Eve Office party, which precluded incorporation of our quarterly report in the last issue of PLACE. Taking solace from the fact that it was the previous, rather than the last, issue, he was inspired to make this report a halfterly—rather than quarterly, to sustain continuity.

Competition, in their unremitting endeavor to encroach upon the domain of the vast BunaB Empire by making long-bacon at our esteemed Founder, his works, our great humanitarian project and especially at our institutional year's-end institutional good will observance, has again failed to infiltrate our current festival. Although armed with cleverly forged certification, the guards at the conditioning booths in the foyer leading to the grand banquet hall have forestalled those agents and confiscated cameras, tape-recorders, pans, pencils and paper. Bona fide key personnel are well aware of the restrictions and bring only a change of raiment and tags to be pinned on a visible portion of their anatomy bearing their names and addresses in order that they may be returned to their posts after the festivities have waned. As is the usual custom, outsiders are supplied with bounteous quantities of the old burnished emphatic and when they have achieved optimum apogee, are quietly escorted to a movie theater and abandoned. Thus the decorum and privacy of our party is sustained.

During a meeting of the bigger and better betterment council a paper was read by the chief of our research division. For obvious reasons, the names and dates have been altered, but not the facts.

One of our distaff key personnel in the field confessed that she had endowed her husband with a flacon of our BunaB No. 3 (Between-Shave Lotion, for the critical 23-hours, 45-minutes between applications of the "After . . ." and "Before . . ." chop-goup purveyed by pushers who can only visualize the small end of the cornucopia). She reported that there was an unaccountable time-variable, and entreated an explanation or recourse. Her alleged husband was spending approximately 45 minutes in the john, ostensibly shaving. As laboratory time studies, and field testing had clearly indicated that a maximum of fifteen minutes was required to mow jaw-stubble, the lady was informed that she had best make an investigation. Suggesting keyhole observation, and possibly bugging of the chandeliers, in order to ascertain just what the tea-whistlin' Hey! was going on in there.

We received a report from her that she had followed our Founder's advice and had been shocked to learn that her spouse had indeed required only the prescribed time to shave, but that he was addicted to eating Clark Bars in secret. Our beloved Mentor responded to her confession with a letter of sympathy. Local key personnel were admonished to abjure further conjecture.

Huzzas and dancing in the aisles greeted the report made by our distribution wing that serial numbers on the prime fruit of the near-genius of the venerable Wizard of Lime Creek had passed the critical 37,403 mark. As our most recent December XVth Mailing Orgy was unique in that it was the first to include more of yet another of our aids to nicer living than the old reliable Improved No. 7 BunaB, our accounting department had feared that demand might be on the wane. However, it was learned that Yuletide gifting unto remaining friends of key personnel of our new ECA KIT was due to the fact that our Mk.VII had already been bestowed upon a goodly number of those fortunate individuals, and that the ECA KIT was yet another manifestation of their unselfish beneficence.

Special dispensation was invoked by our beloved Mentor in granting PLACE permission to offer an Improved No. 7 BunaB as a prize in the "Name The Planet" contest, providing that it would not be FIRST PRIZE. Our Mr. Snav felt that the distinction of having created a new name for the only known sphere infested with allegedly thinking indigini, plus a softball, would be adequate. That a BunaB would be the only appropriate consolation prize for one who came so close to winning the contest.

To key personnel unable to attend our current year's-en festival through restrictions placed by parole officers or wives the venerable Wizard of Lime Creek extends his BEST WISHES FOR MANY HAPPY RETURNS OF 1972, or the good parts thereof, and

> Fraternally,
> ORVILLE K. SNAV & ASSOCIATES
> Al Crowder, Assistant to the President

★

dropped her glasses. but one must learn in roaming to spare only those rods which connect or spoil the yellow sun which seeds the petals as any smuck does it in roads leading to bigger question marks in the friendly neighborhood washerteria or buy a six-park of three point two in time. she licked her feet, and moaned to pace the floor.

later that same, the serenity of KANSAS became us and we could approach their knowledge of the flatness of that other world with varying degrees of sureness in the GREEN surrounding the mill without a wheel kept turning into yellow black butterflies crawling into black serpents beneath our feet.

arriving from the north in blackness we found amidst the green hills of exploitation which could turn only at the last into multicolored squares of sameness wherever man with his real estate of the nation could clear and burn with smoke of stacks and mufflers into the pasteurization of that other place which came in t.v. tubes of those antennas atop those outhouses & unpainted barns; we snuck into the armed camp of birthday party celebrants who tossed their fireworks & cans into the night lake of wall-to-wall pick-up trucks & motor boats of every smuck, and once again she trembled.

we drove all day and into th' heat of the swamp afternoon until five miles before we got "there," we could no more, so rested with loaves and fishes 'neath the shade of a real estate sign until we could, and left the mad tea party to go on, but "they" said we could go no more, so i swallowed my desires in the runny perspiration, and returned sadly without to their place, and saw once again a sun set over telephone poles and garbage cans. the sign said SOLD and marble tombs with concrete crosses and plastic cherubs stood up above their sea levels 'neath the shade of an old television antenna, where brewry towers changed neon colors as the weather changed from sweating heat to thundering storm, and days dragged down upon our backs like camels's knock-kneed legs across the sands. you see, there was no olive tree.

she stepped daintily across the rice krispy floors in an effort not to arouse the beasts within. but, i smelt her lyings and found myself amassed at the presence, and so prodingly i devoured with the only tools to be found at hand, and found her wanten in softness of the damp. lifting until i could, we entered thee gates where i spun in goldness of the passing hardness which followed the glow. floods came and i knew her space in time and the mirrors made us one, but not for thee. for she lay a seep in the jungles of BEING, but i had. then went. we looking for other trees of whiteness.

they have printed black words in imitation of poetry across my desert sunrise and the beauty of the morning is now obscured by somebody else's supposed loneliness as i once wrote upon the matchbook, "DON'T BOTHER TRYING TO CAPTURE THE MOMENT—THERE'LL BE ANOTHER ONE RIGHT AWAY." and if there is a zen to photography it's to be found on the back of that head's bagel and not merely in being open seven days a week or having a nice day in the now or the sweet bye bye.

i looked down at the road for just a second, and lost my rainbow. then i looked up, looking for my lost rainbow, and lost my road.

only soft yellow traces of optical visions remain upon the wet sheets of oil slick puddles as the storm overlaps what was to be. another sunset appears lost but only for those who look, or pizza parlors floating orange peeling's junkies across FLORIDA skies. if only there were strength enough for a purple fart, which the green ferns could in turn grow over, fulfilling their superimposition of TIME over future realities, such as CHANCE dictates. a large white bird flies DOWN and slowly drops into the seas.

James Gross
Selections from a Travel Journal
written at many points between
Anaheim, Calif. and Perry, Fla.

SANTA ANA, CALIFORNIA at seven o'clock on a Saturday mourning is cracked concrete pigeonshit covered street corners lonely figures selling "jesus" or "america" and their respective wars in any language brought fourth in red headlines of AWAKE! pulp empty second hand thrift shops greased duck tails looking for a bus to some WHERE dirty cigarette butted sidewalks GRAYNESS of no liquor in park masking taped windows looking out onto cracks of black spittle.

and then there was a dream of indians surrounding the house .in the black of tossing burning branches thru our terror.

it's now monday morning of which we are to leave california and go somewhere. i'll try to photograph what ever daisyness there IS, if that's what there is.

we went out into the black of the desert where we stayed moving on a treadmill of blackness with black pictures of black places passing our green windows, and an occassional rolling juke box of red & yellow twinkles. a storm trooper stopped us and asked to see our oranges. we had three, but she said we had two, and gave him two of our oranges. he looked at them, gave back to us, and let us go.

a bread truck stopped in front of the SELIGMAN GROCERY STORE, and the trout's eye rolled over and looked at us, until we went the indian curio pharmacy, and couldn't find the tuna.

we slept the desert morning under a white flamingo surrounded by pink lily pads of the jungle nude covered sofa's telephone booth.

they have placed us in a white square cubicle, named "TRINIDAD." the streets were full of western teenagers looking for friday afternoon. we had just driven away from the park where the indians had their apartment buildings a couple of hundred centuries ago, and where an indian named "SAM" had suggested a connibial mating of Esther (a mummy) and George (a general) by way of an explanation of the brown paper coverings, when a massive thunder storm pissed a pun us but we drove on, until we met a hail storm which shit white golf balls a pun us and blanketed our road and whitewashed our windows, but we drove on.

you see, we were only nineteen miles from UTLEYVILLE, when suddenly we saw this windmill. it was a great american windmill, right next to the ruins of something that once was. we had just made a definite decision (TAA! TAA!) that we would not move to SELIGMAN and medusa just kept truckin' along, all strapped in beneath her flies, and ssorg, the nail, was climbing onto the sleeping bag and my black hat. "Let me see what's underneath that hat, BOY," the guard said, and carefully ran his fingers thru my hair.

old granny with the plaid shawl looked out from her bed with fear and trembling, and wiggled her black nose. it seemed that, in spite of the serenity of the green & gold flowing landscape & monoply bored board simpleness of the architectures & the people, the BOOMing VIOLENCE of the sky & the children, not to mention the parents of the children, put fear in the heart of her flute-loving soul. but KANSAS went on and continued even as the hills flowed greenaly and goldaly into the ALL-AMERICAN NIGHT with multi-colored fireworks BOOM! at which blonde-haired children played in preparation for greater wars to come (in christ's name, or address), and at least for one day the red skinned parents in their coveralls gave up their own favorite sport, child beating, to see what fun, as the sky joined with pink on black thunderous applause, and she

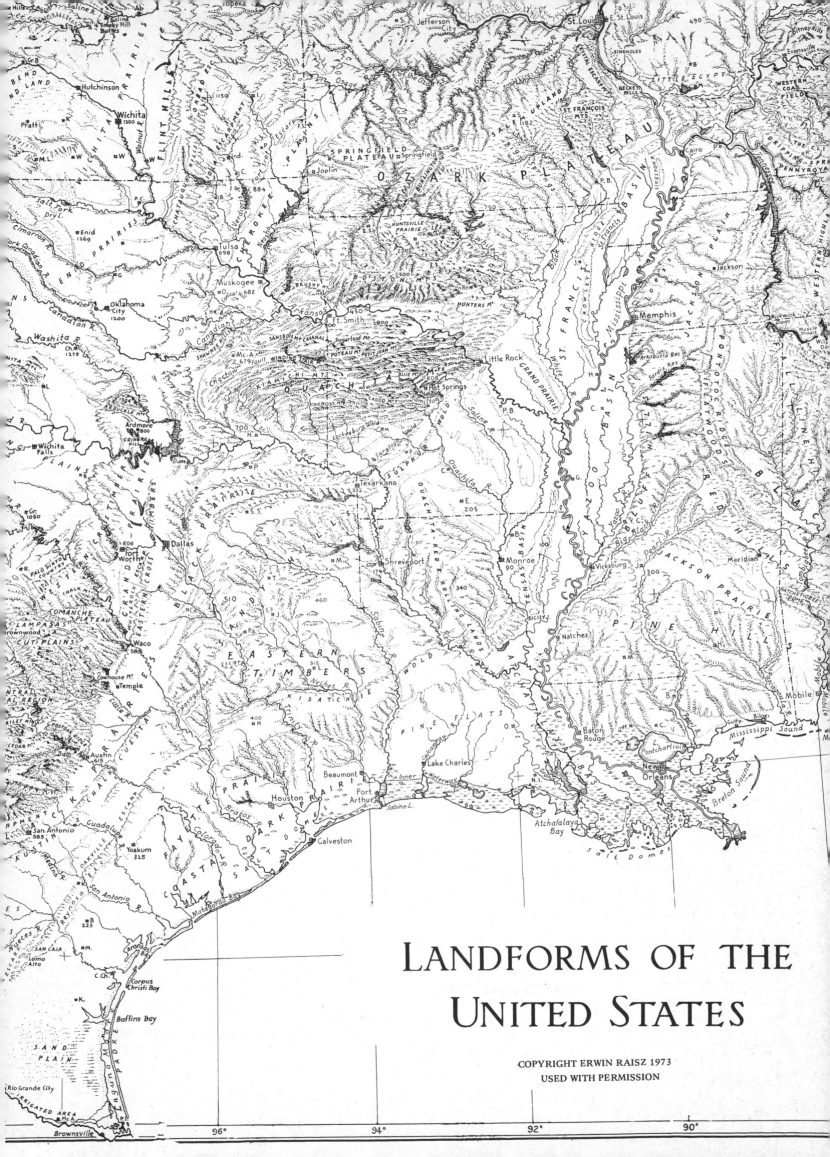

LANDFORMS OF THE
UNITED STATES

still gets done. I slept in their van "Babe a blue Bus" a 64 Ford econoline: Definitely a character car, the engine was held together by epoxy and shredded paper towels. Due to a dead celinoid we had to go through motions that were practically ritualistic to start it.

The year before when I went down to see them we made a "voyage" in their 36' ketch. We started for the Bahamas but ran short of coins so decided to sail down the intra-costal waterways from St. Petersburg to the gulf. Saw some of the most fantastic sunsets anchored in the middle of nowhere; so quiet . . . I love the ocean and sailing it's such an experience. Every day the ocean has something new to bring past your door step. Porpise play in the bow wake in water so clear you can see them, giant sea turtles show themselves occasionally. You never know what to expect in the way of weather, storms are exhilarating and fun to ride out or sail through.

We anchored, among other places, off of Key West. A big tourist trap to those who wish to be trapped. We and the other boat people there played local color for the people in an expensive restaurant with windows over looking the anchorage. The restaurant was and is called Tony's Fish Market. Supposedly "Mafia" run (local legend). Seems the Mafia run businesses quite well and at a more reasonable price. Pantry Pride Food Stores are supposed to be Mafia run too. But they sure are fine stores. So anyway Key West is unique.

There's a place called Lou's Bar on Duval Street that has 15 or 20 cent draft on Tuesdays and huge open windows, ratan chairs and small round tables, the bar curves and twists as it is made of old offset press news printing cylinders cut open you can still see the print. The walls are black and a dude with a straw cowboy hat a poneytail and a bushy mustache tends bar evenings they have live music. One night they had a jug band and people came from every walk of life to stand outside and listen. A vending truck (or whatever) covered with stainless steel diamonds drove up and opened it's lighted jaws and said eat me and the crowd did, watermelon slices sweet and pink with everybody sharing. People laughed and ann and Jerry stoned and looking for each other. In the process Ann saw Lloyd Bridges and he smiled at her, she couldn't get over how beautiful he was. Jerry who also saw him agreed. Jerry and Ann lived on a boat nearby.

I really can't understand why more people haven't turned to sail boats as an alternative to society or whatever. There are quite a few "freak types" sailing around but we also ran into people who were retired and had lived on the ocean all their life. Boats are pretty easy to find and aren't as expensive to buy as a house. One problem is space which is why my sister and brother in law sold their boat they had. There are just so many places you can go by boat like to the Yucatan Peninsula is relatively a short distance away, or South America. So many possibilities.

Ah, but here I am in Ohio digging the grass and the greenery waiting for the fall colors and eventually winter and surfing. Oh boy.

I hope I haven't bored you. I got a bit carried away.

Thanks for your time,

MARY JANE CLARK

★

WAPAKONETA, OHIO

Place;

Maybe you'd like to hear some about Ohio. Ohio is green and flat or hilly (depending on what part of Ohio) loves to grow things from its dark rich soil in the summertime. Trees; maples, oaks and locust (among others) begin to turn green in the spring and explode into the brightest shade of green you've ever seen while your back is turned. It's amazing one can almost see the leaves growing, they change so rapidly in the spring. It's just a great state for growing things. It's not only an agricultural state but industry plays a large part too. I live in a small town called Wapakoneta which most people can't pronounce even after its been patiently pronounced for them several times. The town was named after a Blackfoot Indian chief and his daughter; Wapa, being the chief and Koneta his daughter or wife legend varies. Neil Armstrong (first man on the moon; Apollo something or other) lived here for a while once; his parents still do. The townspeople raised funds and along with a state funding to help, built a museum in his honor which some people think looks like a sewage disposal plant. The person who donated the land (right off interstate 75) just happened to build a holiday Inn, a gift shop & a spiffy restaurant on their remaining property. They get all the business so the townspeople who raised the money for the museum and were expecting more business in town bought ricky ticky souveniers and never sold them. So everywhere the store windows are filled with souveniers that no one except people who live in Wapak (native short name) wanted. So it goes.

We have a courthouse, a newspaper, theater, a million Gas stations, a park and a river that runs behind Au glaize street or the street where all the businesses are located. Wapak has relatively little crime so the "men in Blue" haven't anything to do other than catch speeders and bust kids for drugs. Usually the kids get the charges dropped or very low sentences. People still smile at you and say hi when you walk down the street whether they know you or not. There are a "handful" of longhair people who live on farms and rarely come into town other than for necessities. The temperament of the majority of the people here run from Conservative to Reactionary. However I think that's pretty much the way it is everywhere. It seems the people in this town can handle a person with long hair on a one to one basis and forget appearances but when they see a long hair on the street he is labeled a Commie Hippie or some such Garbage.

All in all it's a pretty nice place to live but it's nice to get away from too. I've been hit by the traveling bug and so am not content to stay long if I can help it. Autumn to spring I spend in school Ohio State University. And summers I spend elsewhere. This summer I drove to Calif and back with my parents and brother in their camper saw alot of really nice country. Also I usually visit my sister & brother in law in Florida at least once a year. They're building a 49' Cross trimoran this summer so I went down and helped build stations and read the table of off sets. Also did some leather work and tie dying. They live in a 17' trailer with an unfinished ferro cement boat 5 feet away. So when you look out the door you see this mass of grey. It's nice cover tho as can't see the trailer from the road so no one knows they're there except friends who drop by at the rate of several a day. Amazingly enough work

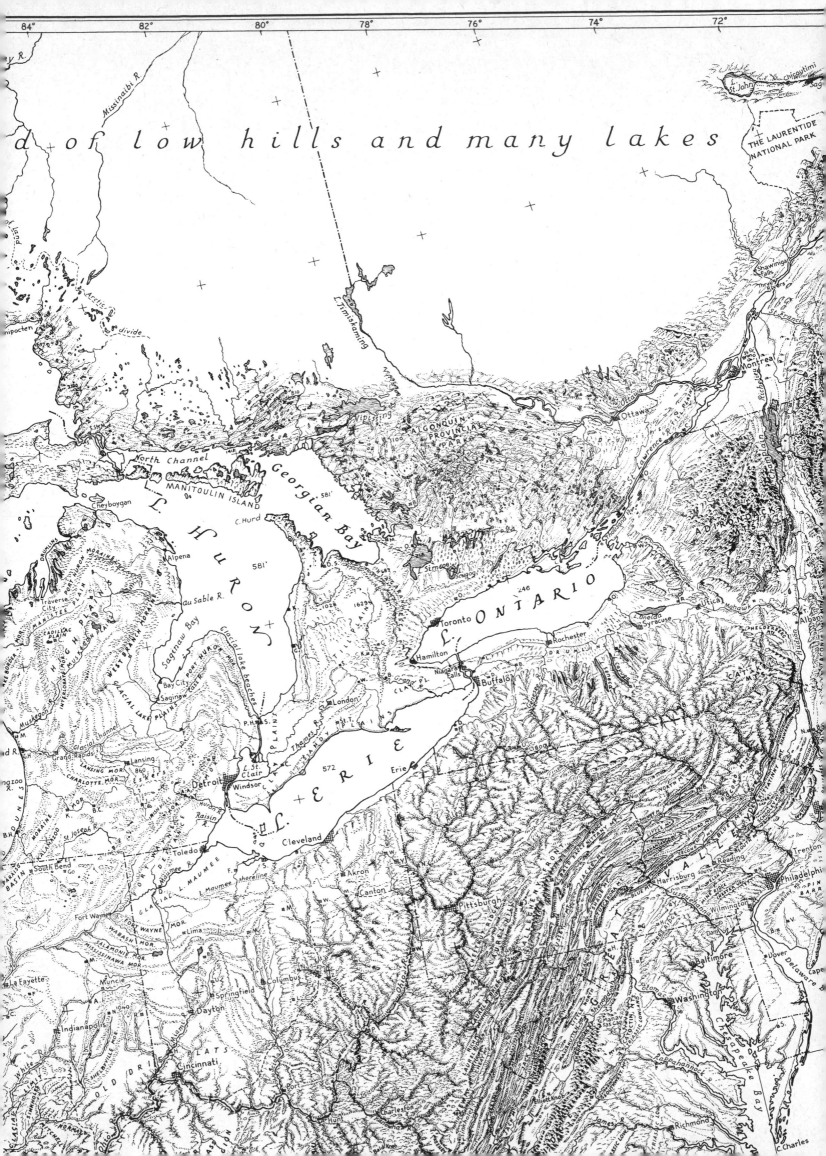

Pears are also picked from New England to the Great Lakes.

WATERMELONS are grown on the black prairies across Central Texas, the Lime Sink region of Central Florida, Georgia, and S. Carolina. Muscatines are grown on an island in the Mississippi.

CANTALOUPES are grown in California's Imperial Valley, Texas, Arizona, and the Rocky Ford Valley of Southeastern Colorado.

CHERRIES are grown extensively on the Michigan shore from Benton Harbor up to Traverse City, and along both sides of Lake Ontario.

GRAPES are principly cultivated in the valleys and hillsides of north central California, also in the Yakima Valley of Central Washington, Southwestern Michigan, under the eastern half of Lake Erie, and into the Finger Lakes of Western New York, with some grapes in Central Missouri, N.W. Arkansas, Upper Georgia and South Carolina.

A quick first crop of **POTATOES** is picked in April-May in Florida, Eastern Louisiana, and the Carolinas (Bayboro and Elizabeth City). Irish potatoes are grown in volume along the Snake River of Eastern Idaho, So. Central Colorado's San Luis Valley, along the Red River between North Dakota and Minnesota, Southern Maryland, New Jersey, the upper edge of Long Island, and in Aroostook County of extreme Northeast Maine.

ENGLISH WALNUTS are orchard grown in Central and Northern California and the Willamette Valley of Oregon. **PECAN** groves are thick in S. Eastern and Central Georgia, and up into the Carolinas, scattered through Alabama, Mississippi, Louisiana, into South Central Texas. Also in a band from the Western Cross Timber Hills of Central Texas up diagonally, through Oklahoma and Western Missouri.

APPLES are grown extensively east of the mountains in Washington's Yakima and Wenatchee Valleys, and scattered further north along the Columbia River. Also the Santa Clara and Sonoma Valleys of Northern California, and the Grand Junction Valley of Western Colorado. Apples are grown throughout the Mid-east and East, with concentrations in S.W. Michigan and all along the bottom of Lake Ontario. From as far south as the hills of Northern Georgia the apple harvest moves north, with a concentration in the upper Shennandoah Valley of Vir., W. Va., Md., and Pennsylvania.

GRAPEFRUIT are grown in the Imperial Valley, the Rio Grande Valley, near Phoenix, and in Central Florida.

LEMONS are grown north of Santa Barbara, in extreme Southwest Arizona (Yuma), and to some degree in Central Florida.

ORANGES are grown among the Santa Ana Mts. (Calif.), near Santa Barbara, in the Southern San Joaquin Valley, near Phoenix, the Rio Grande Valley, and throughout Central Florida, from the Gulf to the Atlantic.

Dr. Herald R. Hoyt,
Placesquirt ★

208

pickers, notice!

LETTUCE, PEAS, and **SNAP BEANS** are grown in the winter gardens of the Imperial Valley of extreme Southern California, the lower Rio Grande Valley of Texas, and on the marshlands to the south of Florida's Lake Okeechobee. With the end of March the Imperial Valley pickers move north, through lettuce and pea fields of San Luis Obispo, Monterey, Alameda, and San Mateo Counties. The largest concentration of summer pea fields is in the Walla Walla Valley of S.W. Washington. Also pea fields along the eastern edge of the Vancouver Sound, Southern Minnesota, S.E. Michigan, No. Illinois, and Western New York. Most **TOMATOES** are grown in the Sacramento and San Joaquin Valleys of N. Central California, with winter crops in the Rio Grande Valley and So. Florida, and summer crops in New Jersey and Maryland.

STRAWBERRIES are winter crops in the Imperial Valley and Southern Florida, and are the earliest fruit ripening up through the country. On the Pacific Coast they are raised in the Salinas Valley of Central California, the Willamette River Valley of N.W. Oregon, and along Vancouver Bay. From Florida, the strawberry picking moves north to Southern North Carolina (Chadbourn), and principly west, to the hill area of Hammond Louisiana, Northeast of Baton Rouge. From there to Chicago the berries ripen successively later, extensively through the St. Francis Basin of N.W. Arkansas into Western Tennessee (Paducah), Ohio, along the Eastern coast of Lake Michigan (Benton Harbor), Western New York, and New Jersey.

PLUM and **PRUNE TREES** are grown principly above and below the San Francisco Bay, the Sacramento Valley and the Lower San Joaquin Valley. Also Western Oregon, So. Central Wash., and the Payette Valley of Western Idaho.

Picking of **APRICOTS** followed by **PEACHES** of Tulare, Kings, and Fresno Cos. of the San Joaquin Valley lasts until August (also asparagas and pea fields here). **PEACHES** also grown near Grand Junction, Colorado, and are scattered throughout the mideast and east, with concentrations in S.W. Michigan and Southern New Jersey. Elberta peaches are grown to perfection within the Pine and Melon Belt (Louisville Plateau and uplands) of Georgia, also the Peach and Grape Belt adjacently northwest.

Some **PEARS** are grown in this Georgian Belt, but the Pacific Slope is the volume leader, and there's pear trees everywhere in the Sacramento-San Joaquin Delta.

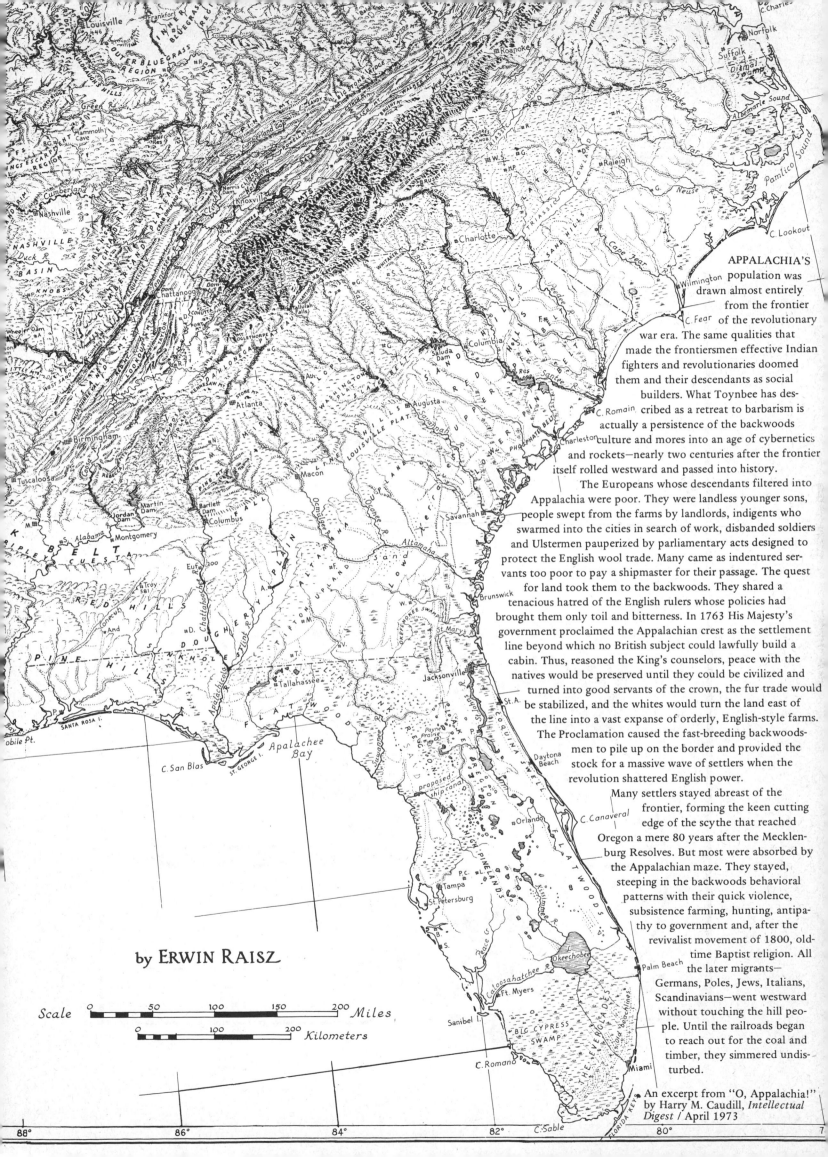

APPALACHIA'S population was drawn almost entirely from the frontier of the revolutionary war era. The same qualities that made the frontiersmen effective Indian fighters and revolutionaries doomed them and their descendants as social builders. What Toynbee has described as a retreat to barbarism is actually a persistence of the backwoods culture and mores into an age of cybernetics and rockets—nearly two centuries after the frontier itself rolled westward and passed into history.

The Europeans whose descendants filtered into Appalachia were poor. They were landless younger sons, people swept from the farms by landlords, indigents who swarmed into the cities in search of work, disbanded soldiers and Ulstermen pauperized by parliamentary acts designed to protect the English wool trade. Many came as indentured servants too poor to pay a shipmaster for their passage. The quest for land took them to the backwoods. They shared a tenacious hatred of the English rulers whose policies had brought them only toil and bitterness. In 1763 His Majesty's government proclaimed the Appalachian crest as the settlement line beyond which no British subject could lawfully build a cabin. Thus, reasoned the King's counselors, peace with the natives would be preserved until they could be civilized and turned into good servants of the crown, the fur trade would be stabilized, and the whites would turn the land east of the line into a vast expanse of orderly, English-style farms. The Proclamation caused the fast-breeding backwoodsmen to pile up on the border and provided the stock for a massive wave of settlers when the revolution shattered English power.

Many settlers stayed abreast of the frontier, forming the keen cutting edge of the scythe that reached Oregon a mere 80 years after the Mecklenburg Resolves. But most were absorbed by the Appalachian maze. They stayed, steeping in the backwoods behavioral patterns with their quick violence, subsistence farming, hunting, antipathy to government and, after the revivalist movement of 1800, old-time Baptist religion. All the later migrants—Germans, Poles, Jews, Italians, Scandinavians—went westward without touching the hill people. Until the railroads began to reach out for the coal and timber, they simmered undisturbed.

An excerpt from "O, Appalachia!" by Harry M. Caudill, *Intellectual Digest* / April 1973

by ERWIN RAISZ

Scale

0   50   100   150   200 Miles

0   100   200 Kilometers

TALKIN' CARTOGRAPHY BY CLARK AKATIFF

We have strayed from the path and hit the road. Our maps are road maps, we are lost without them. Have you looked for yourself in search of America, or has Standard Oil done your looking? If you haven't yet, for god's sake study this map, begin to orient yourself to the reality of the land. Personalize, humanize the map; draw the inroads that you have travelled, the places that you know, and discover the unknown— The Gangplank, The Great Sandy Desert, Cape Flattery, Oldman River, The Crazy Mountains. I have been looking at this map of the U.S. for over a decade, and it a true ally. I expect to never exhaust the form.

I never met Erwin Raisz. What I know of him is gathered from diverse sources and fugitive information about a person whose reputation had grown ledgendary by the time of his death. Erwin Raisz (the name is pronounced Royce by most who knew him) was born into a world that has passed away, a world of Czar and Kaiser, Emporer and King. Out of the maelstrom of the collapse of this world in the First World War, Raisz brought with him to the new world his old world cartographer's skills. His extraordinary ability found long and various employment within American Geography. This map was originally intended to accompany *Feeneman's Two Volume Physiographic Regions of the United States,* a book that is still valuable to read. The map has gone on to be used in many other connections, and the visual grace and clarity of the technique perfected in it has led to a whole school of cartography. To really appreciate his accomplishment, attempt to draw a map yourself. I have done so for many years now and the example of Raisz's work remains a paragon.*

The thing that is most impressive about Raisz is the craftsmanship demonstrated in the execution of his subject. Today much cartography has become automated and conventionalized to the point that individual skill is relatively unimportant and the human touch is little apparent. This, of course results in cheaper, and perhaps more easily readable maps but lower quality. Raisz's work stands as a bulwark against this trend. The ultimate achievement of Raisz's work is that it is the product of one person's vision and skill. Using techniques that are antique (pen and ink) and with an eye as fine as a Paleolithic hunter's, he produces a valid microcosm. And as such, it is an object worthy of contemplation.

Erwin Raisz taught at many of the important American universities, sometimes as a faculty member, often as a visitor. A lecture was often an hour during which time, without his having spoken more than a few words, a magnificent landscape was chalked out on the blackboard. He viewed the mechanical aids to drafting with suspicion and demonstrated in his work the validity of mastering skills that had become obsolete in terms of modern technology. His maps are, in my opinion, among the best examples of caligraphy in the 20th century.

The symbol is never the reality. The map is never the world, and the line is never the object. Rather, all are metaphors which in their spatial arrangement capture the essence of object and earth, place and reality and thereby provide power over object and earth, knowledge of place and reality. We are as good as our maps, and no better. Maps, in the sense of the composite archive of measurement of the earth, have reduced the majority of the surface to a manipulable object. Maps tell us where to drive, to drill, to plant to bomb, and to bury. Maps monitor our existence and chart our future. Good cartography takes time. It takes a lot of time to compile a map, and a lot more to draw it. It takes a lot of time on the part of the viewer, if the tool is to be correctly used. Raisz's work makes us appreciate that fact. If we allow it to, it can settle us into a pace slow enough to appreciate the flow of natural processes.

*See an example of Clark Akatiff's cartography in *Workingman's Guide to the Universe,* page 141.

 BAMA STARSHINE.

trickles: Chattahochee, Tombigbee, Sipsey, Coosa, Conecuh, Cherokee, Black Warrior. Indians and rivers. The waterways were first used by the Indians and facilitated the scattering of the white man (with concurrent destruction of an Aztec—challenging Indian Civilization). Riverboats, steamboats, canoes.

Best of all, the pollution is nil. Clear, sharp nights. You can even still find the big dipper. Night clouds wander in the summer. Hot nights on porches. Quiet talk and ravenous mosquitos. I was visiting 2 months ago and went into shock: at 9 PM, families and couples were strolling the streets "Just out for a walk after suppah." Right. Amazing.

So how come I'm living in California? Family fortunes and college took me away at first. The more disagreeable aspects of living in the 19th century keep me away. Other friends fight the good fight for the environment, down home.

Cheers, ★

LEE MARRS

Berkeley Cal

Dear PLACE—

The enclosed is an Alabama fantascene, drawn cause I am an artist.

Despite Wallace and human equality washouts, Alabama is a beautiful place. If you love the land, the pines alone will drive you drunk. Early conservation and naturally rich soil has kept the state green—the trees being replaced in reverse ratio continually. Therefore most of Bama is woodlands on slooping meadows. Picture postcards in 3D.

The tourist brochures toot for "the growing industry" but forget it—there are 4 cities. 90% of the state are whistlestops, rolling fields and black earth. Oak, mimosa, honeysuckle, magnolia and spanish moss. Isolated gas stations with a general store = a town. Old stale jokes about backwoods hillbillies, cornpone and klu klux klan fade when you're scuffling through fall leaves, meeting the REAL real McCoys and snapping chestnuts.

"More navigable waterways than any other state" is another official gambit. Ponds and puddles, creeks, streams, river and

TALKIN' COLUMBIA

I was down along the river, just sittin' on a rock,
Lookin' at the boats in the Bonneville lock,
An' the gate swing open, the boat sails in,
Toots the whistle, she's go-one again!
    Gasolene goin' up, wheat comin' down.

Filled up my hat-brim, drunk a little taste,
Thought about a river, just goin' to waste,
I thought about the dust, 'n thought about the sand,
I thought about the people, 'n thought about the land
    Ev'rybody runnin' around a-all over creation,
    Just lookin' for some kind of a little place.

Pulled out my pencil 'n I scribbled this song,
Figgered all o'them salmon jes' couldn't be wrong,
C's them salmon fish are mighty shrewd,
    They got senators . . . politicians, too . . .
    Jus' like a president . . . they run ever' four years.

You jes' watch this river 'n pretty soon
E-ev'rybody's gonna be changin' their tune . . .
The big Grand Coulee 'n the Bonneville Dam'll
Build a thousand factories f'r Uncle Sam . . .
    'N ev'rybody else in the world.

Makin' ev'rything from sewin' machines
To a-tomic bedrooms, 'n plastic . . .
E-ev'rything's gonna be made outa plastic.

Uncle Sam needs wool, Uncle Sam needs wheat,
Uncle Sam needs houses 'n stuff to eat,
Uncle Sam needs water 'n power dams,
Uncle Sam needs people 'n the . . . people need land.

Don't like dictators none much myself,
What I think is the whole world oughta be run by
Ee-lectricity . . . .

COMPOSED IN 1939 BY WOODY GUTHRIE

LANDFORM MAPS

of the United States and most other countries,
drawn by ERWIN RAISZ, are available from:

ERWIN RAISZ MAPS
130 Charles Street
Boston, Mass.
02114

Ask for the flyer with map descriptions and prices.
The big maps are the best. There's more to look at.

The Landform map of the United States printed
in this issue is slightly reduced from the 42 x 27"
original which we bought for eighty-five cents (plus
an additional fifty cents for mailing tube and postage).
We've printed the map with overlapping edges so that
92% of the original can be constructed from the ten
map pages of this book. Some suggestions: a) Tests
prove that *Place's* pages can be removed without damage
to the binding. Fold *Neon Rose* flat open and cut with
a sharp pocket or exacto knife directly on the page/
binding junction, cutting into underlying pages and not
the binding. b) Depending on your particular copy
there will be a 1/8 to 1/4" overlap between adjacent
sections of the map. Warm up on the five horizontal,
two-page overlaps. Trim the vertical edges and finish
with the four vertical, four-page overlaps. c) For exact
positioning a light table can be made by placing a lamp
under a glass table top. d) Rubber cement is magic. Any
excess, when dry, can be rolled away with one finger.

TECTONIC COMMENTARY BY MATTHEW CELESTINO

Let's start with the West. Most everything on the map west of a
north-south line through Denver belongs to the *Cordilleran system,*
a "cord" or "chain" of mountainous terrain extending from the South
American Andes through Alaska. The system of geologically youthful
mountains evidences the pushed-up leading edges of continents floating
on a hot, semiplastic layer of the earth's interior. The western states are
on the rise while California collides with and overrides the Pacific Ocean
floor.

California west of the San Andreas Fault is moving northward and
upward out of the present sea, maybe someday to become an island
mountain on its way to the Aleutian Trench south of Alaska's Aleutian
Islands. The Sierra Nevada is lifting: the upturned edge of a granite
block in full tilt, the crest of the Sierra Nevada bears the scars of glaciers
that have resisted its skyward thrust. Also going skyward, but by vol-
canism instead of tilting, are the Cascade Mountains. There's a nice,
continuous line of volcanoes, flanked east and west by masses of volcanic outpourings, starting on the south with Sutter (Marysville) Buttes
in California's Great Central Valley and going straight north through
Washington's Mt. Baker into Canada with Lassen, Shasta, Jefferson,
Hood, Adams, and Rainier, along the way.

The Basin and Range topography looked like "an army of cater-
pillars crawling northward out of Mexico" to Major Clarence E. Dutton,
a worker for John Wesley Powell, the nineteenth-century explorer of
the West. Grove Karl Gilbert, a Berkeley man, saw the basins and ranges
as products of blocks of the earth's crust being uplifted on faults along
their edges. Blocks like the Sierra Nevada, but tilted the other way.
(Orogeny does strange things for both the continent and the mind.)
The ranges drain their water into basins, and not the sea. It's a closed
system, once filled with extensive lakes like Lake Bonneville that
shrank to become the Great Salt Lake. There were great lakes in
Pleistocene times (2-3 million years ago) that filled the Basin-and-
Range valleys while a massive ice sheet scoured the Laurentian Shield
and sea level was 450 feet lower than today's.

The Rockies are almost too damned much to think about . . .
realizing that even the relatively small Sierra Nevada is a lifetime
range for the universal explorer. Anyway, the Rockies rose up through
lowlands, splitting apart the Great Plains and the Colorado Plateaus.
On the western edges of the Colorado Piedmont, the strata underlying
the Great Plains are vividly exposed in "hogback" ridges dragged upward by the uplifting Front Range.

The Great Plains and Central Lowlands are tectonically monotonous.
Flat, gently undulating, or gently dipping strata lie strangely quiet, remembering millions of years of accumulating debris derived from more
active areas, and waiting for the big continental push to fold and break
them into mountains.

The Coastal Plain may be likened to what the Central Lowland, the
Great Plains Province, and the Colorado Plateau once were: deltas and
flats building with the debris washed from mountains. Louisiana is
growing into the Gulf of Mexico using soil and sand from 20-odd other
states, carried at the whims of the Mississippi River drainage system.
Someday, a river cutting down into Coastal Plain sediments may produce
another Grand Canyon.

The Appalachian Mountains once were busy at an ancient continental
front, but gave way to erosional forces during a 70-million year period
beginning some 140 million years ago. Now the mountains are subdued
and rounded, but their structure and that of their surrounds (Appalachian Plateau, Piedmont Province) indicate a long, long past of rugged
activity. Today, the extensive Appalachian chain is partly buried under
the Coastal Plain from Alabama westward into Texas. But the Ouachita
Province and the Stockton Plateau in southwestern Texas still stand as
unburied remnants of the chain.

Reference:
King, Philip B., 1959, *The Evolution of North America:* Princeton
University Press, Princeton, New Jersey, 189 pages and foldout map.
King, Philip B., 1969, *Tectonic Map of North America:* 2 sheets,
40" x 65", scale 1:5,000,000, multi-colored.

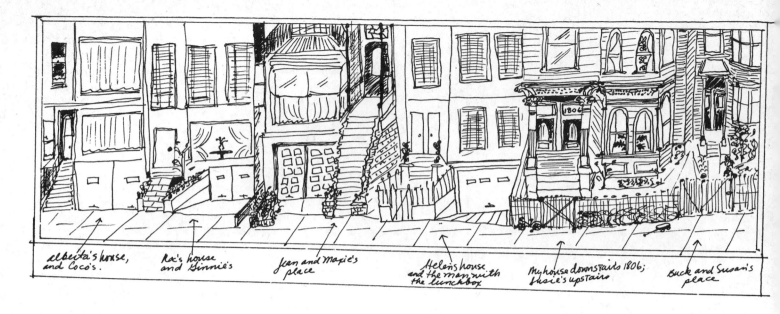

alberta's house, and Coco's.

Ra's house and Ginnie's

Jean and Maxie's place

Helen's house and the man with the lunchbox

My house downstairs 1806; Susie's upstairs

Buck and Susan's place

Put Your Place In Place

Draw your house, or the view from your window, the horizon maybe, or even your room. This is no contest, no winners and no great expectations. Send us your drawings and we'll use the best of them in our next issue. Black ink on white paper, pleeze.

HAPPY CAFE
Our house, Locke, CA.

YOUR HOUSE SHALL BE NOT AS AN ANCHOR BUT AS A MAST. IT SHALL NOT BE A GLISTENING FILM THAT COVERS A WOUND, BUT AN EYELID THAT GUARDS THE EYE.

SUBSCRIBE! RENEW!

One year subscription (4 issues) $8; single issues $2 (supplements) and $4 (216 pp., coated-stock issues). Air subscription rates for anywhere in the US, $14; overseas, $18. Please enclose cash, check, or money order.

THE POST OFFICE doesn't forward fourth-class mail, even if you register your move with them. So please tell us directly. Include your old address.

CONTRIBUTORS

Materials should be *Place* oriented, subject matter ranging from farms to towns to cities, from sumps to mountains, cafes to continents to, in a special sense, places of the mind and spirit, to the skinny little place between your teeth.

Since we're a quarterly, and since any contributions are considered not only for the following issue, but for the one after that, please don't be impatient with our slow replies. We will try to get a letter back to you within 2-3 weeks after we receive your package, but we'd like to be able to hold submissions for 1-3 months.

WHOLESALE INFO

If you're a business, and have a retailer's license, you can order *PLACE* through

> Book People
> 2940 7th Street
> Berkeley, CA 94710

Place issues *Neon Rose* and *See America First* may also be ordered through

> Random House
> Warehouse District Center
> Westminster, MD 21157

Mail will be promptly forwarded to all authors, artists, and photographers published in *Place*.

GOOSEDOWN

We'd like to exchange our product for yours. A pound of goosedown is worth at least a year's subscription—a good homemade quilt should be worth 3 or 4 years. Don't send perishable fruits or vegetables. We send our product 2nd class and bookrate; you'll have to send yours parcel post—so limit yourself to *lightweight* Natural Wonders. No candles, hash pipes, or hotpads, please! *(See Goosedown pp.6-15.)*

I wish to subscribe to *PLACE* for
☐ one year ($8.00)
☐ two years ($14.00)
☐ lifetime ($100.00)

beginning with _____

Also send me:
☐ $4.00 Spring '72, *Workingman's Guide to the Universe*
☐ $2.00 Summer '72, *Star Route One*
☐ $4.00 Fall '72, *See America First*
☐ $2.50 Winter '73, *Rogues Gallery*
☐ $4.00 Spring '73, *Neon Rose*

Name_____

Address_____

City_____State_____zip_____

PLACE Walnut Grove, California 95690

This is a gift subscription from_____

_____

Asleep at the Wheel...

THE STAFF . . .

Barbara DeZonia
Dudley DeZonia
H. Yale Ehresh
Ann Marie Gretsch

Doug Gunesch
Terri Gunesch
James Holdorf
Herald R. Hoyt
Baine Kerr
Margaret Phillips
Dick Schuettge
Pam Frierson
Balkan Sobrannie
Vicky White

The work of editing *NEON ROSE* fell to James, Baine and Herald, with Vicky on Poetry and Terri on the Dreambook. Barbara, Terri, Yale, Pam and Margaret designed it and laid it out. Doug handled the map pages and the Songbook (Peter Music, calligraphy, Annie Bonney, graphics). Dudley organized the production and he and Barbara selected the photographs. Trudy of the golden fingers typeset the bulk of the issue.

Ann Marie edited and laid out the astrological material; Gurney Norman edited the Mountain Eagle selections and wrote an introduction; Fred Pfeil interviewed Wright Morris; Genny Haskell did most of the proofing; and Balkan Sobrannie drew the title page and handled the subscriptions. Dick Schuettge assisted on the book production.

Place moves to the Delta

PLACE is moving its home office to Walnut Grove, California, the heart of the Sacramento Delta. (See "Delta Incidents" pp. 14-23 for a *real* introduction to our new home.) Contributors and friends are urged to stop and visit our new office there and we've included a map to help guide you. After June 1, please address all correspondence to: PLACE, Walnut Grove, CA 95690. Telephone: (916) 776-1619

Next Issue

Pam Frierson (Smith) is handling this summer's on-th-road issue from the Salmon River wilderness in Idaho, where the staff will be hiding out from the Delta heat in August. If you've got anything you've been wanting to say about mountains, this is your chance; send it in to the Mountain Issue. Special features will include explorations of the Salmon River area, the mind of Daniel Boone, the B.L.M. and big sheep.